21

Print and Cover Design: Nora Pauwels

Cultural Critique

EDITOR

Donna Przybylowicz, *University of Minnesota*

ASSOCIATE EDITOR

Abdul R. JanMohamed, *University of California, Berkeley*

ASSISTANT EDITOR

Jean Martin, *University of Minnesota*

EDITORIAL ASSISTANT

Jonathan Kahana, *University of Minnesota*

EDITORIAL COLLECTIVE

Henry Louis Gates, Jr., *Harvard University*
Nancy Hartsock, *University of Washington*
Martin Jay, *University of California, Berkeley*
David Lloyd, *University of California, Berkeley*
Elisabeth Lyon, *Hobart and William Smith Colleges*
Pamela McCallum, *University of Calgary*
Michael McKeon, *Rutgers University*
John Mowitt, *University of Minnesota*
Carolyn Porter, *University of California, Berkeley*
Mark Poster, *University of California, Irvine*
Paul Rabinow, *University of California, Berkeley*
John Carlos Rowe, *University of California, Irvine*
Jochen Schulte-Sasse, *University of Minnesota*
Brackette F. Williams, *Queens College, Graduate Center of CUNY*

Post-Colonial Ruptures and Democratic Possibilities: Multiculturalism as Anti-Racist Pedagogy

Henry A. Giroux

Introduction

Within the last decade, conservatives such as Allan Bloom, Lynne Cheney, Diane Ravitch, Pat Buchanan, and Senator Jesse Helms have placed the issue of culture and difference at the center of the debate about education and democracy. They have asserted the primacy of the political in invoking the language of culture and in doing so have let it be known that culture is a terrain of political and ideological struggle. The ideological and political parameters of this struggle have been made manifest on a number of cultural fronts, including the schools, the arts, and the more blatant attacks aimed at rolling back the benefits of civil rights and social welfare reforms constructed over the last three decades. What is being valorized in the dominant language of the conservative offensive is an undemocratic approach to social authority and a politically regressive move to reconstruct American life within the script of Eurocentrism, racism, and patriarchy. Similarly, within these discourses, the call to define civilization as synonymous with selected aspects of Western tradition is being matched by a fervent attempt to reduce pedagogy to the old transmission model of teaching and learning.

In what follows, I want to analyze the implications that this struggle over culture has for redefining a language of critique and possibility which is capable of challenging the authoritarianism and cultural amnesia that are hallmarks of this new cultural conservatism. In addition, I want to analyze the implications this debate has for reconstructing the purpose and meaning of public and higher education as part of a broader concern for developing a politics of cultural difference in a radical democratic society. First, I will highlight some central elements of the conservative attack on multiculturalism, focusing primarily on the work of Diane Ravitch. Second, I will draw upon some insights provided by post-colonial theorists in order to critically engage various notions of multiculturalism put forth in conservative and liberal discourses. Finally, I will attempt to take up the pedagogical implications of what I call a border pedagogy by focusing on the issue of anti-racist teaching.

The Conservative Cultural Counteroffensive[1]

During the last decade of the Reagan era, various sectors of the Right, including "fundamentalists (anti-obscenity and anti-abortion), nationalists (anti-flagburning and English Only advocates) and political conservatives (anti-affirmative action and anti-civil rights)," have turned their attention to mobilizing a populist campaign against what they allege is a crisis of authority, power, identity, and values in American culture (Yudice 129). Giving a new twist to the relationship between the political and the personal, the conservative backlash has attempted to reverse many of the gains made by women, gays and lesbians, ethnic and racial minorities, and other subordinated groups who have organized around a politics of identity. Alarmed by the challenges posed by these groups to the authority of academic canons, the alleged superiority of Western intellectual tradition, and the refusal to acknowledge that ethnic, racial, gender, and other relations play a significant role in the development and perpetuation of existing hegemonic, social arrangements, conservatives have launched a mass-based cultural offensive in order to radically change public opinion and taste. The conservative offensive has been conducted most recently on two cultural fronts. One attack has focused on both popular and "high" culture. As part of this counteroffensive, fundamentalists and conservatives have waged protests against the public screening of such films as *The Last Temptation of Christ,* they have brought obscenity charges against specific pop and rap musicians claiming that their lyrics were obscene and satanic, and under the auspices of the Meese Commission they have conducted a "war" against pornography.

More recently, conservatives have turned their attention to denouncing public funding of controversial artworks. Rallying against the exhibition of works by photographers Andres Serrano and Robert Mapplethorpe, conservatives have attempted to mobilize public opposition to images depicted as anti-Christian, obscene, and vulgar. The focus on Serrano's and Mapplethorpe's work is not coincidental. Serrano's photograph *Piss Christ* depicted a wood and plastic crucifix in the artist's urine while the Mapplethorpe exhibition contained sexually explicit gay and sadomasochistic photographs.[2] Both exhibits provided the opportunity for conservatives to launch attacks not only on artistic freedom, but more specifically to wage a populist campaign infused with elements of homophobia, fundamentalism, nationalism, and racism. For example, utilizing the discourse of a "sex panic," Senator Jesse Helms has sought to immobilize moderate and liberal opposition by condemning Mapplethorpe's photography on the grounds that "the homosexual theme goes throughout his work" (qtd. in Dowd B6). In addition, Helms has attempted to pass a Senate amendment that would forbid public funding for what he labeled "indecent" and "offensive" art. Helms's bill was modified before it was passed by the Senate, but not because it legitimated a scurrilous attack on the work of gay and lesbian artists. Homophobia aside, liberals rallied against the bill as a result of massive pressure by the arts community. But the compromise bill, which required that the National Endowment for the Arts adhere to legal bans on obscenity in funding public art work, has had the effect of increasing "self-censorship and anxiety in the arts community, spurred by new episodes of formal censorship and McCarthyite witch-hunts" (Vance 49). More specifically, the right-wing attack against the arts has sent a chilling effect through various funding agencies for the arts and, in part, has succeeded in mobilizing a "moral panic" that has a distinctly homophobic and anti-democratic character. At stake in the political and pedagogical struggle over high and popular culture is an attempt by conservatives to dismantle those sectors of the arts that combine artistic freedom with social criticism.[3]

The second thrust of the conservative cultural offensive has expressed itself through a full-fledged attack on higher education and public schooling. This attack has manifested itself in endless diatribes against the so-called evils of political correctness and multiculturalism. Featured in a number of major academic journals and popular magazines, including the *Partisan Review, The New Republic, Newsweek, The New York Review of Books,* and *Forbes,* and in an interminable stream of editorial comments in major American newspapers, the "crisis" on American campuses has been provocatively depicted as "The Chilling of Intellectual Life," "The New Orthodoxy," "Thought Police," and "The Cult of Multiculturalism." It is worth noting some of the assumptions central to this attack, such as

> that the academy is under siege by leftists, multiculturalists, deconstructionists and other radicals who are politicizing the university and threatening to undermine the very foundations of the Western intellectual tradition. These radicals, the theory goes, are the left-wing graduate students of the '60s who sneaked into tenured positions in the '90s and are now promoting an agenda of cultural relativism. Armed with affirmative action admissions and hiring, as well as new French literary theories, the politically correct hope to transform the university into a den of multiculturalism—silencing everyone who would dare dissent by calling them "sexist," "racist" or anti-deconstructionist. (Fraser 6)

Nurtured by conservative organizations such as Accuracy in Academia and the National Association of Scholars, establishment right-wing intellectuals such as Allan Bloom, author of *The Closing of the American Mind,* Roger Kimball, an editor of *New Criterion* and author of *Tenured Radicals,* and Dinesh D'Souza, former editor of *The Dartmouth Review* and author of *Illiberal Education,* have waged a public campaign against leftist radicals in higher education. Wrapping their discourse in a broad-based attack on feminists, radical homosexuals, Marxists, and New Historicists, conservatives such as D'Souza and Fred Siegel claim that "liberal arts students . . . are very likely to be exposed to an attempted brainwashing that deprecates Western learning and exalts a neo-Marxist ideology promoted in the name of multiculturalism" (D'Souza, *Illiberal Education* 35). Siegel extends this criticism by writing about multiculturalists in terms that are as theoretically wooden as they are ideologically extreme. He writes:

> [M]ulticulturalism's hard-liners, who seem to make up the majority of the movement, damn as racism any attempt to draw the myriad of American groups into a common American culture. For these multiculturalists, differences are absolute, irreducible, intractable—occasions not for understanding separation but for separation. (35)

There has been a strong tendency in the conservative view of multiculturalism to separate social criticism from the discourse of cultural difference. That is, any attempt on the part of progressives to use the concept of cultural difference as a basis for social criticism and curricula reform that engage issues of race, class, gender, and ethnicity is dismissed as merely an instance of separatism that threatens nothing less than the very nature of Western civilization itself;[4] or such a position is labeled as a form of "political correctness" and summarily rejected as one that infringes on the academic rights of faculty while simultaneously subjecting liberal arts students "to brainwashing that deprecates Western learning and exalts a neo-Marxist ideology" (D'Souza, "Visigoths" 81).

In the ideology of the NAS, the Madison Center for Education Affairs, and its various ideologues, the curriculum of Western culture is being undermined by the introduction of both popular and non-Western courses (read as trivial), tenured, radical academics are proselytizing a generation of students by introducing them to left-wing, anti-establishment politics, and freedom of speech is being violated on college campuses through the collective actions of left-wing faculty and students who will not tolerate opposing views on race, class, gender, and other political issues. In actuality, all of these charges appear to be bogus.[5] The liberal arts curricula are still dominated by the works of Western culture, radical professors represent a small percentage of college faculties, and it is both patronizing and illogical to suggest that students are indifferent to or uncritical of what they are taught. The political correctness movement seizes upon the issue of free expression in order to undermine social criticism that opposes cultural chauvinism, racism, and gender discrimination. Political correctness is a euphemism used by liberals and neoconservatives to disparage radical professors, cultural workers, and students from displaying ongoing pedagogical interests in fashioning a democratic culture within and outside of higher education. Accordingly, the rallying cry against political correctness is an act of bad faith designed to legitimate and enforce the pedagogical imperative to learn a selected cultural tradition and common culture invented in a monolithic and totalizing discourse.[6]

This attack on difference and cultural diversity by cultural conservatives is not limited to attacks on the arts and higher education. More recently, conservatives such as Diane Ravitch have attempted to counter attempts by educational reformers in New York, Oregon, and California to rewrite public school curricula to include the rich legacies, conflicts, and diverse struggles that characterize the history of the United States.

Ravitch's attempt to silence or marginalize the voices of those who have traditionally been excluded from the school curricula is indicative of how the language of liberalism and pluralism are increasingly being used to give credence to the new nativism and racism that has been resurgent in the last decade in the media, mass culture, and American schools.

Acknowledging the importance of the changing demographic and cultural character of the United States, Ravitch ("Multiculturalism") constructs her argument around a view of pluralism based on a notion of a "common culture" that serves as a referent to denounce any attempt by subordinate groups to challenge the narrow ideological and political parameters by which such a culture both defines and expresses itself.[7] Working as a paid consultant to various task forces that have undertaken curriculum reform, Ravitch has claimed that the language of the multiculturalists is consistently anti-Western and separatist. Arguing against the *Curriculum of Inclusion* report issued by New

York's state commissioner of education, Thomas Sobol, Ravitch wrote in the *New York Daily News:* "It sees nothing in Western culture but racism, greed and intolerance. The task force thinks that white children are too 'arrogant'"(qtd. in Hancock 3). Ravitch's argument is premised on the assumption that multiculturalism represents the equivalent of cultural separatism, ignores the importance of Western culture, and has no language for linking difference to the notion of "common culture."

While Ravitch is quick to recognize that the common culture of the United States is made up of diverse racial and ethnic groups, she glosses over any attempt to designate how dominant configurations of power privilege some cultures over others, or how power works to secure forms of domination that marginalize and silence subordinate groups. Since the notion of common culture is a central theoretical element used by conservatives in attacking multiculturalism, it is important to analyze some of the weaknesses of this position as it is expressed by Ravitch.

In the name of a common culture, Ravitch performs two hegemonic functions. First, she dehistoricizes and depoliticizes the idea of culture. Lost from her perspective is any account of how various social movements have struggled historically to transform a Eurocentric curriculum that, in part, has functioned to exclude or marginalize the voices of women, blacks, and other subordinate groups. For example, there is no mention of how various social movements struggled successfully in the late 1960s and early 1970s to add black, ethnic, and women's studies programs and curricula in both public schools and various institutions of higher learning. Nor does she examine how the relationship between culture and social identity is constituted "through hierarchical knowledge and power relations" within the curriculum (Mohanty 196). In this case, Ravitch erases through her insistence on a common culture the institutional, economic, and social parameters that actively construct deep structural inequalities and forms of domination that characterize relations between privileged and subordinate groups, as well as the challenges that have been waged against such practices.

In Ravitch's worldview, the common culture she constructs denies the necessity of either contesting existing configurations of power or transforming the deep-seated inequalities that characterize institutional and everyday life in the United States. Of course, this is precisely her point. Ravitch invokes pluralism, democracy, and consensus in order to defend a dominant order in which the issues of power, politics, and struggle are coded as forms of disruption and extremism. More importantly, by discrediting the social criticisms and struggles waged by subordinate groups against the dominant culture in the interest of cultural democracy, Ravitch locates the source of oppression and change in individual will and achievement. In this account, the social, economic, cultural, and political centers of power in the United States simply disappear. At the same time, broad-based struggle and political action over the curriculum and related issues of social justice don't simply disappear in Ravitch's account; they are pointedly discredited as a threat to a "sense of common nationhood" ("Diversity" 340).

Second, missing from Ravitch's discourse is a notion of difference and citizenship tied to a project of substantive critical democracy, one which extends the principles of justice, liberty, and equality to the widest possible set of economic and social relations. Employing a comfortable set of oppositions in which those who struggle over extending the meaning of cultural democracy are simply dismissed as particularists, Ravitch utilizes the language of desperation and extremism to wipe out any attempt on the part of subordinate groups to learn about how their identities have been forged in ongoing historical struggles for social justice. For Ravitch, the history of the culture of Otherness should be forged exclusively in positive images organized around events like Black History Month, multicultural dinners, or events celebrating the achievements of women. While such images are pedagogically crucial to any form of critical pedagogy, they cannot be expunged from an ongoing criticism of how the dominant culture has created and sustains the very problems that provided the conditions for such heroic struggles in the first place. Ravitch recognizes that the curriculum needs to become more inclusive in acknowledging the histories, cultures, and experiences of other groups, but she doesn't want students to engage in forms of social criticism aimed at calling into question the Eurocentric nature of the dominant curriculum.

What is important here is not simply the issue of censorship, but a benevolent form of neocolonialism that refuses to hold up to critical scrutiny its own complicity in producing and maintaining specific injustices, practices, and forms of oppression that deeply inscribe its legacy and heritage.

Multiculturalism and the New Politics of Difference

> The language of critique is effective . . . to the extent to which it overcomes the given grounds of opposition and opens up a space of "translation": a place of hybridity, figuratively speaking, where the construction of a political object that is new, neither the one nor the Other, properly alienates our political expectations. (Bhabha, "Commitment to Theory" 10–11)

In opposition to the emerging neoconservative view that defines cultural democracy against difference as part of a politics of empowerment and struggle, I want to provide a rationale for developing a politics of difference and border pedagogy responsive to the imperatives of a critical democracy. In doing so, I want to formulate a nontotalizing response to the challenge that conservatives have raised around the relationship between culture and democracy, on the one hand, and schooling and the politics of difference on the other. In part, my response is formulated in an attempt to develop a theoretical discourse that serves neither to legitimate existing pedagogical practices nor to justify itself by positing some sort of correspondence to an objectively verifiable reality. Such claims for theory belong to paradigms derivative of positivist and empiricist considerations. Instead, I want to construct a theoretical discourse that Homi K. Bhabha calls a space of "negotiation and translation" ("Commitment to Theory" 6). Put another way, I want to develop a theoretical discourse that creates a cartography for creating new boundaries in order to explore, negotiate, and translate between new and old questions, problems, and objects of knowledge.

Creating a theoretical space for new forms of criticism and collective action not only means constructing a discourse that challenges the conservative assault on cultural democracy; it also means demystifying the liberal refusal to link cultural struggle to forms of historical and institutional domination. Liberal notions of multiculturalism affirm difference within a politics of consensus that erases culture as a terrain of struggle constituted within asymmetrical relations of power, knowledge, and experience. Wrapped in the discourse of accommodation, liberal discourses of multiculturalism argue for extending the canon by including minority voices, focusing on the limits of the prevailing structure of the disciplines, and supporting a notion of common culture which "has to be created anew by engaging the cultural differences that are part of American life" (Erickson B3). Clearly liberals offer a view of multiculturalism that challenges the totalizing and often racist views of conservatives, but the central thrust of many of these discourses is that they reproduce the very problems that give rise to their own criticisms. Since the critique of this view has been extensively developed elsewhere, I only want to highlight a few considerations.[8] First, the liberal multicultural position on the academic canon fails to question how the very concept of the canon serves to secure particular forms of cultural and political authority. Adding particular texts or authors to the canon is not the same as analyzing how the structure of the canon in both form and content promotes rather than displaces the effects of the colonial gaze.[9] What is essential here is raising questions regarding how the canon emerged as part of a larger crisis in European history to secure how dominant and oppositional histories are written, produced, and legitimized within the logic of colonization, privilege, and resistance.

Second, the multicultural emphasis on engaging texts differently often ignores how "the ways in which issues of power, political struggle, and cultural identity are inscribed within the form, structures, and content of texts and thereby misses the implicit historical readings of the crisis that circumscribes the texts and to which the texts inescapably and subtly respond" (West, "Minority" 199). To be sure, what is at stake here is not merely articulating the study of texts to broader historical, cultural, and political events, but recognizing that multiculturalism is also about a politics that is attentive to the material and human suffering exhibited in forms of domestic colonialism expressed in racial violence, shameful unemployment among black youth, and the growing numbers of minorities who daily join the ranks of the hungry and the homeless.

Finally, the attempt to accommodate pluralism to a "common culture" rather than to a shared vision grounded in an ongoing struggle to expand the radical possibilities of democratic public life underestimates the legacy of the dominant culture to eliminate cultural differences, multiple literacies, and diverse communities in the name of totalizing and one-dimensional master narratives refigured around issues such as nationalism, citizenship, and patriotism. Furthermore, conservative and liberal discourses that conflate multiculturalism with the imperatives of a "common culture" generally suppress any attempts to call into question the norm of whiteness as an ethnic category that secures its dominance by appearing to be invisible. In this case, emancipatory interests in liberal approaches to multicultural education are generally limited to the call for either assimilation or the demand to reverse negative images of blacks and other ethnic groups as they appear in various forms of texts and images. At work here is the liberal failure to address those post-colonial critiques which not only interrogate forms of European and American culture that situate difference in structures of domination but also analyze race and ethnicity in terms that highlight issues of inequality, injustice, and liberty as part of an ongoing colonial legacy and obstacle to realizing democratic public life.

Conservative and liberal approaches to multiculturalism merge in their refusal to locate cultural differences in a broader examination of how the boundaries of ethnicity, race, and power make visible how "whiteness" functions as a historical and social construction, "an unrecognized and unspoken racial category" that secures its power by refusing to identify culture as "a problem of politics, power, and pedagogy" (Carby 39). As a critical discourse of race and pedagogy, multiculturalism needs to break out of its silence regarding the role it plays in masking how white domination colonizes definitions of the normal.[10] Hence, critical educators need to move their analyses and pedagogical practices away from an exotic or allegedly objective encounter with marginal groups and raise more questions with respect to how their own subjectivities and practices are present in the construction of the margins. As Toni Morrison points out, the very issue of race requires that the bases of Western civilization will require rethinking. This means that the central question may not be why Afro-Americans are absent from dominant narratives, but "What intellectual feats had to be performed by the author or his critic to erase [blacks] from a society seething with [their] presence, and what effect has that performance had on the work? What are the strategies of escape from knowledge?" (11).

I would argue that the issue is not to privilege difference through an appeal to a common culture, but to construct differences within social relations and a notion of public life that challenges networks of hierarchy, systemic injustice, and economic exploitation.

It is crucial for critical educators and cultural workers to link a politics and pedagogy of difference to a theory of social welfare and cultural democracy. At the very least, this means that educators can work to insert the idea of difference into the curriculum as part of an attempt to rearticulate the ideas of justice and equality. A politics of difference not only offers students the opportunity for raising questions about how the categories of race, class, and gender are shaped within the margins and center of power, but it also provides a new way of reading history as a way of reclaiming power and identity. This is no small matter for those students who have generally been either marginalized or silenced by the dominant ideologies and practices of public and higher education. This suggests that educators acknowledge that the radical responsibility of a politics of difference and public life necessitates an ongoing analysis by students of the contradictions in American society between the meaning of freedom, the demands of social justice, and the obligations of citizenship, on the one hand, and the accumulated suffering, domination, force, and violence that permeate all aspects of everyday life on the other. Such an analysis necessitates forms of learning grounded in the ethical imperative both to challenge the prevailing social order while simultaneously providing the basis for students to deepen the intellectual, civic, and moral understanding of their role as agents of public formation.

I am suggesting that the debate over the politics of cultural difference and the curriculum might be reconstructed to engage the broader issue of how the learning that goes on in public and higher education is truly attentive to the problems and histories that construct the actual experiences students face in their everyday lives. A pedagogy of difference is not based merely on providing students with conflicting paradigms or the dispassionate skills of rhetorical persuasion.[11] In fact, it is imperative that a pedagogy of difference move beyond forms of semiotic and deconstructive criticism that dismiss central concerns of power, politics, and ideology. A critical pedagogical approach might begin by both engaging "how the school functions as an institution to produce the available discourses and knowledge" and analyzing the "way students enter into textuality—the way discourse addresses, and, in Althusser's term, 'interpellates' students as subjects" (Clark 127). A pedagogy of difference points to pedagogical practices that offer students the knowledge, skills, and values they will need to negotiate critically and to transform the world in which they find themselves. The politics of cultural difference is not about a pluralism cleansed of the discourse of power, struggle, and equity; instead, it contains all of the problems that make democracy messy, vibrant, and dangerous to those who believe that social criticism and social justice are inimical to both the meaning of education and the lived experience of democratic public life. This is precisely why critical educators cannot let the politics and discourse of difference be subordinated to cleansing and comforting self-righteous appeals made in the name of a common culture or the false equality of a pluralism devoid of the trappings of struggle, empowerment, and possibility.

In what follows, I want to provide a brief analysis of some of the central theoretical assumptions that characterize the diverse work of a number of post-colonial theorists.[12] In doing so, my aim is to appropriate selectively a number of critical assumptions as part of an effort both to enter into dialogue with this body of work and to engage its criticisms as part of an attempt to challenge some of the primary categories that construct current forms of radical educational theory dealing with multiculturalism, race, and pedagogy. At the same time, I want to use some of the central insights of post-colonial theories to problematize and extend the possibilities for developing what I call the politics of border pedagogy. Finally, I want to develop an approach to anti-racist teaching through some of the central categories that inform the theoretical boundaries and practices of a border pedagogy.

Post-Colonial Ruptures/Democratic Possibilities

> The choice of language and the use to which it is put is central to a people's definition of themselves in relation to their natural and social environment, indeed in relation to the entire universe. (Ngugi 4)

The challenge presented by Ngugi and other post-colonial critics offers a new theoretical discourse to address the political and pedagogical crises in culture, difference, and authority that have beset many of the Western democracies in the 1990s. In part, post-colonial critics challenge the authority and discourses of those practices wedded to the legacy of a colonialism that either directly constructs or is implicated in social relations that keep privilege and oppression alive as active constituting forces of daily life within the centers and margins of power. Most specifically, post-colonial discourses have pushed against the boundaries of the liberal and conservative debate on multiculturalism by asserting that politics and struggle are central to the discourse of difference. That is, they scan the surface language that constructs the alleged crisis of multiculturalism and ask: which crisis, for whom is there a crisis, and who speaks in the name of such a crisis?

Post-colonial discourses have also made clear that the old legacies of the political Left, Center, and Right can no longer be so easily defined. Indeed, post-colonial critics have gone further and provided important theoretical insights into how such discourses either actively construct colonial relations or are implicated in their construction. From this perspective Robert Young argues that post-colonialism is a dislocating discourse that raises theoretical questions regarding how dominant and radical theories "have themselves been implicated in the long history of European colonialism—and, above all, the extent to which [they] continue to determine both the institutional conditions of knowledge as well as the terms of contemporary institutional practices—

practices which extend beyond the limits of the academic institution" (viii). This is especially true for many of the theorists in a variety of social movements who have taken up the language of difference and a concern with the politics of the Other. In many instances, theorists within these new social movements have addressed political and pedagogical issues through the construction of binary oppositions that not only contain traces of theoretical vanguardism but also fall into the trap of simply reversing the old colonial legacy and problematic of oppressed vs. oppressor. In doing so, they have often unwittingly imitated the colonial model of erasing the complexity, complicity, diverse agents, and multiple situations that constitute the enclaves of colonial/hegemonic discourse and practice.[13]

Post-colonial discourses have both extended and moved beyond the parameters of this debate in a number of ways. First, post-colonial critics have made it clear that the history and politics of difference are often informed by a legacy of colonialism that warrants analyzing the exclusions and repressions that allow specific forms of privilege to remain unacknowledged in the language of Western educators and cultural workers. At stake here is deconstructing forms of privilege that benefit males, whiteness, and property as well as those conditions that have disabled others to speak in places where those who are privileged by virtue of the legacy of colonial power assume authority and the conditions for human agency. This suggests, as Gayatri Spivak has pointed out, that more is at stake than problematizing discourse; more importantly, educators and cultural workers must be engaged in "the unlearning of one's own privilege. So that, not only does one become able to listen to that other constituency, but one learns to speak in such a way that one will be taken seriously by that other constituency" (41). In this instance, post-colonial discourse extends the radical implications of difference and location by making such concepts attentive to providing the grounds for forms of self-representation and collective knowledge in which the subject *and* object of European culture are problematized, though in ways radically different from those taken up by Western radicals and conservatives (Tiffin, "Post-Colonialism").

Second, post-colonial discourse rewrites the relationship between the margin and the center by deconstructing the colonialist and imperialist ideologies that structure Western knowledge, texts, and social practices. In this case, there is an attempt to demonstrate how European culture and colonialism "are deeply implicated in each other" (R. Young 119). This suggests more than rewriting or recovering the repressed stories and social memories of the Other; it means understanding and rendering visible how Western knowledge is encased in historical and institutional structures that both privilege and exclude particular readings, specific voices, certain aesthetics, forms of authority, specific representations, and forms of sociality. The West and Otherness relate not as polarities or binarisms in post-colonial discourse but in ways in which both are complicitous and resistant, victim and accomplice. In this instance, criticism of the dominating Other returns as a form of self-criticism. Linda Hutcheon captures the importance of this issue with her question: "How do we construct a discourse which displaces the effects of the colonizing gaze while we are still under its influence?" ("Circling" 176). While it cannot be forgotten that the legacy of colonialism has meant large-scale death and destruction as well as cultural imperialism for the Other, the Other is not merely the opposite of Western colonialism, nor is the West a homogeneous trope of imperialism.

This perspective suggests a third rupture provided by post-colonial discourses. The current concern with the "death of the subject" cannot be confused with the necessity of affirming the complex and contradictory character of human agency. Post-colonial discourse reminds us that it is ideologically convenient and politically suspect for Western intellectuals to talk about the disappearance of the speaking subject from within institutions of privilege and power. This is not meant to suggest that post-colonial theorists accept the humanist notion of the subject as a unified and static identity. On the contrary, post-colonial discourse agrees that the speaking subject must be decentered, but this does not mean that all notions of human agency and social change must be dismissed. Understood in these terms, the post-modernist notion of the subject must be accepted and modified in order to extend rather than erase the possibility for creating the enabling conditions for human agency. At the very least, this would mean coming to understand the strengths and limits of

practical reason, the importance of affective investments, the discourse of ethics as a resource for social vision, and the availability
of multiple discourses and cultural resources that provide the
very grounds and necessity for agency (Giroux, *Border*).

What do post-colonial discourses suggest for the ways in
which educators and other cultural workers take up the issue of
race and difference? In part, they provide a theoretical foundation for deconstructing the master narratives of white supremacist
logic and for redrawing the boundaries between the construction
of experience and power. In the first instance, by challenging the
concept of master narratives, post-colonial discourses have
opened up the possibility for launching a renewed attack on the
underlying assumptions that have allowed the dominant culture
to enforce its own authority and racist practices through an unproblematic appeal to the virtues of Western civilization. In challenging the notions of universal reason, the construction of a
white, humanist subject, and the selective legitimation of high
culture as the standard for cultural practice, post-colonial criticism has illuminated how Eurocentric-American discourses of
identity suppress difference, heterogeneity, and multiplicity in
their efforts to maintain racist hegemonic relations of power. Not
only do post-colonial theorists offer new ways to understand how
power works in constructing racist identities and subjectivities, but
they redefine culture and experience within multiple relations of
difference that propose a range of subject-positions from which
people can struggle against racist ideologies and practices. By
calling into question the themes of "degraded Otherness and subaltern marginality" post-colonial discourses suggest new theoretical tools for attacking "notions of exclusionary identity, dominating heterogeneity, and universality—or in more blunt language,
White supremacy" (West, "Black" 90).

Rather than either celebrate or dismiss the master narratives
of the West, post-colonial theorists raise important questions
about how such narratives are constructed, what they mean, how
they regulate particular forms of moral and social experience,
and how they affirm or transgress particular discourses of ethnicity, community, and cultural democracy. Similarly, post-colonial
theorists not only delineate how borders are named and constructed as sites of terror, resistance, and possibility, but they also

attempt to redraw the very maps of meaning, desire, and difference, inscribing the social and individual body with new intellectual and emotional investments, and calling into question traditional forms of power and their accompanying modes of legitimation. For educators interested in developing an anti-racist pedagogy, post-colonialism offers new epistemologies for rethinking the broader and specific contexts in which democratic authority is defined; it offers a healthy skepticism not only toward all forms of boundary-fixing but also regarding existing definitions of what is central and what is marginal, what is included and what is excluded, particularly in dominant discourses of ethnicity and difference. Isaac Julien and Kobena Mercer state the issue well:

> One issue at stake . . . we suggest, is the potential break-up or deconstruction of structures that determine what is regarded as culturally central and what is regarded as culturally marginal. . . . Rather than attempt to compensate the "structured absences" of previous paradigms, it would be useful to identify the relations of power/knowledge that determine which cultural issues are intellectually prioritized in the first place. The initial stage in any deconstructive project must be to examine and undermine the force of the binary relation that produces the marginal as a consequence of the authority invested in the centre. (3)

All of these developments redefine theory by moving it far beyond—and in opposition to—the concerns embodied in the ideologies and questions that have defined the underlying racist principles which have remained unchallenged as a central aspect of conservative and liberal educational discourses.

Post-colonial discourses represent a space in which to retheorize, locate, and address the possibilities for a new politics based on the construction of new identities, zones of cultural difference, and forms of ethical address that allow cultural workers and educators alike to transform the languages, social practices, and histories that are part of the colonial inheritance. This position offers new hope for expanding both the practice of cultural work and the liberatory possibilities of crossing borders that open up new political and pedagogical possibilities. It is to these issues that I will now turn.

Border Pedagogy and the Politics of Anti-Racist Teaching

[T]he border is not an abyss that will have to save us from threatening otherness, but a place where the so-called otherness yields, becomes us, and therefore comprehensible. (Gómez-Peña qtd. in Joselit 122)

Central to the notion of border pedagogy is the political project that informs it. In this case, the concept of border pedagogy is grounded in the imperatives of a radical public philosophy that respects the notion of difference as part of a common struggle to extend the quality of democratic public life (Laclau and Mouffe 114–93). In short, the notion of border pedagogy presupposes an acknowledgment of the shifting borders that both undermine and reterritorialize different configurations of culture, power, and knowledge.

I believe that the concept of border pedagogy has important implications for redefining radical educational theory and practice. The category of border signals in the metaphorical and literal sense how power is inscribed differently on the body, culture, history, space, land, and psyche. Borders elicit a recognition of those epistemological, political, cultural, and social margins that distinguish between "us and them," delineate zones of terror from locations that are safe, and create new cartographies of identity and difference.[14] The concept of borders when defined as part of a politics of cultural difference can be used heuristically to make problematic specific authorial positions secured in monolithic views of culture, nationalism, and difference.

The category of border also prefigures cultural criticism and pedagogical processes as a form of border crossing. That is, it signals forms of entrance and transgression in which existing borders forged in domination can be challenged and redefined, while borders that offer humane and democratic possibilities can be secured. It also speaks to the need to create pedagogical conditions in which students become border crossers in order to un-

derstand Otherness in its own terms, and further to create bor-
derlands in which diverse cultural resources allow for the
fashioning of new identities within existing configurations of
power. In this sense, border crossing becomes a metaphor for
inviting students and teachers to cross over into different cultural
zones in order to "map the politics of their forays into other
cultures" (JanMohamed, "Worldliness" 3). This type of pedagogical cartography can illuminate and make problematic the historically and socially constructed strengths and limitations of those
places and borders we inherit and which frame our discourses
and social relations as intellectuals, students, and citizens. Moreover, as part of a broader politics of difference, border pedagogy
makes primary the language of the political and ethical. It stresses
the political by examining how institutions, knowledge, and social
relations are inscribed differently in power; it highlights the ethical by examining how the shifting relations of knowing, acting,
and subjectivity are constructed in spaces and social relationships
based on judgments which demand and frame "different modes
of response to the other; that is, between those that transfigure
and those that disfigure, those that care for the other in his/her
otherness and those that do not" (Kearney 369).

As part of a radical pedagogical practice, border pedagogy
points to the need for conditions that allow students to write,
speak, and listen in a language in which meaning becomes multi-
accentual and dispersed, and resists permanent closure. This is a
language in which one speaks with rather than exclusively for
others. Border pedagogy necessitates combining an emphasis on
the capacity of individuals to use critical reason to address the
issue of public life with a concern with how we might experience
agency in a world constituted in differences unsupported by tran-
scendent phenomena or metaphysical guarantees.

In opposition to conservative and liberal pedagogical practices, border pedagogy does not refuse to call into question the
dominating aspects of white culture or to engage the oppositional
potential of difference as a site of struggle. This becomes more
clear in moving from an analysis of the general attributes of border pedagogy to analyzing how it might be taken up or developed
as an approach to anti-racist teaching.

Central to an anti-racist notion of border pedagogy is the

need to provide a language and set of pedagogical practices that offer educators the opportunity to rethink the relations between the centers and the margins of power. That is, such a pedagogy must address the issue of racism as one that calls into question not only forms of subordination that create inequities among different groups as they live out their lives, but, as I have mentioned previously, also challenges those institutional and ideological boundaries that have historically masked their own relations of power behind complex forms of distinction and privilege. What does this suggest for the way we develop the basic elements of an anti-racist pedagogy?

First, the notion of border pedagogy offers students the opportunity to engage the multiple references that constitute different cultural codes, experiences, and languages. This means providing learning opportunities for students not only to analyze how cultural texts produce and are produced by various discursive racial codes, but also how students "read" themselves intellectually and affectively into those cultural identities and subject-positions offered by dominant and oppositional representations. This suggests developing pedagogical practices that address texts as social and historical constructions which presuppose particular cultural identities; it also suggests developing pedagogical practices that allow students to analyze texts in terms of their presences and absences; and most importantly, such practices should provide students with the opportunity to read texts dialogically through a configuration of many voices, some of which offer up resistance, some of which provide support.

Within this discourse, students engage knowledge as border crossers, by moving in and out of borders constructed around coordinates of difference and power (Hicks). These are not only physical borders; they are ideological, psychological, and cultural borders historically constructed and socially organized within maps of rules and regulations that serve to either limit or enable particular identities, individual capacities, and social forms. In this case, students cross over into borders of meaning, maps of knowledge, social relations, and values that are increasingly being negotiated and rewritten as the codes and regulations which organize them become destabilized and reshaped. Border pedagogy decenters as it remaps.

At one level this means giving students the opportunity to speak, to locate themselves in history, and to become subjects in the construction of their identities and the wider society. It also means defining voice not merely as an opportunity to speak, but to engage critically with the ideology and substance of speech, writing, and other forms of cultural production. In this case, "coming to voice" for students from both dominant and subordinate cultures means engaging in rigorous discussions of various cultural texts, drawing upon one's personal experience, and confronting the process through which ethnicity and power can be rethought as a political narrative that challenges racism as part of a broader struggle to democratize social, political, and economic life. In part, this means looking at the various ways in which race implicates relations of domination, resistance, suffering, and power within various social practices and how these are taken up in multiple ways by students who occupy different ethnic, social, and gender locations. In this way, race is never discussed outside of broader articulations nor is it merely about people of color.

Second, an anti-racist border pedagogy needs to do more than educate students to perform ideological surgery on master narratives based on white, patriarchal, and class-specific interests. If the master narratives of domination are to be deterritorialized effectively, it is important for educators to understand how such narratives are taken up as part of an investment of feeling, pleasure, and desire. There is a need to rethink the syntax of learning and behavior outside of the geography of rationality and reason. For example, this means that racism cannot be dealt with in a purely limited, analytical way. An anti-racist pedagogy must engage how and why students make particular ideological and affective investments and occupy particular subject-positions that give students a sense of meaning, purpose, and delight. As Stuart Hall argues, this means uncovering both for ourselves as teachers as well as for the students we are teaching "the deep structural factors which have a tendency persistently not only to generate racial practices and structures but to reproduce them through time which therefore account for their extraordinarily immovable character" (61). In addition to engaging racism within a politics of representation, ideology, and pleasure, it is also important to stress that any serious analysis of racism also has to be historical and structural. It has to chart out how racist practices develop, where they come from, how they are sustained, how they affect dominant and subordinate groups, and how they can be challenged. This is not a discourse about personal preferences or dominant tastes but a discourse about economics, culture, politics, and power.

Third, a border pedagogy offers the opportunity for students to air their feelings about race from the perspective of the subject-positions they experience as constitutive of their own identities. Ideology in this sense is treated not merely as an abstraction but as part of the student's lived experience. This does not mean that teachers reduce their role to that of an intellectual voyeur or collapse their authority into a shabby form of relativism. Nor does it suggest that students merely express or assess their own experiences. Rather, it points to a particular form of teacher authority grounded in a respect for a radically decentered notion of democratic public life. This is a view of authority that rejects the notion that all forms of authority are expressions of unwarranted power and oppression. Instead, it argues for forms of authority that are rooted in democratic interests and emancipatory social relations, forms of authority that, in this case, begin from a standpoint from which to develop an educational project that rejects politics as aesthetics, that retains instead the significance of the knowledge/power relationship as a discourse of criticism and politics necessary for the achievement of equality, freedom, and struggle. This is not a form of authority based on an appeal to universal truths; it is a form of authority that recognizes its own partiality while simultaneously asserting a standpoint from which to engage the discourses and practices of democracy, freedom, and domination. Put another way, this is a notion of authority rooted in a political project that ties education to the broader struggle for public life in which dialogue, vision, and compassion remain critically attentive to the liberating and dominating relations that organize various aspects of everyday life.[15]

This suggests that educators and other cultural workers use their authority to establish pedagogical conditions in which different views about race can be aired but not treated as simply an expression of individual views or feelings (Mohanty 194–95). Andrew Hannan rightly points out that educators must refuse to treat racism as a matter of individual prejudice and counter such a position by addressing the "structural foundations of [the] culture of racism" (127). An anti-racist pedagogy must demonstrate that the views we hold about race have different historical and ideological weight, forged in asymmetrical relations of power, and that they always embody interests that shape social practices in particular ways. In other words, an anti-racist pedagogy cannot treat ideologies as simply individual expressions of feeling, but as historical, cultural, and social practices that serve to either undermine or reconstruct democratic public life. These views must be engaged without silencing students, but they must also be interrogated next to a public philosophy that names racism for what it is and calls racist ideologies and practices into account on political and ethical terms.

Fourth, educators need to understand how the experience of marginality at the level of everyday life lends itself to forms of oppositional and transformative consciousness. For both privileged and subordinate students, this suggests the ethical and political imperative to both reclaim and remake their histories, voices, and visions as part of a wider struggle to change those material and social relations that deny radical pluralism as the basis of democratic political community. It is only through such an understanding that teachers can develop a border pedagogy which opens up the possibility for students to reclaim their voices as part of a process of empowerment and not merely what some educators have called an initiation into the culture of power (Delpit 282–83). It is not enough for students to learn how to resist power which is oppressive, which names them in a way that undermines their ability to govern rather than serve, and prevents them from struggling against forms of power that subjugate and exploit. For example, Lisa Delpit's call for educators to integrate black students into what she unproblematically addresses as "the culture of power" appears to be linked to how such power is constructed in opposition to democratic values and used as a force for domination (292). This is not to suggest the authority of white dominant culture is all of one piece, nor is this meant to imply that it should not be the object of study. What is at stake here is forgoing a notion of power that does not collapse into a form of domination but rather is critical and emancipatory, one that allows students both to locate themselves in history and to appropriate critically, not slavishly, the cultural and political codes of their own and other traditions. Moreover, students who have to disavow their own racial heritage in order to succeed are not becoming "raceless," as Signithia Fordham has argued; they are being positioned to accept subject-positions that are the source of power for a white, dominant culture (57–58). The ability of white, male, Eurocentric culture to normalize and universalize its own interests works so well, in this case, that Fordham underemphasizes how whiteness as a cultural and historical construction, as a site of dominant narratives, exercises the form of authority which prevents black students from speaking through their own memories, histories, and experiences. Delpit and Fordham are right in attempting to focus on issues of powerlessness as they relate to pedagogy and race, but they both obscure this relation by not illuminating more clearly how power works in this society within the schools to secure and conceal various forms of racism and subjugation. Power is multifaceted and we need a better understanding of how it works not simply as a force for oppression but also as a basis for resistance and self and social empowerment. Educators need to fashion a critical and democratic notion of authority, one that decenters essentialist claims to power while simultaneously fighting for relations of authority and power that allow many voices to speak so as to initiate students into a culture that multiplies rather than restricts democratic practices and social relations as part of a wider struggle for democratic public life.

Fifth, educators need to analyze racism not only as a structural and ideological force, but also in the diverse and historically specific ways in which it emerges. This is particularly true of the most recent and newest expressions of racism developing in the United States and abroad among youth, in popular culture, and in its resurgence in the highest reaches of the American government. This also suggests that any notion of anti-racist pedagogy must arise out of specific settings and contexts. Such a pedagogy must allow its own character to be defined, in part, by the historically specific and contextual boundaries in which it emerges. At the same time, such a pedagogy must disavow all claims to scientific method or for that matter to any objective or transhistorical claims. As a political practice, an anti-racist pedagogy has to be constructed not on the basis of essentialist or universal claims but on the concreteness of its specific encounters, struggles, and engagements. Roger Simon outlines some of the issues involved here in his discussion of critical pedagogy:

> Such a form of educational work is at root contextual and conditional. A critical pedagogy can only be concretely discussed from within a particular "point of practice"; from within a specific time and place and within a particular theme. This means doing critical pedagogy is a strategic, practical task, not a scientific one. It arises not against a background of psychological, sociological, or anthropological universals—as does much educational theory related to pedagogy—but from such questions as: "How is human possibility being diminished here?" (2)

Sixth, an anti-racist border pedagogy must redefine how the circuits of power move in a dialectical fashion among various sites of cultural production.[16] That is, we need a deeper understanding of how ideologies and other social practices which bear down on classroom relations emerge from and articulate with other spheres of social life. As educators, we need a clearer understanding of how the grounds for the production and organization of knowledge are related to forms of authority situated in political economy, the state, and other material practices. We also need to understand how circuits of power produce forms of textual authority that offer readers particular subject-positions, that is, ideological references that provide but do not rigidly determine particular views of the world.[17] In addition, educators need to explore how the readings of texts are linked to the forms of knowledge and social relations that students bring into the classroom. In other words, we need to understand in terms of function and substance those social and cultural forms outside of the classroom that produce the multiple and often contradictory subject-positions that students learn and express in their interaction with the dominant cultural capital of American schools.

Finally, central to the notion of border pedagogy are a number of important pedagogical issues regarding the role that teachers might take up in making a commitment to fight racism in their classrooms, schools, communities, and the wider society. The concept of border pedagogy also helps to locate teachers within social, political, and cultural boundaries that define and mediate in complex ways how they function as intellectuals who exercise particular forms of moral and social regulation. Border pedagogy calls attention to both the ideological and the partial as central elements in the construction of teacher discourse and practice. In part, this suggests that to the degree that teachers make the construction of their own voices, histories, and ideologies problematic they become more attentive to Otherness as a deeply political and pedagogical issue. By deconstructing the underlying principles which inform their own lives and pedagogy, educators can begin to recognize the limits underlying the partiality of their own views. They can interrogate Otherness as a set of practices and relationships which, from different vantage points and positions of power, inscribe their own identity rather than unproblematically point to individuals or groups that appear remote and removed from a sense of place, identity, and authority that secures their own identity, comfort, and authority, especially if one is white, male, and middle-class. Such a recognition offers the promise of allowing teachers to restructure their pedagogical relations in order to engage in an open and critical fashion fundamental questions about the knowledge they teach, how it relates to students' lives, how students can engage with such knowledge, and how such practices actually relate to empowering both teachers and students.

Within dominant models of pedagogy, teachers are often silenced through a refusal or inability to problematize for students the values that inform how they teach and engage the multifaceted relationship between knowledge and power. Without the benefit of dialogue and understanding of the partiality of their own beliefs, they are cut off from any understanding of the effects their pedagogies have on students. In effect, their infatuation with certainty and control serves to limit the possibilities inherent in their own voices and visions. In this case, dominant pedagogy serves not only to disable students, but teachers as well. In short, teachers need to take up a pedagogy that provides a more dialectical understanding of their own politics and values; they need to break down pedagogical boundaries that silence them in the name of methodological rigor or pedagogical absolutes; more importantly, they need to develop a power-sensitive discourse that allows them to open up their interactions with the discourses of various Others so that their classrooms can engage rather than negate the multiple positions and experiences that allow teachers and students to speak in and with many complex and different voices.

What border pedagogy makes undeniable is the relational nature of one's own politics and personal investments. But at the same time, border pedagogy emphasizes the primacy of a politics in which teachers assert rather than retreat from the pedagogies they utilize in dealing with the various differences represented by the students who come into their classes. For example, it is not enough for teachers merely to affirm uncritically their students' histories, experiences, and stories. To take student voices at face value is to run the risk of idealizing and romanticizing them. It is equally important for teachers to help students find a language for critically examining the historically and socially constructed forms by which they live. Such a process involves more than allowing students to speak from their own histories and social formations; it also raises questions about how teachers use power to cross over borders that are culturally strange and alien to them.

At issue here is not a patronizing notion of understanding the Other, but a sense of how the self is implicated in the construction of Otherness, how exercising critical attention to such a relationship might allow educators to move out of the center of the dominant culture to its margins in order to analyze critically the political, social, and cultural lineaments of their own values and voices as viewed from different ideological and cultural spaces. It is important for teachers to understand both how they wield power and authority and how particular forms of authority are sedimented in the construction of their own needs along with the limited subject-positions offered them in schools. Border pedagogy is not about engaging just the positionality of our students but the nature of our own identities as they have and are emerging within and between various circuits of power. If students are going to learn how to take risks, to develop a healthy skepticism toward all master narratives, to recognize the power relations that offer them the opportunity to speak in particular ways, and to be willing to confront critically their role as critical citizens who can animate a democratic culture, they need to see such behavior demonstrated in the social practices and subject-positions that teachers live out and not merely propose.

If an anti-racist pedagogy is to have any meaning as a force for creating a democratic society, teachers and students must be given the opportunity to put into effect what they learn outside of the school. In other words, they must be given the opportunity to engage in anti-racist struggles in their effort to link schooling to real life, ethical discourse to political action, and classroom relations to a broader notion of cultural politics. The school curriculum should make anti-racist pedagogies central to the task of educating students to animate a wider and more critically engaged public culture; it should not merely allow them to take risks but also to push against the boundaries of an oppressive social order. Such projects can be used to address the relevance of the school curriculum and its role as a significant public force for linking learning and social justice to the daily institutional and cultural traditions of society and reshaping them in the process. All schools should have teachers and students participate in anti-racist curricula that in some way link up with projects in the wider society. This approach redefines not only teacher authority and student responsibility, but places the school as a major force in the struggle for social, economic, and cultural justice. In this case, a post-colonial pedagogy points to challenging not only the oppressive boundaries of racism, but all of those barriers that undermine and subvert the construction of a democratic society.

In short, border pedagogy is grounded in a politics of difference that moves beyond the colonizing discourse of the "common culture" that is so central to conservative discourses; at the same time, it rejects the appeal to a facile pluralism that is at the heart of liberal approaches to multiculturalism. Neither approach engages how the legacy of colonialism is produced and rewritten in the texts, institutions, and social practices that contextualize relations between and within the margins of American society. A border pedagogy formed in post-colonial ruptures and democratic possibilities must rethink the relationship between power and culture. This suggests making the pedagogical more political and the political more pedagogical. This means that cultural workers and educators need to work to provide the conditions for students and others to develop the knowledge and skills that enable them as collective agents to recognize not only their own historical locations and subject-positions, but also to shape history within rather than outside of a political imaginary in which differences are both affirmed and transformed as part of a broader struggle for a radical, cultural democracy.

Notes

1. This section draws on a number of ideas in Giroux (1991).

2. In both cases, right-wing critics ignored the contexts of the photographs in question and selectively read them as an attack on the issues of moral decency and Christianity. Serrano's photograph is especially relevant here since it was accompanied by a text in which he points out that the photo represents a critique of evangelical media ministers who debase (piss on) the figure of Christ through the processes of commodification and sensationalism. In effect, Serrano's work celebrated rather than debased Christianity. Serrano's text was generally ignored by the major mass media.

3. For two excellent commentaries on this issue, see Wallis and Mattick.

4. Of course the most prominent group that has taken up this position is the National Association of Scholars, bankrolled by corporate foundations such as Coors, Mobil, Smith-Richardson, Earhart, and Scaife and Olin. For an analysis which historically contextualizes the various groups that set the ideological and political groundwork for the emergence of the NAS, see Diamond and Soley. Some of the most public spokespersons for this position include Bloom, Hirsch, and Ravitch.

5. The outright lies, distortions, and misrepresentations produced by conservatives such as D'Souza, the National Association of Scholars, and other George Will "wannabees" have been well documented. For instance, see Beers's account of the alleged disruption by left-wing students at the State University of New York at Binghamton on 14 March 1991 (35, 64). Furthermore, the conservative claim that 1960s radicals have taken over university faculty is a rather egregious overstatement considering that a "recent poll of 35,478 professors at 392 institutions nationwide, conducted by the Higher Education Research Institute at UCLA" indicated that only "4.9 percent of all college instructors rate themselves 'far left,' while the vast majority, 94.8 percent, call themselves 'liberal,' (38.8 percent), 'moderate' (40.2 percent), or 'conservative' (17.8 percent)" (Duster 63). Conservative academic journals, such as the *Partisan Review*, have attempted to interrogate these issues concerning the canon, radical social theory, etc., with a bit more care, but the endless claims to objectivity, timeless truths, and universal standards invoked in the defense of conservative positions are not only ideological but politically self-serving. See especially the special issue of the *Partisan Review* (1991) on the changing culture of the university.

6. Outside of the arts community, the Left has not responded with the degree of urgency that is warranted to the attacks on multiculturalism waged by the Right. Some exceptions include Jay, Mohanty, Giroux and Trend, Aronowitz

and Giroux, Giroux, Erickson, Hancock, and Martínez. For an exceptional text that addresses the relationship between multiculturalism and the politics of representation, see Lippard.

7. In his own attack on multiculturalism, Roger Kimball cites and elaborates Ravitch's notion of common culture as a basis for dismissing any criticism of Western culture. He is worth quoting at length:

> Implicit in the politicizing mandate of multiculturalism is an attack on the idea of common culture, the idea that, despite our many differences, we hold in common an intellectual, artistic, and moral legacy, descending largely from the Greeks and the Bible, supplemented and modified over centuries by innumerable contributions from diverse hands and peoples. It is this legacy that has given us our science, our political institutions, and the monuments of artistic and cultural achievement that define us as a civilization. Indeed, it is this legacy, insofar as we live up to it, that preserves us from chaos and barbarism. And it is precisely this legacy that the multiculturalist wishes to dispense with. ("Postscript" 6)

8. For examples of the liberal approach to multiculturalism in education, see Jeffcoate; Glazer and Moynihan, *Beyond the Melting Pot* and *Ethnicity*; Banks; and Treuba. For a radical critique of conservative and liberal approaches to multiculturalism, see Trend; McCarthy, esp. ch. 3; Sleeter; Jon Young; Simonson and Walker; Wallace, esp. chs. 21 and 22; and Sivandan, esp. chs. 3–5.

9. For an elaboration of this position, see Spivak, "The Making of Americans," and West, "Minority Discourse."

10. On the radical imperative to engage whiteness as a central racial category in the construction of moral power and political/cultural domination, see Dyer, West ("New Cultural Politics" 105), and Ferguson.

11. The chief proponent of this position is Graff. As Bruce Henricksen points out, Graff does not sufficiently "contextualize his model as a class and power-allocating activity"; nor does he move beyond the relativism of a dialogic model in which there is "no firm ground, nothing to believe in but the conversation itself" (31, 35).

12. The literature on anti-colonialism and post-colonialism is far too vast to cite here, but it would include some of the following: Fanon, *The Wretched of the Earth* and *Black Skin, White Masks*, Nkrumah; Memmi; Freire; Ngugi Wa Thiong'O; JanMohamed, "The Economy of Manichean Allegory"; Carew; Said; Guha and Spivak; Clifford; Ashcroft, Griffiths, and Tiffin; Adams; Bhabha, *Nation and Narration*, Spivak, *The Post-Colonial Critic*; Adam and Tiffin; Torgovnick; and Robert Young.

13. For an excellent discussion of these issues as they specifically relate to post-colonial theory, see Parry; JanMohamed, *Manichean Aesthetics*; and Spivak, *The Post-Colonial Critic*. For a particularly revealing demonstration of how polarizing binarisms can undermine a text that calls for openness, partiality, and multiple perspectives, see Lather, esp. 41–49. For an example of how the legacy of colonialism has influenced the ways in which North American scholars treat the work of Paulo Freire, see Giroux, "Paulo Freire."

14. This theme is developed in Anzaldúa; Rosaldo; and JanMohamed, "Worldliness."

15. I have taken up this issue in *Schooling*, esp. chs. 2 and 3; also see two excellent pieces on authority and pedagogy by Bizzell, "Classroom" and

"Power." For an insightful analysis of the dialectics of authority and its importance to feminist and radical social practice, see Jones.

16. For thorough analyses of the discourse of cultural politics and its relationship to various circuits of power, see Johnson and Grossberg.

17. These issues are taken up in Belsey; Bennett; and Aronowitz and Giroux.

Works Cited

Adam, Ian, and Helen Tiffin, eds. *Past the Last Post: Theorizing Post-Colonialism and Post-Modernism.* Calgary: U of Calgary P, 1990.

Adams, Howard. *Prison of Grass: Canada From a Native Point of View.* Saskatoon: Fifth House, 1989.

Anzaldúa, Gloria. *Borderlands/La Frontera: The New Mestiza.* San Francisco: Spinsters/Aunt Lute, 1987.

Aronowitz, Stanley, and Henry A. Giroux. *Postmodern Education: Politics, Culture, and Social Criticism.* Minneapolis: U of Minnesota P, 1991.

Ashcroft, Bill, Gareth Griffiths, and Helen Tiffin, eds. *The Empire Writes Back: Theory and Practice in Post-Colonial Literatures.* New York: Routledge, 1989.

Banks, James. *Multiethnic Education.* 2nd ed. Boston: Allyn, 1988.

Beers, David. "P.C.? B.S." *Mother Jones* Sept.–Oct. 1991: 34 + .

Belsey, Catherine. *Critical Practice.* New York: Methuen, 1980.

Bennett, Tony. "Texts in History: The Determinations of Readings and Their Texts." *Post-Structuralism and the Question of History.* Ed. Derek Atridge, Geoff Bennington, and Robert Young. New York: Cambridge UP, 1987. 63–81.

Bhabha, Homi K. "The Commitment to Theory." *Social Formations* 5 (1988): 5–22.

Bizzell, Patricia. "Classroom Authority and Critical Pedagogy." *American Literary History* (forthcoming).

——. "Power, Authority, and Critical Pedagogy." *Journal of Basic Writing* (forthcoming).

Bloom, Allan. *The Closing of the American Mind: How Higher Education Has Failed Democracy and the Souls of Today's Students.* New York: Simon, 1987.

Carby, Hazel. "The Canon: Civil War and Reconstruction." *Michigan Quarterly Review* 28.1 (1989): 35–43.

Carew, Jan. *Fulcrums of Change.* Trenton: Africa World, 1988.

Clark, Suzanne. "Discipline and Resistance: The Subjects of Writing and the Discourses of Instruction." *College Literature* 18.2 (June 1991): 119–34.

Clifford, James. *The Predicament of Culture: Twentieth-Century Ethnography, Literature, and Art.* Cambridge: Harvard UP, 1988.

Delpit, Lisa. "The Silenced Dialogue: Power and Pedagogy in Educating Other People's Children." *Harvard Educational Review* 58.3 (1988): 280–98.

Diamond, Sara. "Readin', Writin' and Repressin'." *Z Magazine* Feb. 1991: 45–48.

Dowd, Maureen. "Jesse Helms Takes No-Lose Position on Art." *New York Times* 28 July 1989: A1 + .

D'Souza, Dinesh. *Illiberal Education: The Politics of Race and Sex on Campus.* New York: Free, 1991.

——. "The Visigoths in Tweed." *Forbes* 147.7 (1 April 1991): 81–86.

Duster, Troy. "They're Taking Over!" *Mother Jones* Sept.–Oct. 1991: 30 + .

Dyer, Richard. "White." *Screen* 29.4 (1988): 44–64.

Erickson, Peter. "Rather than Reject a Common Culture, Multiculturalism Advocates a More Complicated Route by Which to Achieve It." *Chronicle of Higher Education* 26 June 1991: B3.

Fanon, Frantz. *Black Skin, White Masks.* New York: Grove, 1967.

———. *The Wretched of the Earth.* New York: Grove, 1963.

Ferguson, Russell. "Introduction: Invisible Center." *Out There: Marginalization and Contemporary Culture.* Ed. Russell Ferguson, et al. Cambridge: MIT P, 1991. 9–14.

Fordham, Signithia. "Racelessness as a Factor in Black Students' School Success: Pragmatic Strategy or Pyrrhic Victory?" *Harvard Educational Review* 58.3 (1988): 54–82.

Fraser, Laura. "The Tyranny of the Media Correct: The Assault on the 'New McCarthyism.'" *Extra* 4.4 (1991): 6–8.

Freire, Paulo. *Pedagogy of the Oppressed.* Trans. Myria Bergman Ramos. New York: Seabury, 1973.

Giroux, Henry A. *Border Crossings: Cultural Workers and the Politics of Education.* New York: Routledge, 1992.

———. "Democracy and the Discourse of Cultural Difference: Towards a Politics of Border Pedagogy." *British Journal of Sociology of Education* 12.4 (1991): 501–20.

———. "Paulo Freire and the Politics of Post-Colonialism." *Journal of Advanced Composition* (forthcoming).

———. *Schooling and the Struggle for Public Life.* Minneapolis: U of Minnesota P, 1988.

Giroux, Henry A., and David Trend. "Cultural Workers, Pedagogy, and the Politics of Difference: Beyond Cultural Conservatism." *Cultural Studies* (forthcoming).

Glazer, Nathan, and Daniel Patrick Moynihan. *Beyond the Melting Pot.* Cambridge: Harvard UP, 1963.

———, eds. *Ethnicity: Theory and Experience.* Cambridge: Harvard UP, 1975.

Graff, Gerald. "Teach the Conflicts." *South Atlantic Quarterly* 89.1 (1990): 51–68.

Grossberg, Lawrence. *We Gotta Get Out of This Place: Popular Conservatism and Postmodern Culture.* New York: Routledge (forthcoming).

Guha, Rinajit, and Gayatri Spivak, eds. *Selected Subaltern Studies.* New York: Oxford UP, 1988.

Hall, Stuart. "Teaching Race." *The School in Multicultural Society.* Ed. Alan Jones and Robert Jeffcoate. London: Harper, 1981. 58–69.

Hancock, LynNell. "Whose America Is This, Anyway?" *Rethinking Schools* May–June 1991: 3–4.

Hannan, Andrew. "Racism, Politics, and the Curriculum," *British Journal of Sociology of Education* 8.2 (1987): 119–32.

Henricksen, Bruce. "Teaching Against the Grain." *Reorientations: Critical Theories and Pedagogies.* Ed. Bruce Henricksen and Thais E. Morgan. Urbana: U of Illinois P, 1990. 28–39.

Hicks, D. Emily. "Deterritorialization and Border Writing." *Ethics/Aesthetics: Post-Modern Positions.* Ed. Robert Merrill. Washington: Maisonneuve, 1988. 47–58.

Hirsch, E. D., Jr. *Cultural Literacy: What Every American Needs to Know.* Boston: Houghton, 1987.

Hutcheon, Linda. "Circling the Downspout of Empire." *Past the Last Post: The-*

orizing Post-Colonialism and Post-Modernism. Ed. Ian Adam and Helen Tiffin. Calgary: U of Calgary P, 1990. 167–89.

JanMohamed, Abdul. "The Economy of Manichean Allegory: The Function of Racial Difference in Colonialist Literature." *Critical Inquiry* 12.1 (1985): 59–87.

———. *Manichean Aesthetics: The Politics of Literature in Colonial Africa.* Amherst: U of Massachusetts P, 1983.

———. "Worldliness-without-World, Homelessness-as-Home: Toward a Definition of the Border Intellectual." Unpublished ms.

Jay, Gregory. "The End of 'American' Literature: Toward a Multicultural Practice." *College English* 53.3 (1991): 264–81.

Jeffcoate, Robert. *Positive Images: Towards a Multicultural Curriculum.* London: Writers and Readers Cooperative, 1979.

Johnson, Richard. "What is Cultural Studies Anyway?" *Social Text* 16 (Winter 1986–87): 38–80.

Jones, Kathleen B. "The Trouble with Authority." *Difference* 3.1 (1991): 104–27.

Joselit, David. "Living on the Border." *Art in America* 77 (1989): 121–28.

Julien, Isaac, and Kobena Mercer. "Introduction: De Margin and De Centre." *Screen* 8.2 (1988): 2–10.

Kearney, Richard. *The Wake of the Imagination.* Minneapolis: U of Minnesota P, 1988.

Kimball, Roger. *Tenured Radicals: How Politics Has Corrupted Higher Education.* New York: Harper, 1990.

———. "*Tenured Radicals*: A Postscript." *New Criterion* (Jan. 1991): 4–13.

Laclau, Ernesto, and Chantal Mouffe. *Hegemony and Socialist Strategy.* London: Verso, 1985.

Lather, Patti. *Getting Smart.* New York: Routledge, 1991.

Lippard, Lucy. *Mixed Blessings: New Art in a Multicultural Society.* New York: Pantheon, 1990.

Martínez, Elizabeth. "Willie Horton's Gonna Get Your Alma Mater." *Z Magazine* July–Aug. 1991: 126–30.

Mattick, Paul, Jr. "Arts and the State." *Nation* 1 Oct. 1990: 348–58.

McCarthy, Cameron. *Race and Curriculum: Social Inequality and the Theories and Politics of Difference in Contemporary Research on Schooling.* New York: Falmer, 1991.

Memmi, Albert. *The Colonizer and the Colonized.* Boston: Beacon, 1965.

Mohanty, Chandra T. "On Race and Voice: Challenges for Liberal Education in the 1990s." *Cultural Critique* 14 (Winter 1989–90): 179–208.

Morrison, Toni. "Unspeakable Things Unspoken: The Afro-American Presence in American Literature." *Michigan Quarterly Review* 28.1 (1989): 1–34.

Ngugi Wa Thiong'O. *Decolonizing the Mind.* Portsmouth, Eng.: Heinemann, 1966.

Nkrumah, Kwame. *Consciencism.* New York: Monthly Review, 1964.

Parry, Benita. "Problems in Current Theories of Colonial Discourse." *Oxford Literary Review* 9.1–2 (1989): 205–25.

Partisan Review. A Special Issue. "The Changing Culture of the University." 2 (1991).

Ravitch, Diane. "Diversity and Democracy: Multicultural Education in America." *American Educator* (Spring 1990): 16+.

———. "Multiculturalism: E Pluribus Plures." *The American Scholar* 59.3 (1990): 337–54.

Rosaldo, Renato. *Culture and Truth*. Boston: Beacon, 1989.

Said, Edward W. *Orientalism*. New York: Vintage, 1986.

Siegel, Fred. "The Cult of Multiculturalism." *New Republic* 18 Feb. 1991: 35+.

Simon, Roger I. "For a Pedagogy of Possibility." *Critical Pedagogy Networker* 1.1 (1981): 1–4.

Simonson, Rick, and Scott Walker, eds. *Multicultural Literacy: Opening the American Mind*. Saint Paul: Graywolf, 1988.

Sivandan, A. *Communities of Resistance*. London: Verso, 1991.

Sleeter, Christene, ed. *Empowerment Through Multicultural Education*. Albany: SUNY P, 1981.

Soley, Lawrence. "Right Thinking Conservative Think Tanks." *Dissent* (Summer 1991): 418–20.

Spivak, Gayatri C. "The Making of Americans, the Teaching of English, and the Future of Cultural Studies." *New Literary History* 21.1 (Autumn 1990): 781–98.

———. *The Post-Colonial Critic: Interviews, Strategies, Dialogues*, ed. Sarah Harasym. New York: Routledge, 1990.

Tiffin, Helen. "Post-Colonialism, Post-Modernism, and the Rehabilitation of Post-Colonial History." *Journal of Commonwealth Literature* 23.1 (1988): 169–81.

Torgovnick, Marianna. *Gone Primitive: Savage Intellects, Modern Lives*. Chicago: U of Chicago P, 1990.

Trend, David. *Cultural Pedagogy: Art/Education/Politics*. New York: Bergin, 1992.

Treuba, H. "Culturally Based Explanations of Minority Students' Academic Achievement." *Anthropology and Education Quarterly* 19 (1988): 270–81.

Vance, Carol. "Misunderstanding Obscenity." *Art in America* 78 (1990): 49–55.

Wallace, Michele. *Invisibility Blues: From Pop to Theory*. London: Verso, 1990.

Wallis, Brian. "Bush's Compromise: A New Form of Censorship." *Art in America* 78 (1990): 57–63.

West, Cornel. "Black Culture and Postmodernism." *Remaking History*. Ed. Barbara Kruger and Phil Mariani. Seattle: Bay, 1989. 87–96.

———. "Minority Discourse and the Pitfalls of Canon Formation." *Yale Journal of Criticism* 1.1 (1987): 193–201.

———. "The New Cultural Politics of Difference." *October* 53 (1990): 93–109.

Young, Jon, ed. *Breaking the Mosaic: Ethnic Identities in Canadian Schooling*. Toronto: Garamond, 1987.

Young, Robert. *White Mythologies: Writing History and the West*. New York: Routledge, 1990.

Yudice. George. "For a Practical Aesthetics." *Social Text* 25–26 (1990): 129–45.

CHICAGO

An Invitation to Reflexive Sociology

Pierre Bourdieu and Loïc J. D. Wacquant

The first and only comprehensive introduction to, and overview of, the work of Pierre Bourdieu. Systematic and accessible, this book is the ideal entree into the core of his wide-ranging oeuvre.

**Paper $13.95 (est.) 336 pages (est.)
Library cloth edition $38.95 (est.)**

Make Room for TV

Television and the Family Ideal in Postwar America

Lynn Spigel

Combining an analysis of the growth of electronic culture with a social history of family life during the postwar era, *Make Room for TV* provides a fascinating account of how television became a medium for so many of American society's hopes and fears.

**Paper $15.95 288 pages
Library cloth edition $42.00**

Forests

The Shadow of Civilization

Robert Pogue Harrison

A richly allusive account of how Western civilization cleared its space in the midst of forests — and found in the woods a stage for the shaping of its cultural imagination.

"Harrison writes with a passionate desire to see more intelligent, more ethical, more farseeing treatment of the earth's steadily dwindling forests. . . . There is a fine spirit animating this book, although one must confess that the ecological message is quite terrifying." — Yves Bonnefoy
Cloth $24.95 304 pages 8 halftones

THE UNIVERSITY OF CHICAGO PRESS

5801 S. Ellis Ave., Chicago, IL 60637

"The Aesthetic Ideology" as Ideology; or, What Does It Mean to Aestheticize Politics?

Martin Jay

In 1930, Walter Benjamin reviewed a collection of essays edited by the conservative revolutionary Ernst Jünger and entitled *War and Warrior*. Noting its contributors' avid romanticization of the technology of death and the total mobilization of the masses, he warned that it was "nothing other than an uninhibited translation of the principles of *l'art pour l'art* to war itself" (122). Six years later, in the concluding reflections of his celebrated essay "The Work of Art in the Era of Mechanical Reproduction," Benjamin widened the scope of his analysis beyond war to politics in general. Fascism, he charged, meant the aestheticization of politics, the deadly consummation of *l'art pour l'art*'s credo *"Fiat ars-pereat mundus"* (244).

Like much else in Benjamin's remarkable corpus, the reception and dissemination of these ideas was delayed for a generation or so after his suicide in 1940. By then his remedy—the politicization of art by Communism in the 1936 piece,[1] the transformation of war into a civil war between classes in the earlier review—was forgotten by all but his most militant Marxist interpreters. But the fateful link between aesthetics and politics was eagerly seized on in many quarters as an invaluable explanation for the seductive fascination of fascism.

In such works as Bill Kinser and Neil Kleinman's *The Dream That Was No More a Dream,* Nazism was explained by the fact that "German consciousness treated its own reality—developed and lived its history—as though it were a work of art. It was a culture committed to its aesthetic imagination" (7). Hitler's personal history as an artist *manqué* was recalled by commentators like J. P. Stern, who saw the legacy of Nietzsche's conflation of artistic form-giving and political will in Nazism (45).[2] The confusion between reality and fantasy in films like Leni Riefenstahl's *Triumph of the Will* was taken as emblematic of the illusory spectacle at the heart of fascist politics by critics like Susan Sontag.[3] Similar inclinations were discerned in French fascism by Alice Yaeger Kaplan, who successfully solicited the admission from one of her subjects, the film historian Maurice Bardèche, "there is, if you like, a link between aestheticism and fascism. We were probably mistaken to connect aesthetics and politics, which are not the same thing" (184). Even the contemporary representation of the fascist past has been accused of being overly aestheticized, albeit in the sense of kitsch art, by Saul Friedländer.[4]

As a result of these and similar analyses, the connection between "the aestheticization of politics" and fascism has become firmly established. In fact, it has become such a commonplace that some of its affective power has wandered from the historians' treatment of the issue into a related, but not identical discussion carried on mainly by literary critics over what is called "the aesthetic ideology." The term was coined by Paul de Man, whose interest in ideology critique seems to have been increasing shortly before his death in 1983.[5] The concept has been taken up by his defenders in the controversy that followed the disclosures of his wartime journalism, for reasons to be examined shortly.[6] And it has also appeared in the recent writings of the Marxist critics David Lloyd and Terry Eagleton, whose agenda is very different from that of most of de Man's supporters.[7]

The displacement of the discussion from historical to literary critical circles has involved, however, a significant, but not always acknowledged reevaluation of the aesthetics whose imposition on the political is damned as pernicious. The change has also meant a concomitant reattribution of the original culprits allegedly responsible for the crime. In what follows, I want to explore the implications of the shift and ask if the critique of "the aesthetic ideology" in certain of its guises may itself rest on mystifications, which allow us to call it ideological in its turn.

Any discussion of the aestheticization of politics must begin by identifying the normative notion of the aesthetic it presupposes. For unless we specify what is meant by this notoriously ambiguous term, it is impossible to understand why its extension to the realm of the political is seen as problematic. Although a thorough review of the different uses in the literature cited above is beyond the scope of this essay, certain significant alternatives can be singled out for scrutiny.

As Benjamin's own remarks demonstrate, one salient use derives from the *l'art pour l'art* tradition of differentiating a realm called art from those of other human pursuits, cognitive, religious, ethical, economic, or whatever. Here the content of that realm apart—often, but not always, identified with something known as beauty—is less important than its claim to absolute autonomous and autotelic self-referentiality. For the obverse of this claim is the exclusion of ethical, instrumental, religious, etc. considerations from the realm of art.

A politics aestheticized in this sense will be equally indifferent to such extra-artistic claims, having as its only criterion of value aesthetic worth. Moreover, the definition of that worth implied by such a rigid differentiation usually suppresses those aspects of the aesthetic, such as sensuous enjoyment and bodily pleasure, which link art and mundane existence; instead, formal considerations outweigh "sentimental" ones. On a visit to Paris in 1891, Oscar Wilde was reported to have said: "When Benvenuto Cellini crucified a living man to study the play of muscles in his death agony, a pope was right to grant him absolution. What is the death of a vague individual if it enables an immortal word to blossom and to create, in Keats' words, an eternal source of ecstasy?" (Raynaud 397). Another classical expression of this attitude appeared in the notorious response of the Symbolist poet Laurent Tailhade to a deadly anarchist bomb thrown into the French Chamber of Deputies in 1893: "What do the victims mat-

ter if the gesture is beautiful?"[8] Not long after, F. T. Marinetti's
Futurist Manifesto echoed the same sentiments in glorifying, along
with militarism, anarchistic destruction, and contempt for
women, "the beautiful ideas which kill" (182). Moving beyond the
Futurists' flatulent rhetoric, Mussolini's son-in-law and foreign
minister Ciano would confirm the practical results of its imple-
mentation when he famously compared the bombs exploding
among fleeing Ethiopians in 1936 to flowers bursting into bloom.

The aestheticization of politics in these cases repels not
merely because of the grotesque impropriety of applying criteria
of beauty to the deaths of human beings, but also because of the
chilling way in which nonaesthetic criteria are deliberately and
provocatively excluded from consideration. When restricted to a
rigorously differentiated realm of art, such antiaffective, formal-
ist coldness may have its justifications; indeed, a great deal of
modern art would be hard to appreciate without it. But when then
extended to politics through a gesture of imperial dedifferentia-
tion, the results are highly problematic. For the disinterestedness
that is normally associated with the aesthetic seems precisely what
is so radically inappropriate in the case of that most basic of human interests, the preservation of life. Benjamin's bitter observation that mankind's "self-alienation has reached such a degree
that it can experience its own destruction as an aesthetic pleasure
of the first order" ("Work of Art" 244) vividly expresses the dis-
gust aroused by this callous apotheosis of art over life.

A related, but somewhat different use of the term *aesthetic*
derives from the elitist implications of the artist who expresses his
or, far more rarely, her will through the shaping of unformed
matter. A characteristic expression of this use appeared in
Nietzsche's claim in *The Genealogy of Morals* that the first politicians
were born rulers "whose work is an instinctive imposing of forms.
They are the most spontaneous, most unconscious artists that
exist. . . . [T]hese men know nothing of guilt, responsibility, consideration. They are actuated by the terrible egotism of the artist
. . ." (220). The fascist adoption of this stance is plainly evident in
Mussolini's boast that "when the masses are like wax in my hands,
or when I mingle with them and am almost crushed by them, I
feel myself to be a part of them. All the same there persists in me
a certain feeling of aversion, like that which the modeler feels for

the clay he is molding. Does not the sculptor sometimes smash his block of marble into fragments because he cannot shape it into the vision he has conceived?" (Smith 82). What makes this version of aestheticized politics so objectionable is its reduction of an active public to the passive "masses," which is then turned into pliable material for the triumph of the artist/politician's will.

Still another use draws on the perennial battle between the image and the word. Insofar as the aesthetic is identified with the seductive power of images, whose appeal to mute sensual pleasure seems to undercut rational deliberation, the aestheticization of politics in this sense means the victory of the spectacle over the public sphere. Russell Berman, in his foreword to Alice Yaeger Kaplan, faults the fascist critics Robert Brasillach and Maurice Bardèche for praising silent films over talkies and compares their celebration of the cinema with Benjamin's:

> The fascist film theoreticians contrast the organic—and organizing!—homogeneity of the silent image with the introduction of speech that dissolves the nation through individuation and criticism. . . . Bardèche and Brasillach value the pure image, popularized aestheticism, in order to produce the fascist folk, while the iconoclast Benjamin applauds the shattering of the image in montage in order to call the masses (for him at this point the communist masses) to language. (xix)[9]

Taking seriously the religious underpinnings of the taboo on images, he further claims that "Benjamin's account of an aestheticization of politics consequently appears as a civilizational regression to graven images of the deity, as in Riefenstahl's representation of Hitler's descent from the clouds in *Triumph of the Will*" (xxi). In short, politics has to be saved from its reduction to spellbinding spectacle and phantasmagoric illusion in order to allow a more rational discourse to fill the public space now threatened with extinction by images and simulacra of reality.

In this cluster of uses, the aesthetic is variously identified with irrationality, illusion, fantasy, myth, sensual seduction, the imposition of will, and inhumane indifference to ethical, religious, or cognitive considerations. If any pedigree is assumed, it is found in the writings of Nietzsche in certain of his moods and in

aesthetic modernists like Tailhade or Marinetti. Scarcely beneath
the surface is an appreciation of the links between decadence,
aestheticism, and elitism, which suggest that the seedbed of fascism was fin-de-siècle bourgeois culture in crisis. We are, in other
words, very much in the world whose decline was so powerfully
chartered by Thomas Mann from *Death in Venice* through "Mario
the Magician" to *Doctor Faustus.*

In the case of the "aesthetic ideology" criticized by de Man,
Eagleton, and other contemporary literary critics, the target is
constructed, however, very differently. The aesthetic in question
is not understood as the opposite of reason, but rather as its
completion, not as the expression of an irrational will, but as the
sensual version of a higher, more comprehensive notion of rationality, not as the wordless spectacle of images, but as the realization of a literary absolute. In short, it is an aesthetic that is understood to be the culmination of Idealist philosophy, or perhaps
even Western metaphysics as a whole, and not its abstract negation. Bourgeois culture at its height rather than at its moment of
seeming decay is thus taken as the point of departure for aestheticized politics.

An early version of this argument appeared in *The Literary
Absolute* by the French theorists Philippe Lacoue-Labarthe and
Jean-Luc Nancy, published in 1978 and translated into English a
decade later.[10] Discussing the Jena Romantics' redemptive notion
of art, they claim that it represents the displacement of Platonic
eidetics, the search for essential forms, into a new realm, which
they call "eidaesthetics." This quasi-religious metaphysics of art is
responsible for an absolute notion of literature, whose task is the
overcoming of differences, contradictions, and disharmonies.
Although implicitly challenged by a counterimpulse they call
"romantic equivocity," the telos of eidaesthetics is the closure
of a complete work produced by an omnipotent subject, who
realizes the Idea in sensual form. Jena Romanticism's desire for
poetic perfection is thus derived from an ultimately metaphysical project, which has political implications as well. The
Romantic fascination with the fragment, they contend, is
premised on the possibility of an "ideal politics . . . an organic
politics" (44–45). As Europe's first self-conscious intellectual
avant-garde, the Jena Romantics thus set the agenda for the

conflation of art and politics pursued by so many later intellectuals.

What we might call the "eidaestheticization of politics" is even more explicit in one of the main instigators of the aesthetic ideology as de Man describes it, Friedrich Schiller. According to de Man, "the aesthetic, as is clear from Schiller's formulation [from a passage in *Letters on the Aesthetic Education of Mankind*], is primarily a social and political model, ethically grounded in an assumedly Kantian notion of freedom" ("Aesthetic Formalization" 264).[11] Its effect on writers like Heinrich von Kleist, whose *Über das Marionettentheater* de Man reads with alarm, was pernicious. The dance of Kleist's puppets, so often admired as a utopian state of grace in which purposiveness without purpose is brilliantly realized, turns out to have a very different implication. "The point is not that the dance fails and that Schiller's idyllic description of a graceful but confined freedom is aberrant," de Man darkly warns. "Aesthetic education by no means fails; it succeeds all too well, to the point of hiding the violence that makes it possible" ("Aesthetic Formalization" 289). That violence is directed against all the cultural impulses, especially those in language, which resist coerced totalization and closure.

In a later piece on "Kant and Schiller," de Man teased out the implications of this argument for fascism. Although in many ways appreciative of Kant's resistance to metaphysical closure and epistemological overreaching, de Man nonetheless identified in him the potential to sanction, however unintentionally, a sinister tradition. Citing a passage from Goebbels's novel *Michael*, which includes the claim that "politics are the plastic art of the state," he concedes that "it is a grievous misreading of Schiller's aesthetic state."[12] But he then adds, "the principle of this misreading does not essentially differ from the misreading which Schiller inflicted on his predecessor, namely Kant." In other words, for all their emancipatory intentions, Kant and even more so Schiller spawned a tradition that contained the potential to be transformed into a justification for fascism.

Lest the specific antifascist purposes of de Man's critique of the aesthetic ideology be missed, Jonathan Culler spells them out in his defense of de Man in the controversy over the wartime journalism. "Walter Benjamin called fascism the introduction of aesthetics into politics," Culler writes. "De Man's critique of the aesthetic ideology now resonates also as a critique of the fascist tendencies he had known" (780). That critique was carried out in the name of a notion of literature very different from that Lacoue-Labarthe and Nancy saw as complicitous with eidaesthetics. For de Man, it was precisely literary language's resistance to closure, transparency, harmony, and perfection that could be pitted against the aesthetic ideology. According to Culler, de Man's realization of this opposition demonstrates his rejection of his earlier collaborationist position: "The fact that de Man's wartime juvenilia had themselves on occasion exhibited an inclination to idealize the emergence of the German nation in aesthetic terms gives special pertinence to his demonstration that the most insightful literary and philosophical texts of the tradition expose the unwarranted violence required to fuse form and idea, cognition and performance" (783).

Whether or not this apology is fully convincing, it nonetheless clearly expresses one way the concept of the aesthetic ideology functions for deconstruction. Another concerns the sensual dimension of aesthetic pleasure, which we've also seen evident in the critique of images in the name of words made by Kaplan and Berman. In a telling passage in his essay on Hans Robert Jauss's "reception aesthetics," de Man claims that "the aesthetic is, by definition, a seductive notion that appeals to the pleasure principle, a eudamonic judgment that can displace and conceal values of truth and falsehood likely to be more resilient to desire than values of pleasure and pain" ("Reading and History" 64).[13] Ironically, here aesthetics is attacked not because it is formally cold and antihumane, but rather because it is human-all-too-human.

De Man's ascetic resistance to eudamonism and desire fits well with his frequent insistence that language is irreducible to perception and provides none of its easy pleasures. It also jibes nicely with his hostility to natural metaphors of organic wholeness, which, as Christopher Norris correctly notes, he saw as a major source of the aesthetic ideology (xii). By implication, an aestheticized politics would thus be seductively promising sensual pleasures, such as oneness with an alienated nature, it could never deliver (or at least so the resolutely antiutopian and austerely self-abnegating de Man thought).[14]

A similar, but less one-dimensionally negative analysis of this very dimension of the aesthetic ideology has recently been advanced by Terry Eagleton. He begins by noting the importance of the body and materiality in aesthetic discourse beginning with Alexander Baumgarten in the eighteenth century. It is not so much the realization of the Idea that is crucial as its concrete manifestation in the "feminine" register of sensuous form. Aesthetics thus expresses the need to leave behind the lofty realm of logical and ethical rigor for the rich if confusing realm of particular experience.

But despite what may seem to be progress in the detranscendentalization and demasculinization of reason, Eagleton reads the political implications of the ideology of the aesthetic with no less suspicion than de Man. It marks, he claims, "an historic shift from what we might now, in Gramscian terms, call coercion to hegemony, ruling and informing our sensuous life from within while allowing it to thrive in all its relative autonomy" (328).[15] Once again the culprit is Schiller, who was "shrewd enough to see that Kant's stark imperatives are by no means the best way of subjugating a recalcitrant material world. . . . What is needed instead is what Schiller called the 'aesthetic modulation of the psyche,' which is to say a full-blooded project of fundamental ideological construction" (329). The modern subject is thus more aesthetic than cognitive or ethical; he is the site of an internalized, but illusory reconciliation of conflicting demands, which remain frustratingly in conflict in the social world. As such, the aesthetic functions as a compensatory ideology to mask real suffering, reinforcing what the Frankfurt School used to call "the affirmative character of culture."[16]

Eagleton remains, to be sure, enough of a Marxist to interpret the aesthetic dialectically, and thus acknowledges its subversive potential. "Aesthetics are not only incipiently materialist," he writes, "they also provide, at the very heart of the Enlightenment, the most powerful available critique of bourgeois possessive individualism and appetitive egoism. . . . The aesthetic may be the language of political hegemony and an imaginary consolation for a bourgeoisie bereft of a home but it is also, in however idealist a vein, the discourse of utopian critique of the bourgeois social order" (337). Eschewing the deconstructionist assumption that all dreams of autonomous and autotelic life are recipes for totalitarianism, he lyrically concludes that Marx himself was an aesthetician: "For what the aesthetic imitates in its very glorious futility, in its pointless self-referentiality, in all its full-blooded formalism, is nothing less than human existence itself, which needs no rationale beyond its own self-delight, which is an end in itself and which will stoop to no external determination" (338).

Although Eagleton's recuperation of the aesthetic moment in Marxism may seem excessively starry-eyed, and indeed is rejected by more uncompromising Marxist critics of the aesthetic ideology like David Lloyd,[17] it nonetheless reopens the question of how unequivocally evil the link between aesthetics and politics must be. Fortunately, a new and magisterial history of the problem has just appeared, which provides ample evidence for a more nuanced judgment: Josef Chytry's *The Aesthetic State*.[18] Although he acknowledges the usefulness of Benjamin's interpretation of fascism, Chytry is at pains to disentangle the earlier advocates of aesthetic politics from their alleged fascist progeny. Rather than positing an essentially unified narrative of fateful misreadings from Schiller and Kleist up to Goebbels, as did de Man, he stresses discontinuities instead, going so far as to argue that even Richard Wagner's version of the aesthetic state should not be confused with that of twentieth-century totalitarians. Having read Benjamin's essay on the Jünger collection, he knows how important the experience of the First World War was in giving an irrationalist aesthetic gloss to mass mobilization and the violence of the new technologies. There is a difference, he implicitly suggests, between the brutality committed by Kleist's dancing marionettes and that celebrated in Jünger's "storm of steel."

After a learned prologue on Greek, Renaissance, and other antecedents, Chytry's overview of the German tradition of the aesthetic state begins with Winckelmann's mid-eighteenth-century recovery of the myth of an aesthetic Hellenic polis. He painstakingly traces its fortunes through the Weimar Humanists, Schiller, Hölderlin, Hegel, Schelling, Marx, Wagner, Nietzsche, Heidegger, and Marcuse. His account ends with an appreciation of Walter Spies, the German modernist artist who escaped in the 1920s to Bali, where he found—or helped create—a stunning realization of the "magic realism" that had been his artistic credo.

Clifford Geertz's celebrated discussion of the Balinese theater state derived from ancient Hindu-Buddhist religion serves Chytry as scholarly support for the plausibility of Spies's vision.[19]

However idealized Spies's interpretation of Bali may seem, it is clear that Balinese aesthetic politics is a far cry from Riefenstahl's *Triumph of the Will* or Ciano's callous reduction of bombed humans to blossoming flowers. Nor is it reducible to the nightmare of seductive sensuality that appears to have kept de Man restlessly tossing and turning in his bed of linguistic austerity. Chytry's book, moreover, has another lesson worth heeding by those who want to avoid hastily turning all aesthetic politics into a prolegomenon to tyranny. In his discussion of Schiller's *Letters on the Aesthetic Education of Mankind,* he tacitly contests the critical reading we have seen in de Man. Schiller, he writes, "does not identify the moral with the aesthetic. Schiller fully recognizes the dangers of untrammeled aestheticism, but he interprets these pitfalls as resulting from an *inadequate* experience of beauty. The free play of faculties characteristic of aesthetic awareness ought to lead to awareness of the power of reason and the notion of a moral law, and any equation of this free play with the moral law itself reflects a serious misunderstanding of the experience" (90).[20] In other words, rather than yearning to create a fully aestheticized form of life in which all differentiations were collapsed, Schiller was cognizant of the need to maintain certain distinctions. Rather than seek a complete totalization based on the eidaesthetic fiat of a dominating artist/politician, Schiller was sensitive to the value of preserving the nonidentical and the heterogeneous.

Another dimension of Schiller, as Chytry reads him, concerns the universalizing impulse in his notion of the aesthetic, which he connects to Winckelmann's emphasis on the Greek polis's democratic character. The aesthetic state in this sense is profoundly anti-Platonic and thus less the outcome of eidaesthetics than of the alternative Greek notion of *phronesis* or practical wisdom. "Against 'the most perfect Platonic republic' [Schiller] gives precedence to consent, and against what will be the German romantics' staple argument of individual sacrifice on behalf of the greater whole based on the metaphor of the formal artwork, he points out the basic categorical fallacy behind such arguments"

(86). According to Schiller, the lesson of learning to appreciate natural beauty is transferable to intersubjective relations; in both cases, individuals come to respect the otherness of different objects and subjects, rather than dominating them. Even if Schiller withdrew at the end of the *Letters* into a pessimistic acknowledgment of the likely realization of his ideal by only a small elite,[21] his legacy was flexible enough to sanction a variety of aesthetic states, some more sympathetic than others.

Another way to express the more benign implications of aestheticizing politics in certain of its guises concerns the thorny issue of judgment, which takes us away from producing works of art (or their political correlates) to the problem of how we appreciate and evaluate them.[22] It was, of course, in Kant's Third Critique that the link between judgment and aesthetic taste was classically forged. Aesthetic (or what he also called reflective) judgment is not cognitive (or determinant) because it does not subsume the particular under the general. Rather, it judges particulars without presupposing universal rules or a priori principles, relying instead on the ability to convince others of the rightness of the evaluation. When, for example, I call a painting beautiful, I assume my taste is more than a personal quirk, but somehow expresses a judgment warranting universal assent. I imaginatively assume the point of view of the others, who would presumably share my evaluation. Aesthetic judgment thus cannot be legitimated by being brought under a concept or derived from a universal imperative; it requires instead a kind of uncoerced consensus building that implies a communicative model of rationality as warranted assertability.

Kant's critique of judgment has been itself criticized by those hostile to the aesthetic ideology. In *The Truth in Painting*, for example, Jacques Derrida claims that its dependence on the principle of analogy (as opposed to induction and deduction) means it tacitly privileges an anthropocentric law-giver, who relentlessly reduces difference to sameness (117).[23] Like de Man, he sees the aesthetic as thus complicitous with violence. He also claims that the very attempt to restrict aesthetic judgment to autotelic works of art necessarily fails because the boundary between the work (*ergon*) and the frame (*parergon*) is always permeable, so that it is impossible to distinguish one form of judgment from another so categorically.

This last argument, however, can be turned against the critics of the aestheticization of politics, who want to maintain a rigid demarcation between the two allegedly separate spheres. If the boundary is always to be breached (although not completely effaced), what will the results look like? The negative answers have already been spelled out above. Are there more attractive alternatives? Three come to mind. The first draws on, but doesn't fully accept, the absoluteness of the distinction between the aesthetic and the literary in de Man; whereas the former tends toward closure, mastery, control and the deceptive hiding of violence, the latter means heightened sensitivity to everything in language that resists such an outcome. De Man himself drew political consequences from this contrast in one of his last essays, in which he invoked no less an authority than Marx as a model for his own work: "[M]ore than any other mode of inquiry, including economics, the linguistics of literariness is a powerful and indispensable tool in the unmasking of ideological aberrations, as well as a determining factor in accounting for their occurrence. Those who reproach literary theory for being oblivious to social and historical (that is to say ideological) reality are merely stating their fear at having their own ideological mystifications exposed by the tool they are trying to discredit. They are, in short, very poor readers of Marx's *German Ideology*" (*Resistance to Theory* 11). The implication of this argument is that a politics informed by the skills of reading literature deconstructively will be less prone to tyranny than one that is not. Although the target is the aesthetic ideology, the remedy is thus a kind of extension of certain tools of aesthetic analysis into the realm of politics. How, of course, anything beyond ideology critique, anything constructive, will emerge is not very clear.

Two more promising defenses of a benign version of the link between aesthetics and politics have drawn on the lessons of Kant's Third Critique, which critics like de Man dismissively assimilated to the totalizing, analogizing impulse they so disliked. The first of these can be found in the political musings of Jean-François Lyotard, most notably his dialogue with Jean-Loup Thébaud, *Just Gaming*.[24] For Lyotard, both politics and art, or at least postmodern art, are realms of "pagan" experimentation in which no general rule governs the resolution of conflicts. Kant's exposure of the dangers of grounding politics in transcendental illusions, of falsely believing that norms, concepts, or cognition can provide a guide to action, is for Lyotard a valuable corrective to the terroristic potential in revolutionary politics in particular. The recognition that we must choose case by case without such criteria, that the conflicts Lyotard calls *differends* cannot be brought under a single rule, means that political, like aesthetic practice, is prevented from becoming subservient to totalizing theory. Rightly understood, it also prevents us from embracing a more problematic version of aestheticized politics, which draws on the mistaken belief that the political community can be fashioned or fabricated like a work of art.[25]

For Lyotard, the result is a politics that can be called aestheticized in the sense of an aesthetics of the sublime. That is, insofar as the sublime acknowledges the unpresentability of what it tries to present, it stops short of attempting to realize theoretically inspired blueprints for political utopias. Rather than trying to instantiate Ideas of Reason or the Moral Law, it follows aesthetic judgment in arguing from analogies, which preserve differences even as they search for common ground. As David Carroll, one of Lyotard's admirers, puts it, "the sublime serves to push philosophy and politics into a reflexive, critical mode, to defer indefinitely the imposition of an end on the historical-political process" (182).

There are, to be sure, potential problems in this version of an aesthetic politics. Not all political problems, after all, allow the luxury of an indefinitely deferred solution. The sublime may be useful as a warning against violently submitting incommensurable differends to the discipline of a homogenizing theory, but it doesn't offer much in the way of positive help with the choices that have to be made. Lyotard's anxiety about introducing any criteria whatsoever into political judgment opens the door, as Eagleton has noted, for a politics of raw intuition, which fails to register the inevitable generalizing function of all language (396ff.).

A more promising version of the claim that aesthetic judgment can be a model of a politics that avoids the imposition of rational norms from without can be found in the work of Hannah Arendt.[26] Aesthetics in her sense is also not the imposition of an artist's arrogant will on a pliable matter, but rather the building of a *sensus communis* through using persuasive skills comparable to those employed in validating judgments of taste. Here the recognition that politics necessitates a choice among a limited number of imperfect alternatives, which are conditioned by history, replaces the foolhardy belief that the politician, like the creative artist, can begin with a clean canvas or a blank sheet of paper. It also means, however, acknowledging the intersubjective basis of judgment, which Lyotard's strong hostility to communication tends to obscure.[27]

As Arendt put it, "that the capacity to judge is a specifically political ability in exactly the sense denoted by Kant, namely, the ability to see things not only from one's own point of view but in the perspective of all those who happen to be present; even that judgment may be one of the fundamental abilities of man as a political being insofar as it enables him to orient himself in the public realm, in the common world—these are insights that are virtually as old as articulated political experience" ("Crisis in Culture" 221). Because judgment operates by invoking paradigmatic examples rather than general concepts, it avoids reducing all particulars to instantiations of the same principle. Instead, it involves the faculty of imagination, which allows participants in the process to put themselves in the place of others without reducing the others to versions of themselves. The "enlarged mentality," as Kant called it, that results from imagination produces a kind of intersubjective impartiality that is different from the alleged God's-eye view of the sovereign subject above the fray (Arendt, *Lectures* 42ff.). Although not transcendental, it is nonetheless more than the validation of infinite heterogeneity and the paradoxical sublime representation of the unpresentable; it mediates the general and the particular rather than pitting one against the other, as Lyotard would prefer.

Arendt's exploration of judgment is, to be sure, more suggestive than fully worked out. Even friendly commentators like Richard Bernstein have faulted her for failing to resolve the implicit tension between her stress on the virtues of action, on the one hand, and her praise of the spectatorial role of judging, on the other (237).[28] And her problematic segregation of a putatively political realm from its socioeconomic other, which has troubled many of her critics, is not resolved by her desegregating the political and the aesthetic.

But whatever their inadequacies, both Lyotard's and Arendt's thoughts on the potentially benign links between aesthetic judgment and politics serve as useful reminders that not every variant of the aestheticization of politics must lead to the same dismal end.[29] The wholesale critique of "the aesthetic ideology," to return to our initial question, can thus be itself deemed ideological if it fails to register the divergent implications of the application of the aesthetic to politics. For ironically, when it does so, it falls prey to the same homogenizing, totalizing, covertly violent tendencies it too rapidly attributes to "the aesthetic" itself.

Notes

1. In the original version of the essay, which appeared in the *Zeitschrift für Sozialforschung* 5.1 (1936): 40–66, the word *Communism* was replaced by the euphemism *les forces constructives de l'humanité* (66). When the essay was republished in the 1960s, the original word was restored and appears in the English translation.

2. For another account of Nietzsche's influence on aestheticized politics in the milieu which spawned Hitler, see William J. McGrath, *Dionysian Art and Populist Politics in Austria.*

3. See her "Fascinating Fascism."

4. See Saul Friedländer, *Reflections of Nazism.*

5. See Paul de Man, *The Resistance to Theory.* This volume includes one of de Man's last essays, which dealt with Benjamin's "The Task of the Translator." In his foreword, Wlad Godzich notes the forthcoming appearance of another collection to be called *The Aesthetic Ideology*, edited by Andrzej Warminski. The concept's importance for de Man has been underlined in Christopher Norris, *Paul de Man.*

6. See, for example, Jonathan Culler, "'Paul de Man's War' and the Aesthetic Ideology," and J. Hillis Miller, "An Open Letter to Professor Jon Weiner."

7. See David Lloyd, "Arnold, Ferguson, Schiller" and "Kant's Examples," and Terry Eagleton, "The Ideology of the Aesthetic."

8. For a recent account of Tailhade and other Symbolists involved with anarchist politics, see Richard D. Sonn, *Anarchism and Cultural Politics in Fin de Siècle France.* The links between anarchist and fascist politics have often been made because of their shared aestheticization of violence.

9. In a subsequent piece on Ernst Jünger, Berman makes a similar charge of the fetishization of images. See his "Written Right Across Their Faces." Inter-

estingly, the same assumption was held by a very different figure, the logical positivist and avid socialist Otto Neurath, who claimed that *"Words divide, pictures unite"* (217).

10. In a later work on Heidegger and Nazism, Lacoue-Labarthe returned to the issue of "the aestheticization of politics." See chapter seven of his *Heidegger, Art and Politics.*

11. The fairness of de Man's reading of Schiller has been powerfully challenged by Stanley Corngold in "Potential Violence in Paul de Man."

12. It should be noted that misreading was not simply a pejorative term in de Man's vocabulary, for all interpretations were inevitably misreadings in the sense that no reading could claim to be the only correct one. The adjective *grievous,* however, indicates that he wanted to distinguish between misreadings, perhaps in terms of their pragmatic implications.

13. See also his remark in "Phenomenality and Materiality in Kant": "morality and the aesthetic are both disinterested, but this disinterestedness becomes necessarily polluted in aesthetic representation: the persuasion that [such] judgments are capable of achieving is linked, in the case of the aesthetic, with positively valorized sensual experiences" (137–38). I will leave de Man's more psychoanalytically inclined interpreters to muse on the implications of his anxiety about sensual pollution.

14. Although this is not the place to launch yet another analysis of the links between de Man's wartime writing and his later work, it may be conjectured that the ascetic, antieudamonistic rigor of the latter was in some sense a reaction to—perhaps even a self-punishment for—his having fallen for the seductions of an organic ideology of aesthetic redemption.

15. David Lloyd also claims that it functioned in the transition from coercion to hegemony; see "Arnold, Ferguson, Schiller," 155.

16. See Herbert Marcuse, "The Affirmative Character of Culture."

17. Lloyd's greater hostility is perhaps explained by his interest in the way that the ideology of the aesthetic functions in the relations between hegemonic and marginal cultures, such as the English and Irish. He notes its role in establishing the canon of great texts, which works to exclude "minor works" that fail to fit the hegemonic model.

18. See also Luc Ferry, *Homo Aestheticus: L'invention du goût a l'âge démocratique.*

19. See his *Negara: The Theatre State in Nineteenth-Century Bali.*

20. For a similar analysis of Schiller, see Jürgen Habermas, *Der philosophische Diskurs der Moderne,* 61f.

21. For a less generous interpretation of this withdrawal, see Lloyd, "Arnold, Ferguson, Schiller," where he writes, "since the realization of the aesthetic state is perpetually deferred and can be found in only a few representative individuals, the aesthetic education of individuals towards participation in the ethical State is likewise deferred in a process which requires the order guaranteed by the dynamic State of rights, that is, by the force of the natural State once again" (167).

22. For a recent and very thorough consideration of the issue, see Howard Caygill, *The Art of Judgement.*

23. In *Paul de Man,* Norris also spells out the problematic implications of analogy in Kant's discussion of both the beautiful and the sublime. The former analogizes between the realm of sensual experience and the faculty of the Understanding, the latter between sensual experience and Reason (56ff.).

For a subtle response to Derrida's analysis, see Caygill, *The Art of Judgement,* 395.

24. See also Lyotard, *The Differend,* 140ff., and "Lessons in Paganism." For sympathetic accounts of Lyotard's political thought and its relation to aesthetics, see David Carroll, *Paraesthetics,* chapter seven, and Bill Readings, *Introducing Lyotard.*

25. In his April 1987 interview with Willem van Reijen and Dick Vreeman, Lyotard explicitly draws on Lacous-Labarthe and Nancy's rejection of politics as a work of art. The critique of this version of aesthetic politics appears on 296f.

26. Arendt's discussion of judgment was unfortunately cut short by her sudden death in 1975, which prevented her from adding a volume on it to the planned trilogy that began with "Thinking" and "Willing." These are included in *The Life of the Mind.* Her most extensive early discussion can be found at the end of her essay "The Crisis in Culture," in *Between Past and Future.* Her last thoughts on the subject are collected as *Lectures on Kant's Political Philosophy.* For analyses of Arendt on judgment, see Michael Denneny, "The Privilege of Ourselves," and Richard J. Bernstein, "Judging—the Actor and the Spectator." Despite the clear similarities in their work, Lyotard never acknowledges Arendt's earlier use of Kant's Third Critique as a model for politics. For a comparison of Arendt and Lyotard, see David Ingram, "The Postmodern Kantianism of Arendt and Lyotard."

27. According to Lyotard, even if aesthetic judgments contain a pretension of universality, they are still

> exempt from the domain of conversation. Even if my taste for a work or for a landscape leads me to discuss it with others (taking that last term in the sense, this time, of an empirical group), it is no less true that any assent that I can obtain from them has nothing to do with the validity of my aesthetic judgment. For the conditions of validity of this judgment are transcendental and are clearly not subject to the opinions of any others whatsoever. The communicability, and even, to speak rigorously, the communion of aesthetic sentiments, cannot be obtained *de facto,* empirically, and much less by means of conversation. . . . [A]esthetic judgment does not proceed through concepts, it cannot be validated by argumentative consensus. ("Interview" 306)

28. Ronald Beiner too wrestles with this tension. See, in particular, Arendt, *Lectures* 135f. One example of the difficulties of her position appears in her citation of Kant's treatment of war, in which he claims that it expresses something sublime that is lost in a long peace. "This is the judgment," she writes, "of the spectator (i.e., it is aesthetical)" (*Lectures* 53). Here we are not that far from Ciano admiring the formal beauty of bombing Ethiopians. What needs to be done to make the political implications of aesthetic judgment attractive is to close the gap between the actors and the spectators of action, and thus reverse Arendt's curious claim that "the public realm is constituted by the critics and the spectators, not by the actors or the makers" (63).

29. Still another possible version might be sought in an unexpected place, the work of Jürgen Habermas. Although the role of the aesthetic is less central in his system than in Lyotard's and Arendt's, it might be argued that his recent interest in aesthetic rationality suggests interesting avenues of inquiry. For an account

that stresses their importance, see David Ingram, *Habermas and the Dialectic of Reason.*

Works Cited

Arendt, Hannah. "The Crisis in Culture." *Between Past and Future: Six Exercises in Political Thought.* Cleveland: Faber, 1961. 197–226.
——. *Lectures on Kant's Political Philosophy.* Ed. with an interpretive essay by Ronald Beiner. Chicago: U of Chicago P, 1982.
——. *The Life of the Mind.* New York: Harcourt, 1978.
Benjamin, Walter. "Theories of German Fascism: On the Collection of Essays *War and the Warrior.*" *New German Critique* 17 (1979): 120–28.
——. "The Work of Art in the Era of Mechanical Reproduction." *Illuminations.* Ed. Hannah Arendt. Trans. Harry Zohn. New York: Schocken, 1968. 217–51.
Berman, Russell. "Foreword: The Wandering Z: Reflections on Kaplan's Reproductions of Banality." *Reproductions of Banality.* By Alice Yaeger Kaplan. xi–xxiii.
——. "Written Right Across Their Faces: Ernst Jünger's Fascist Modernism." *Modernity and the Text: Revisions of German Modernism.* Ed. Andreas Huyssen and David Bathrick. New York: Columbia UP, 1989. 60–80.
Bernstein, Richard J. "Judging—the Actor and the Spectator." *Philosophical Profiles: Essays in a Pragmatic Mode.* Philadelphia: U of Pennsylvania P, 1986. 221–37.
Carroll, David. "The Aesthetic and the Political." *Paraesthetics: Foucault, Lyotard, Derrida.* New York: Routledge, 1987. 155–84.
Caygill, Howard. *The Art of Judgement.* Cambridge: Basil Blackwell, 1989.
Chytry, Josef. *The Aesthetic State: A Quest in Modern German Thought.* Berkeley: U of California P, 1989.
Corngold, Stanley. "Potential Violence in Paul de Man." *Critical Review* 3.1 (1989): 117–37.
Culler, Jonathan. "'Paul de Man's War' and the Aesthetic Ideology." *Critical Inquiry* 15.4 (1989): 777–83.
de Man, Paul. "Aesthetic Formalization: Kleist's *Über das Marionettentheater.*" *The Rhetoric of Romanticism.* New York: Columbia UP, 1984. 263–90.
——. *The Aesthetic Ideology.* Ed. Andrzej Warminski. Minneapolis: U of Minnesota P, forthcoming.
——. "Kant and Schiller." *The Aesthetic Ideology.*
——. "Phenomenality and Materiality in Kant." *Hermeneutics: Questions and Prospects.* Ed. Gary Shapiro and Alan Sica. Amherst: U of Massachusetts P, 1984. 121–44.
——. "Reading and History." *The Resistance to Theory.* 54–72.
——. *The Resistance to Theory.* Minneapolis: U of Minnesota P, 1986.
Denneny, Michael. "The Privilege of Ourselves: Hannah Arendt on Judgment." *Hannah Arendt: The Recovery of the Public World.* Ed. Melvyn A. Hill. New York: St. Martin's, 1979. 245–74.
Derrida, Jacques. *The Truth in Painting.* Trans. Geoff Bennington and Ian McLeod. Chicago: U of Chicago P, 1987.

Eagleton, Terry. *The Ideology of the Aesthetic*. Cambridge: Blackwell, 1990.

Ferry, Luc. *Homo Aestheticus: L'invention du goût à l'âge démocratique*. Paris: Grasset, 1990.

Friedländer, Saul. *Reflections of Nazism: An Essay on Kitsch and Death*. Trans. Thomas Weyr. New York: Harper, 1984.

Geertz, Clifford. *Negara: The Theatre State in Nineteenth-Century Bali*. Princeton: Princeton UP, 1980.

Habermas, Jürgen. *Der philosophische Diskurs der Moderne*. Frankfurt: Suhrkamp, 1985.

Hillach, Ansgar. "The Aesthetics of Politics: Walter Benjamin's 'Theories of German Fascism.'" *New German Critique* 17 (1979): 99–119 (preface to Benjamin, "Theories").

Ingram, David. *Habermas and the Dialectic of Reason*. New Haven: Yale UP, 1987.

———. "The Postmodern Kantianism of Arendt and Lyotard." *The Review of Metaphysics* 42.1 (1988): 51–77.

Kaplan, Alice Yaeger. *Reproductions of Banality: Fascism, Literature and French Intellectual Life*. Minneapolis: U of Minnesota P, 1986.

Kinser, Bill, and Neil Kleinman. *The Dream That Was No More a Dream: A Search for Aesthetic Reality in Germany, 1890–1945*. New York: Harper, 1969.

Lacoue-Labarthe, Philippe. *Heidegger, Art and Politics: The Fiction of the Political*. Trans. Chris Turner. New York: Blackwell, 1990.

Lacoue-Labarthe, Philippe, and Jean-Luc Nancy. *The Literary Absolute: The Theory of Literature in German Romanticism*. Trans. Philip Barnard and Cheryl Lester. Albany: State U of New York P, 1988.

Lloyd, David. "Arnold, Ferguson, Schiller: Aesthetic Culture and the Politics of Aesthetics." *Cultural Critique* 2 (1985–86): 137–70.

———. "Kant's Examples." *Representations* 28 (1989): 34–54.

Lyotard, Jean-François. *The Differend: Phrases in Dispute*. Trans. Georges Van Den Abbeele. Minneapolis: U of Minnesota P, 1988.

———. "Interview with Jean-Francois Lyotard." By Willem Van Reijen and Dick Vreeman. *Theory, Culture and Society* 5 (1988): 277–309.

———. "Lessons in Paganism." *The Lyotard Reader*. Ed. Andrew Benjamin. Oxford: Blackwell, 1989. 122–54.

Lyotard, Jean-François, and Jean-Loup Thébaud. *Just Gaming*. Trans. Wlad Godzich. Minneapolis: U of Minnesota P, 1985.

Marcuse, Herbert. "The Affirmative Character of Culture." *Negations: Essays in Critical Theory*. Trans. Jeremy J. Shapiro. Boston: Beacon, 1968. 88–133.

Marinetti, F. T. *The Futurist Manifesto*. Rpt. in James Joll, *Three Intellectuals in Politics*. New York: Pantheon, 1960. 179–84.

McGrath, William J. *Dionysian Art and Populist Politics in Austria*. New Haven: Yale UP, 1974.

Miller, J. Hillis. "An Open Letter to Professor Jon Weiner." *Responses: On Paul de Man's Wartime Journalism*. Ed. Werner Hamacher, Neil Hertz, and Thomas Keenen. Lincoln: U of Nebraska P, 1989. 334–42.

Neurath, Otto. *Empiricism and Sociology*. Trans. Paul Foulkes and Marie Neurath. Ed. Marie Neurath and Robert S. Cohen. Dordrecht: Reidel, 1973.

Nietzsche, Friedrich. *The Birth of Tragedy and The Genealogy of Morals*. Trans. Francis Golffing. New York: Doubleday, 1956.

Norris, Christopher. *Paul de Man: Deconstruction and the Critique of the Aesthetic Ideology*. New York: Routledge, 1988.

Raynaud, Ernest. *Souvenirs sur le symbolisme*. Paris: Payot, 1895.

Readings, Bill. *Introducing Lyotard: Art and Politics*. London: Routledge, 1991.

Smith, Denis Mack. "The Theory and Practice of Fascism." *Fascism: An Anthology*. Ed. Nathanael Greene. New York: Crowell, 1968. 73–112.

Sonn, Richard D. *Anarchism and Cultural Politics in Fin de Siècle France*. Lincoln: U of Nebraska P, 1989.

Sontag, Susan. "Fascinating Fascism." *Under the Sign of Saturn*. New York: Farrar, Straus, Giroux, 1980. 73–108.

Stern, J. P. *Hitler; The Führer and the People*. Berkeley: U of California P, 1976.

Cryptonormativism and Double Gestures:
The Politics of Post-Structuralism

Amanda Anderson

Much post-structuralist cultural criticism takes for its topic the processes of othering, both subtle and blatant, that underwrite economies of power and inform discursive practices. Like-
wise, the tasks of historical and cultural recovery in the contemporary human sciences often aim to reconstruct and thereby "give
voice" to the suppressed or negated experiences of historically
subordinated groups, groups defined through hierarchies of gender, race, class, and sexuality. To take a central example, the
movement of cultural studies in Britain and North America
largely derives from the felt need to reconstitute the lived practices of subcultures, social groups, and variously positioned subjectivities. But these new disciplinary practices of course do more
than redraw the topical map: they make a moral and political
appeal. Indeed, in his recent survey of cultural studies, Patrick
Brantlinger offers the following as the main "lesson" that cultural
studies has to offer: "in order to understand ourselves, the discourses of 'the Other'—of all the others—is that which we most
urgently need to hear" (3).

In this essay I wish to render explicit and to theorize the normative ideals that underlie contemporary critiques of hegemonic constructions of otherness. I will approach the topic through an examination of what is widely regarded as the primary impasse or, in less skeptical formulations, the constitutive tension of post-structuralist thought: the incommensurability between its epistemological stance and its political claims, between its descriptions and its prescriptions, between the pessimism of its intellect and, if not the optimism, at least the intrusiveness of its moral and political will. Of course "post-structuralism" is a wide and varied terrain, but the shared tenets of its several manifestations—deconstructive, psychoanalytic, Marxist, Foucauldian—form something of a generalizable paradigm. Post-structuralism in its various guises forwards a critique of humanism and the unified subject of modern liberalism, and casts Enlightenment conceptions of truth, rationality, and autonomy as at once deluded and oppressive, as derivatives of a mistaken conception of human subjectivity, and as dangerously complicit in wider forms of power and domination. The critiques of power and domination, however, entail implicit normative claims that remain external to the overarching antifoundationalist epistemology. Ever-encroaching and self-extending power networks in Foucault, the violence of metaphysics in deconstruction, the painstaking analyses of reified or suppressed otherness in cultural and literary criticism—all of these make appeal at some level to a vision of unalienated relations and undamaged forms of social life. As Jürgen Habermas writes in discussing the critique of reason as it has been waged through negative dialectics, deconstruction, and genealogy,

> Whether modernity is described as a constellation of life that is reified and used, or as one that is technologically manipulated, or as one that is totalitarian, rife with power, homogenized, imprisoned—the denunciations are constantly inspired by a special sensitivity for complex injuries and subtle violations. Inscribed in this sensitivity is the picture of an undamaged intersubjectivity that the young Hegel first projected as an ethical totality. (*Philosophical Discourse* 337)

The same normative appeal attends post-structuralist cultural criticism, which has itself grown out of the earlier critiques of modernity. In post-structuralist criticism, this normative appeal also only fleetingly or awkwardly appears, since it is characteristically subordinated to a perspective which construes human subjects as the effects of larger forces and structures: as the point through which language speaks, as the site of unconscious disruptions, or as a position within a social grid traversed by the constitutive forces of gender, race, and class. This third-person perspective—what might best be called the residual objectivism of post-structuralism—relegates morality to the status of assertion or intimation and casts into question its own viability as critique, since, as Peter Dews points out, the philosophical position of poststructuralism "assumes the foundations of the classical forms of critique to be necessarily and oppressively identitarian" (xvi).

[Many who subscribe to the post-structuralist paradigm dismiss the problems of grounding one's critique or being able properly to account for one's own account, either by adopting a pragmatic stance compatible with the antifoundationalist credo, or by self-consciously embracing the idea that their own critique is necessarily complicit with those forms of power it purports to "unmask."[1] But the problem of political will and normative assertion has generated a more elaborate and sustained debate. Approaches to the issue take several distinct forms, though many critics and theorists employ a combination of the forms. Some theorists posit a politically efficacious resistance or disruption that is guaranteed as a systems-effect, thereby avoiding the rhetoric of voluntarism. Examples of this first approach include deconstructionist intimations about the inherent subversiveness of linguistic undecidability and psychoanalytic claims for the disrupting effects of the unconscious.[2] Others actively embrace the tension between epistemology and politics, affirming a "double gesture" that simultaneously avows a theoretical antihumanism and a political humanism. This approach is represented by theorists who have followed Gayatri Spivak's endorsement of "strategic essentialism."[3] Foucault's own shifts in perspective from the systemic to the local (as the site of resistances and "reverse discourses") also rely on a similarly motivated double move.[4] Still others, due in part to dissatisfaction with the double gesture, have sought to articulate political strategies that derive more directly from constructionist critique: Judith Butler is a prime example here, as are the proponents of various oppositional politics.[5]

I will argue here that none of these approaches adequately theorizes the normative appeals informing post-structuralist critique; and I hope to forward the discussion of post-structuralist politics and ethics by placing the debate in dialogue with Habermas's theory of communicative action. Habermas's project calls for a turn to "intersubjectivity" as a means of overcoming the impasse between a subject-centered paradigm and the theoretical and ethical failures of systems-theories. For Habermas, the logocentrism of Western thought and the powerful instrumentality of reason are not absolute but rather constitute "a systematic foreshortening and distortion of a potential always already operative in the communicative practice of everyday life." The potential he refers to is the potential for mutual understanding "inscribed into communication in ordinary language" (*Philosophical Discourse* 311). Habermas recognizes the dominance and reach of instrumental reason—his project is largely devoted to a systematic analysis of the historical conditions and social effects of that dominance—yet at the same time he wishes to retrieve an emancipatory model of *communicative* reason derived from a linguistic understanding of intersubjective relations. Versions of the Habermasian call for a turn to "intersubjectivity" or dialogism have also characterized important work by Seyla Benhabib, Richard J. Bernstein, and Drucilla Cornell.[6]

Ironically, those accounts which remain unable to mediate between the systemic and intersubjective perspectives, and which fundamentally privilege the former, end up reifying subjectivity and otherness in a manner analogous to those forms of exclusion that are typically the object of critique. Habermas's announced shift from the paradigm of the philosophy of consciousness to the linguistically conceived paradigm of mutual understanding, by contrast, cogently addresses and resolves the problems generated by the impasse of post-structuralism as I outlined it above. It makes possible a nonmetaphysical grounding of critique by means of those very emancipatory communicative ideals that already inhere in acts of linguistic exchange. It renders explicit the ideal of undamaged intersubjectivity that the critique of systemic distortion necessarily implies and invokes. And it mediates between the prescriptive and descriptive in its employment of dialogic reciprocity as a regulative ideal that can guide political practices. It suggests, in other words, that if various forms of domination undermine, distort, or even foreclose the communicative ideal incipient in dialogical relations, then our task is not only to analyze those distortions but also to nurture the communicative ideals of recognition and respect. This is by no means to imply that such an ideal could ever be fully actualized or that "learning to listen" is an antidote adequate in and of itself to massive, structurally embedded inequalities. As Bernstein writes,

> It would be a gross distortion to imagine that we might conceive of the entire political realm organized on the principle of dialogue or conversation, considering the fragile conditions that are required for genuine dialogue and conversation. Nevertheless, if we think out what is required for such a dialogue based on mutual understanding, respect, a willingness to listen and risk one's opinions and prejudices, a mutual seeking of the correctness of what is said, we will have defined a powerful regulative ideal that can orient our practical and political lives. (162–63)

The theories of communicative reason and ethics profoundly shift the terms of the debate as they have been elaborated by the other approaches to the normative impasses of post-structuralism. The first approach is inadequate insofar as it locates subversion and transformation entirely beyond individual or collective agency. The double gesture, in calling for an oscillation between local acts of will and a systemic view of the social grid, objectifies social identities and fails to show how or why we should want to privilege certain acts of will over others. The more consistent models of subversive or oppositional politics redress problems in the other two approaches, yet still lack a positive normative dimension. In this essay, I will argue that the Habermasian theory not only overcomes the impasses of the other approaches but also can itself be reformulated so as to accommodate less exclusively rationalistic conceptions of intersubjective reciprocity *and* so as to acknowledge more fully the indeterminacy of social relations. In order to make the case for a revised Habermasian model, I will first examine in some detail the call for a "double gesture" which embraces both a theoretical antiessentialism and a "strategic essentialism." I want to begin here because the double gesture self-consciously attempts to resolve the tension between theory and politics, and hence in certain ways might be seen as redressing the cryptonormativism that characterizes other approaches.[7]

Risks Necessary and Unnecessary

Back in 1978, in a long and influential article about sexual difference, politics, and the cinema, Stephen Heath wrote that the project of exposing the constructed character of sexual difference need and perhaps should not be defined in opposition to the project of reconstructing the woman's gaze, or of attempting to "distinguish positively feminine elements in particular film practices." In a phrase which was to be taken up by academic cultural critics and literary theorists in the mid- to late-eighties, Heath surmised that "the risk of essence may have to be taken" (99). In a similar vein, Gayatri Chakravorty Spivak began in interviews and essays in the mid-eighties to elaborate a concept of "strategic essentialism" which, from the vantage point of a deconstructive antihumanism, both justified and endorsed political uses of humanist categories such as the will, autonomy, rights, consciousness, and identity.[8] Numerous post-structuralist critics and theorists—aligned with feminism, cultural studies, and gay and lesbian studies—have in turn advocated some form of alliance between constructionism and essentialism, or between antihumanist theory and humanist claims and practices.[9] The double gesture that characterizes this paradoxical practice accepts and renders explicit the post-structuralist tension between theory and politics. It also seeks to redress a perceived problem of agency: rather than locating subversion and transformation entirely beyond individual or collective agency, it obtrusively insists on a kind of voluntarism, though one that remains informed by the antifoundationalist critique of the will.

An understanding of strategic essentialism cannot be gained simply from analyzing the origins of the term and its subsequent citations, for there are many manifestations of a similarly motivated double gesture that do not employ the term. In fact, within feminism, a version of strategic essentialism began to appear along with the first sympathetic appropriations of post-structuralist thought. In *Sexual/Textual Politics*, for example, Toril Moi endorses Kristeva's "'deconstructed' form of feminism" but warns at the same time that "it still remains *politically* essential for feminists to defend women *as* women in order to counteract the patriarchal oppression that precisely despises women *as* women" (13).[10] Moi does not make clear precisely what she means by "as women"; rhetorically, she enacts the very affirmation of unified identity for which the statement calls. One might also view the looseness of her formulation as a deliberate eclipsing of theoretical precision by political demand.

Moi's position exemplifies what has become a primary version of strategic essentialism, that is, the argument that a political pragmatism must accompany post-structuralist strategies of demystification and critique. Within this framework, however, essentialist categories are often cast as imperative in more than a narrowly pragmatic way. It isn't simply the case that we need categories such as rights and the subject of those rights in order to achieve distinct political goals; we also need myths of community and identity in order to counter dominant ideologies and underwrite collective forms of political practice. The more narrow approach assumes simply that we need to work within the existing system; the broader one makes a more fundamental claim about the role of myth and identity in human praxis. It makes a claim about a common human need (though usually not so baldly as that). As Ann Snitow writes: "Whatever the issue, feminists have gained a great deal by saying, 'We are "women," and this is what "women" want.' This belief in some ground of shared experience is the social basis from which any sustained political struggle must come" (12).

The argument for the political necessity of identity thinking thus claims that we must deliberately choose certain strategies whose abandonment in the name of post-structuralist rigor would be grossly misguided. Another version of strategic essentialism—or sometimes just another moment within a strategic essentialism argument—concentrates not so much on the future as on the past, arguing that, despite itself, essentialism has produced progressive political effects in the past. More a practice of reading than a plan of action, this approach revises and recuperates not only the past but also what are often too quickly dismissed as anachronistic or naive textual practices in the present. Spivak's approach to the Subaltern Studies project, a postcolonial historical reconstruction of Indian colonial "experience," exemplifies this particular facet of strategic essentialism. While Spivak sees an important constructionist emphasis in much of the work of these historians, she seeks also to explain and recuperate what her Western antihumanist training has caused her to view with considerable suspicion: an investment in the will, consciousness, and effective agency of the subaltern, a commitment to reconstructing the lost, negated, or covered-over experience of Indian colonial subjects. She accounts for this by positing an unavoidable asymmetry between her work and the work of the historians, one constituted through the displacing axis of the "international division of labor": "[T]he discourse of the unified consciousness of the subaltern *must* inhabit the strategy of these historians, even as the discourse of the micrologized or situated subject must mark that of antihumanists on the other side of the international division of labor" ("Subaltern Studies" 210). Spivak not only explains but also privileges the work of these historians: by casting the subaltern as "the subject of his own history," the Subaltern Studies project importantly reveals "the *limits* of the critique of humanism as produced in the West" (209, my emphasis). What Spivak means here is that the critique of humanism remains blind to the ways in which the reconstruction of subjectivity, experience, and identity are of vital importance to groups who have been colonized.

Spivak's reading thus seems to grant the Subaltern Studies project a kind of autonomous critical function, insofar as she credits the historians with revealing the limits of antihumanism. Yet she simultaneously feels compelled to rescue the project from its own naïveté by reading it as a "*strategic* use of positivist essentialism in a scrupulously visible political interest" (205). Strangely, this formulation retains the notion of a strategy in a case where the effects seem not to have been calculated from a thoroughgoing post-structuralist vantage point. It's one thing to say that the historians' emphasis on humanist categories has a corrective effect on post-structuralist paradigms: that places their work in productive dialogue with Western deconstruction. But it's quite another thing to reinscribe their operative concepts as *strategies*, when they simply don't evince any attitude toward them as such.[11] The strategy here lies in the critic's reading of the historians, not with the historians themselves. In a similar way, Diana Fuss recasts Irigaray's essentialist language as an intentional strategy: "The point, for Irigaray, of defining women from an essentialist standpoint is not to imprison women within their bodies but to rescue them from enculturating definitions by men" (61). Essentialism here becomes a brillantly conceived escape from oppressive constructions, or constructionism *tout court*. That such an escape is within her own terms necessarily deluded does not trouble Fuss, for she believes it does political good to "believe" otherwise.[12]

Thus far I have laid out two different approaches to essentialism. The first, the politically pragmatic approach, endorses deliberate appropriations of essentialist and humanist categories: it is anticipatory and voluntaristic. The second, the recuperative, retroactive version, rereads and revises what have hitherto been dismissed as failed or faulty practices. It is backward looking rather than forward looking, a way of reading rather than a political prescription. The third and final approach to essentialism that I will examine here paradoxically modifies the notion of intentional strategy altogether; it insists instead that essentialism is entirely *unavoidable*, and hence something we must affirm and use. I want first to examine the way this argument appears in Spivak's work, and then to move on to more recent feminist assertions that some form of double gesture is in fact inescapable.[13]

For Spivak, whose political criticism is strongly influenced by deconstruction, essentialism is not something that we could ever jettison or have done with, since it is a function of language—or logocentrism—itself. Let me begin by quoting a representative statement from a 1986 interview: "Since one cannot not be an essentialist, why not look at the ways in which one is essentialist, carve out a representative essentialist position, and then do politics according to the old rules whilst remembering the dangers in this? That's the thing deconstruction gives us; an awareness that what we are obliged to do, and must do scrupulously, in the long run is not OK" ("Strategy, Identity, Writing" 45). It's not OK, because essentialism enacts the violence of metaphysics generally and a host of exclusions historically, exclusions primarily of race and gender. Thus, although deconstructive critique must be supplemented by political practice, practice itself must be continually corrected by theory. Or, as Spivak puts it, not only does practice norm theory, but "theory always norms practice" (44).

While Spivak argues for the necessity of essentialism from within the paradigm of deconstruction, others such as Ann Snitow and Denise Riley have argued, in somewhat different terms, that the double gesture is simply constitutive of the history of feminism, or of feminism itself. In the opening paragraph of *"Am I That Name?": Feminism and the Category of "Women" in History*, Riley states, "both a concentration on and a refusal of the identity of 'women' are essential to feminism. This its history makes plain" (1). Similarly, Ann Snitow, in her thoughtful and enormously helpful essay, "A Gender Diary," offers the following argument:

> Feminism is inevitably a mixed form, requiring in its very nature such inconsistencies. In what follows I try to show first, that a common divide keeps forming in both feminist thought and action between the need to build the identity "woman" and give it solid political meaning and the need to tear down the category "woman" and dismantle its all-too-solid history. (9)

Snitow's essay carefully works through the way this divide informs a number of classic debates within feminism, not only the essentialism/constructionism debate, but also the equality/difference debate, and the tension between cultural feminism and post-structuralism. Snitow argues that the divide cannot be overcome through thought alone, and that it will only be overcome in a historical process. On this basis, she dismisses any attempt at what she calls "third course thinking" and asserts instead that "'Embracing the paradox' is just what feminism cannot choose but do" (19).[14]

I want to suggest that Snitow fails to make a crucial distinction here. Recognizing the importance of a divide within the history of feminism, and understanding the powerful ways that divide informs the contemporary moment, does not mean that one is obliged to embrace that divide theoretically.[15] Indeed, transmuting the historical debate into a theoretical postulate generates a series of problems, both practical and theoretical. At the least, a certain irony attends this position, insofar as it aims to get beyond debate and disagreement by insisting that we *all* affirm a contradiction. But as we shall see, the call to "embrace the paradox" is itself elaborated from, and fundamentally privileges, the poststructuralist position. In some ways this position reinscribes the problem of rescue and recuperation that marks the revisionist approach to essentialism. The recuperative stance harbors within itself, however, a more fundamental problem. By associating essentialism with practice, and antiessentialism with an ultimate theoretical truth, the articulation of strategic essentialism generates a theory/practice split. In turning to Habermas, I will argue for a conception of theory that can render explicit, rather than undermine, the norms and self-understandings that are internal to practice. That is, theory need not be other than (and superior to) practice; ideally, it is practice itself as self-reflexive.

To further elaborate my critique of the double gesture, however, I must return to Spivak, who made the apparently even-handed claim that practice norms theory and theory norms practice, that each corrects the excesses or blindnesses of the other. In her reading of the Subaltern Studies project, as we have seen, Spivak argues for the importance of essentialist categories insofar as they point up a "limit" in the Western critique of humanism. But two things then crucially modify, if not altogether undermine, that point. First, as I mention above, Spivak feels compelled to rescue the historians' practice by designating it as a strategy. Second, this retrieval is complemented by Spivak's own antihumanist reading of the subaltern's "identity" as "no more than a theoretical fiction to entitle the project of reading": "what had seemed the historical predicament of the colonial subaltern can be made to become the allegory of the predicament of *all* thought, *all* deliberative consciousness, though the elite profess otherwise" ("Subaltern Studies" 204). This formulation should sound familiar to feminists, insofar as Lacanian feminism reads precisely in this fashion. The scapegoated feminine predicament reveals the truth of the whole: nobody has the phallus. Here, the negated subaltern reveals the truth of the whole: nobody has autonomous deliberative consciousness. In my view, however, to read historically disempowered or negated subject-positions as figures for an

What about JHL?

abstractly decentered subjectivity is to distort our understanding
of *both* the decentered subject and the condition of specific oppressed groups. More importantly, Spivak generates a false dualism between a higher theoretical truth—the truth of decentered
subjectivity—and what ultimately must then be seen as an enabling practical *lie*. That is, her conception of a strategic essentialism that both guarantees practice and then obligingly acts as a
target for a knowing antihumanism ultimately works to disar-
ticulate practice from theory, subordinating the former to the
latter.

The idea that practice only works through what are ultimately dangerous fictions diminishes the extent to which the critique of naturalized identities can itself inform political practice.
In terms less ominous than Spivak's, for example, Snitow nonetheless similarly suggests that those engaging in political activism
are required to foster a forgetfulness of the kind of constructionist critique that led them to understand the workings of power in
the first place:

Fishian ... can't be self-reflexive + an advocate

> We begin: The category "woman" is a fiction; then poststruc-
> turalism suggests ways in which human beings live by fictions;
> then, in its turn, activism requires of feminists that we elab-
> orate the fiction "woman" as if she were not a provisional
> invention at all but a person we know well, one in need of
> obvious rights and powers. Activism and theory weave to-
> gether here, working on what remains the same basic cloth,
> the stuff of feminism. (19)

The problem I have with this formulation lies in the way
constructionism *belongs to* post-structuralism, while activism requires the bracketing of constructionist critique (*pace* the weaving
metaphor).[16] In a refusal of these kinds of double gestures, some
cultural critics have insisted that we derive our politics more directly from constructionist critique. For example, Judith Butler
argues for a feminist politics "that will take the variable construction of identity as both a methodological and normative prerequisite, if not a political goal" (5). For Butler, the affirmation of
unified identity is not a political prerequisite; on the contrary, the
disruption of naturalized conceptions of identity should serve as

the model for political practice as such.[17] Butler thus aims to reconcile the normative and the theoretical, and does not insist on their irreducible opposition. Yet Butler's theory remains limited insofar as it fails to account sufficiently for the political ideals and values that inform progressive practice, ones that extend beyond the recognition of constructedness. Because for Butler, the point is not simply to show that all subjectivity is constructed, but also to show that it is constructed within a dominant and oppressive heterosexual matrix. And in characterizing the heterosexual matrix as dominant and oppressive, Butler means to emphasize, one can only assume, its failure to recognize and respect other sexualities and subjective practices. But this is a normative claim that only cryptically informs her account. Subverting identity constitutes the methodology and the goal of feminist political practice; recognition and respect inform the discussion but are not given theoretical primacy. She introduces the ideas of coalition and dialogue, but only to argue against the possibility of formulating any notion of solidarity, which she in an unwarranted move equates with unity: "Despite the clearly democratizing impulse that motivates coalition building, the coalitional theorist can inadvertently reinsert herself as sovereign of the process by trying to assert an ideal form for coalitional structures *in advance*, one that will effectively guarantee unity as the outcome" (14). But there's a difference between giving theoretical explicitness to tacitly supposed intersubjective ideals, and decreeing what "unity" will be. While I am entirely in accord with Butler's idea that we should expect "divergence, breakage, splinter, and fragmentation" as part of the dialogical process of democratization, I think that she makes this point only to swerve away from giving theoretical prominence to the intersubjective ideals that inform this very point (14).

Spivak's own reconsiderations on the topic of strategic essentialism revealingly devolve on the issue of dialogue and intersubjectivity. In an interview with Ellen Rooney for the journal *Differences*, Spivak expresses surprise as well as regret at the way that strategic essentialism has been so widely heralded as a solution to theory's political impasses, suggesting that we must shift toward a new terrain, that of "building for difference" ("In a Word" 128). Over the course of the questioning, Spivak manifests a repeated impatience with the very term *essentialism* and with the attempt to refine a theory about it. Arguing that we must talk of deconstructive practice in more "mundane" terms, she calls for "a sort of deconstructive homeopathy, a deconstructing of identity by identities" (130). Partly Spivak is answering the charge that she talks too much about herself:

> I believe that the way to counter the authority of either objective, disinterested positioning or the attitude of there being no author (and these two opposed positions legitimize each other) is by thinking of oneself as an example of certain kinds of historical, psycho-sexual narratives that one must in fact use, however micrologically, in order to do deontological work in the humanities. When one represents oneself in such a way, it becomes, curiously enough, a deidentification of oneself, a claiming of an identity from a text that comes from somewhere else. . . . To an extent, the way in which one conceives of oneself as representative or as an example of something is this awareness that what is one's own, supposedly, what is proper to one, has a history. That history is unmotivated but not capricious and is larger in outline than we are, and I think this is quite different from the idea of talking about oneself. (130–31)

A self-reflexive form of autobiographical historicizing will thus enable productive deidentifications without the pretense of a rigid antiessentialism: "being obliged to graph one's bio is very different from the attitude of claiming anti-essentialism" (131). In the interview Spivak thus reelaborates the concept of a necessary essentialism, one which, if accompanied by a "persistent critique," will prompt efficacious (homeopathic) deidentifications, thereby successfully curing people of the impulse to naturalize their histories and identities (126). We are back, then, to a more basic claim about deconstruction's capacity for demythologizing critique, and hence back to a claim about the political efficacy of deconstruction. Yet despite the holistic connotations of the homeopathic metaphor, the form of the double gesture is still discernible as the internal oscillation, within the individual, between identification and deidentification. All the same, Spivak has abandoned the sharp opposition between strategic local practices and a demystifying theoretical deconstruction practiced "elsewhere";

and there is quite a difference between a persistent self-critique modeled on hermeneutic self-awareness (which her reformulation suggests) and an endorsement of decisionist essentializing.

Spivak's reconsiderations thus only partly recapitulate her earlier position. What I am more interested in, however, is the extent to which the category of otherness seems to have prompted her impulse to revise. That is, a redirective toward dialogical relations frequently accompanies Spivak's admission of the earlier argument's inadequacy. For example, in an attempt to derail what she takes to be a misguided emphasis on the theoretical question of a pristine antiessentialism, she introduces the new goal of "building for difference." And at the very end of the interview there is a sudden call for the importance of transactions with an audience:

> [M]any of the changes I've made in my position are because the audience has become a co-investigator and I've realized what it is to have an audience. You know what I'm saying? An audience is part of one. An audience shows us something. Well, that is the transaction, you know, it's a responsibility to the other, giving it faces. It's not . . . I don't see this de-essentializing particularly, but really deconstructing the binary opposition between investigator and audience. (153)

When one coinvestigates by inviting an audience to respond, then "positionality is shared with it" (153).

The realization of what it is to have an audience has disrupted and rendered inadequate Spivak's earlier position, and in fact prompted her toward a conception of "shared positionality." I want to suggest, however, that "shared positionality" can only function as a threshold concept in Spivak's overall account, an account that still subordinates intersubjectivity to a systems-perspective. Spivak makes an appeal to mutual understanding, but the form of *self*-understanding that underlies mutual understanding is conceived exclusively from a systemic perspective. In recognizing one's positionality, in "thinking of oneself as an example of certain kinds of historical, psycho-sexual narratives," one undergoes the salutary process of deidentification. In sharing positionality, presumably, one recognizes the other as similarly constructed, as equally an example of certain larger narratives without which self-representation remains impossible, and as equally capable of homeopathic deidentifications. One could presumably undergo a dialogue in which such forms of self-understanding were exchanged, mutually prompted, and critically examined. However, it still remains the case that such a conception of intersubjectivity is radically truncated insofar as it is routed only through the systemic perspective. The form of self-understanding embraced is one whereby the subject sees him or herself not as constituted through intersubjective relations but rather as a member of an atomized, post hoc "community" of systems-effects.

In response to the potentially reified conceptions of subjectivity that derive from a too-atomized version of positionality, some critics have focused instead on the individual as the site of heterogeneous, multiple identities. Thus, as a white lesbian working-class student, or as a black middle-class heterosexual law professor, one becomes the site of intersecting and often conflicting positions that one is always "negotiating." Yet as Diana Fuss argues, risks of essentialism and reification inhabit both singular and multiple conceptions of positionality, insofar as "the essentialism in 'antiessentialism' inheres in the notion of place or positionality" (29). Fuss herself endorses the Lacanian conception of identity as radically destabilizing, as at once necessary and impossible, "alienated and fictitious" (102). According to Fuss, a nonpsychoanalytic conception of constructed identity, whether singular or multiple, does not acknowledge the "subversive and destabilizing potential of the Unconscious" and engages in an unanxious taxonomy of "identifiable and unitary," even if ultimately conflicting, notions of identity (105, 103).[18]

Unlike Fuss, I am concerned here less with the charge that social constructionist discourse can lend itself to fixed conceptions of identity than I am in the objectivism, or systems-perspective, that often dominates the elaboration of subject positionality. Indeed, the notion of subject-positions ironically partakes of an inverted Cartesianism: the various anti-cogitos of post-structuralism simply define the human subject as *res extensa* rather than *res cogitans*, and thereby reinstate a curiously scientistic model. Such a dualistic framework precludes the possibility of an intersubjective perspective that would define the human subject not as purely autonomous and self-present, nor as a mere place on intersecting grids, but rather as constituted through its ongoing relations to others as they are mediated by language, social systems, and history. The Lacanian paradigm of split subjectivity, while it may avoid the essentialism of place, does not further such an understanding, but rather insists on an internally destabilized or "precarious" subject. Moreover, that internal destabilization is the product of a dualistic subject-structure model. Coherent self-identity is disrupted by a systemic force: the unconscious as the symbolic order or the "transindividual dimension of language" (Dews 83). For Lacan, language remains in crucial ways an interruptive and not an enabling medium.

both?

It is certainly true that many post-structuralist accounts have attempted to forward nonmechanistic theories of subject-constitution, particularly by emphasizing that subjects perform, enact, or participate in their own constructions. A kind of participation does for example emerge in Foucault's accounts of constructed subjectivity, but it subordinates intersubjective relations to the workings of a systemic form of power. In his very last works on the classical period in Greece Foucault significantly shifted his attention precisely to ethical relations; however, the highly influential *Discipline and Punish* and *The History of Sexuality, Volume I* focus overwhelmingly on the singular subject's participation in his or her own construction, the various means by which modern individuals "willingly" internalize the workings of disciplinary power. Spivak's own conception of "being obliged to graph one's bio" follows in the wake of this project to understand the drama of subject-constitution, as does Judith Butler's emphasis on the potential for adopting a parodic relation toward the construction one is "in." To conceive of the subject as a participant in its own constructions, however, is not the same as conceiving of the subject as a participant in social communities.[19] The self-disciplining, self-inscribing, or self-parodic subject is one whose most fundamental relation is to the system and not to other subjects. Indeed, Foucauldian as well as Lacanian models fundamentally tend to read intersubjective relations as displaced confrontations between the subject and the system. The Lacanian rewriting of the Oedipal scenario as a confrontation with the Law partakes of this displacement, as does the Foucauldian account of the Panopticon and the

qualifier

self-disciplining subject. In the Panopticon, which Foucault presents as the model of modern disciplinary society, the gaze of the concrete other becomes a mere lieutenant for a structure of anonymous and global surveillance.

Insofar as these forms of dramatizing subjectivity reduce the participatory to the systemic, they only partially describe the social world. We can certainly trace the historical and social determinants of this self-alienating mode of apprehension, which undeniably forms a part of modern self-understandings and powerfully informs the various modernist and postmodernist aesthetics. However, I want to suggest that we have no obligation to reproduce this self-alienating mode as an absolute fact about the social world or modern history. The systemic anti-cogito that characterizes the post-structuralist sensibility ("The system thinks me, therefore I am not") produces an utterly atomized social field, one that precludes entering into the perspective of nonreifying encounters between subjects. In the next section of this essay, I will examine how such dominant theoretical approaches can be challenged through a shift to intersubjectivity and dialogism.

Intersubjectivity: Reconceiving the Subject

The theory of communicative action enables us to resolve the most problematic aspects of those arguments that resort to cryptonormativism or a paradoxical double gesture. It gives due prominence to the intersubjective ideals that inform critiques of othering and calls to respect differences. The accounts that I discussed in the previous section fail to mediate between the systems-perspective and the perspective of intersubjective and transformative praxis. In the case of the double gesture, political and theoretical practice are fundamentally irreconcilable. In the case of those more consistent accounts which attempt to derive practice from post-structuralist theory, accounts of dialogical practice and intersubjective relations are refracted through a systems-perspective.

I will be emphasizing that Habermas's approach can advance the debate over the politics of post-structuralism only if it is significantly revised in a less rationalistic and formalistic direction.

why?

critique...

But I want first to stress the vital importance of the conception of communicative reason for any theory which seeks to advance and justify democratic ideals. Habermas's account of the relations of reciprocity and recognition that are presupposed in any action oriented toward reaching understanding disallows the radical rupture between ethics and epistemology, and between practice and theory, in much post-structuralist and postmodern thought. By bringing to light those aspects of our intersubjective relations that are constituted communicatively, Habermas articulates a discourse ethics. This discourse ethics insists that the higher level of argumentation required in any self-reflexive democratic process is an extension of the more primary mode of action that is oriented toward reaching understanding. Thus, Habermas's theory enjoins us to see in our politics or ethics those regulative ideals of recognition and respect that are already presupposed in ordinary communication, presupposed even as they are simultaneously thwarted and distorted by social hierarchies and systemic domination. For Habermas, an ethics of discourse requires that norms be validated through a procedure of public argumentation between all those who are affected; only those norms which produce a consensus can be said to be valid.

In Habermas's account, there is thus a dialectical and not an incommensurable relation between the systemic and the intersubjective perspectives, and between the theory and the practice. The intersubjective ideal internally prompts systemic critique, and the concept of communicative reason underlies critique's claim to emancipatory and transformative potential. Our status as subjects who are constituted through intersubjective relations is preserved, yet also placed in productive dialogue with an understanding of larger systems and histories. The Habermasian foregrounding of an intersubjective ideal does not mean that we abandon systemic analyses of the social world in favor of a celebratory, local insistence on community, human interrelatedness, or friendly conversation. We can only ensure proper democratic processes if we understand and engage those forces, both historical and structural, that determine the social world and powerfully condition what our capacities and arenas for action will be. The systemic perspective not only allows us to understand the structurally embedded inequities that distort human interaction but also can itself meaningfully inform an intersubjective relation, insofar as it allows us more fully to understand another's history and social situatedness.[20] However, it is practice itself that prompts the move to the systemic-theoretical perspective; and theory has done its work properly only if its account enables a reconfiguring of lived intersubjective relations.

The need to integrate a participatory or first-person perspective into cultural criticism has made itself felt in a number of ways in recent years. In a crucial sense, the attempt to mediate the tension between structural and "lived" accounts has defined the field of cultural studies. As Richard Johnson has written, cultural studies "is about the historical forms of consciousness or subjectivity, or the subjective forms we live by, or, in a rather perilous compression, perhaps a reduction, the subjective side of social relations" (43). For Johnson as well as for Stuart Hall, cultural studies is always concerned to both use and modify structuralist accounts. Likewise, much of the most important work being done in gender studies, postcolonialism, and gay and lesbian theory centers precisely on the reconstruction of experience in light of constructionist and post-structuralist critique. These cultural analyses involve subtle dialectical understandings of the relation between structural positions and subjective experience.[21] Such approaches, insofar as they aim to mediate between systemic and lived perspectives, share an affinity with the dialectical model I'm endorsing here; and they certainly redress the dominance of the systemic perspective that I earlier criticized. However, what the theory of communicative reason would contribute to these approaches is a more explicit and integral normative self-understanding.

If the theory of communicative reason remains central to any consistent elaboration of a democratic or plural politics, it still, as I have suggested, stands in need of substantial revisions if it is to answer adequately to the complex indeterminacies of the social world and to the inseparability of feeling from action oriented toward reaching understanding. As Seyla Benhabib's feminist critique of Habermas has shown, an elaboration of affective interaction can significantly deepen the concept of mutual understanding. As part of a larger analysis of modern theories of justice and moral development, Benhabib argues that Habermas's account is elaborated only from the perspective of the "generalized" and not from that of the "concrete" other. Consequently, Habermas fails to recognize the affective specificity of reciprocal recognition, which in turn provides the basis for the principles of need as opposed to justice. As Benhabib writes, "Human situations are perspectival, and to appreciate such perspectives involves empathy, imagination, and solidarity" (*Critique* 349).[22]

Benhabib's account of the importance of concrete otherness sometimes appears uncritically to reflect a shrinking lifeworld composed of very few concrete others, and based on the model of friendship rather than more widely conceived forms of social and political relations. Partly this derives from a too-sharp dualism generated by her insistence on the equal but separate importance of the perspectives of generalized and concrete otherness. For Benhabib, the perspective of the generalized other serves as the basis for a principle of equality; and the perspective of the concrete other introduces the more concretely realized ethical principles of care, friendship, empathy, solidarity, and intimacy. Benhabib nonetheless redresses the overemphasis on reason in the Habermasian ideal of mutual understanding. Concerned as he is to rescue reason from its detractors, Habermas does not acknowledge the extent to which the norms of mutual understanding and reciprocal recognition are internally dependent on empathy and compassion.

Habermas has met these criticisms only partway, and with an underlying recalcitrance. He acknowledges the importance of empathy to the procedure of role-taking, but this means that its importance is admitted only in the application, and not in the universal justification, of procedural ethics (*Moral Consciousness* 182). Habermas argues that once we move historically from a traditional to a rationalized lifeworld, this enables us to abstract questions of justice from questions of the good life. For Habermas, it is only the former that constitute the proper domain of moral theory; questions of the good life, by contrast, remain imbued with particularity and relativity—they cannot be justified, only adjudicated. Such an overly formalistic and Kantian approach to ethical theory (only seemingly tempered by Hegelian historicizing) ultimately installs an artificial rupture between questions of justice, which for Habermas can be universalized, and questions of the good life, which "are accessible to rational discussion only *within* the horizon of a concrete historical form of life or an individual life style" (*Moral Consciousness* 178). In a subsidiary move, Habermas relegates nonrational dimensions of intersubjectivity to the realm of the concrete, and protects the norm of mutual understanding from any affective resonances or disruptions. Such limiting abstractions must be abandoned in favor of an approach which fully integrates particularity and affect into the norm of mutual understanding.

In response to those moral theorists who argue that an ethics of responsibility or care must accompany an ethics of justice, Habermas has claimed that the only universally justifiable complement to the perspective of justice is *solidarity*, and not benevolence, care, or responsibility. While the justification of solidarity may appear to integrate an affective dimension into the theory, it turns out to refer merely to the necessary maintenance of our life as shared: the principle of solidarity "is rooted in the realization that each person must take responsibility for the other because as consociates all must have an interest in the integrity of their shared life context in the same way" ("Justice and Solidarity" 47). The principle of solidarity thus refers not to the irreducible affective dimensions of our interactions with others but rather conceives of responsibility toward others as an acknowledgment that we must maintain the webs of relation that constitute our social world. But there is no reason why the norm of mutual understanding cannot be amplified so as to embrace the affective forms that accompany and enable recognition and respect. Indeed, to fail to do so is to truncate the conception of intersubjectivity that underlies systemic critique. Here Habermas himself generates distortions that issue in part, one can only surmise, out of blindness to his own biases of gender and culture.

In his attempt to further substantiate his theory of moral justification through appeal to theories in developmental sciences, Habermas has also undermined the more radical implications of his shift from a subject-centered to a communicative paradigm. Of vital importance in the theory of communicative action is the conception of the subject as intersubjectively decentered and inherently relational.[23] Yet in my view Habermas's infatuation with developmental sciences both reflects and reinforces a too-stable conception of individual identity. I think we need to accentuate and further elaborate the ways in which the intersubjective relation itself works against the rigidities of identity thinking, and this despite the seeming stability invoked by the norm of "reaching understanding." As Benhabib has argued, the true negation of identity logic resides precisely in our relation to the other:

> The true negation of identity logic would imply a relation to an "other" who could at every point remind the self that it was not a mere projection or extension of the self, but an independent being, another self. The limits of the compulsion to identity are revealed when the object of identification is itself capable of acting in such a way as to differentiate between identity and difference, between self and other. If identity logic is the attempt to blur limits and boundaries, then those limits can be reestablished via the act of an other self who is capable of rejecting the narcissistic self-extension of the other. The true negation of identity logic would be an epistemological relation in which the object could not be subsumed under the cognitive categories of the self without that it—the object—could also regard these categories as adequate to capture its own difference and integrity. Identity logic can only be stopped when difference and differentiation are internal to the very self-identification of the epistemological object and subject, and this is only the case when our object is another subject or self. (*Critique* 221)

The norms embedded in the speech act need not, and indeed should not, translate into an unproblematic exchange of self-identical meanings by two placeholding consciousnesses. Indeed, as Dews has argued in his analysis of Habermas's conceptions of intersubjectivity, the ideal of reaching understanding is required precisely because of the "constitutive tension of linguistic intersubjectivity," a tension which exists "even in the absence of structural inequalities of power":

> Communication is not simply a matter of the transferral of identical meanings from one consciousness to another, but involves the simultaneous maintenance of the distinct identities of—in other words: the non-identity between—the part-

ners in communication. This non-identity cannot fail to enter
into the interpretation of meaning. (221)

Habermas's primary emphasis on the principle of justice (as
that which enforces relations of equality) and his reconstruction
of moral stages of development have tended to diminish the profound importance of intersubjective tension and social plurality,
even as procedural ethics remains in the service of adjudicating
between concrete individuals and collective constituencies. It also
risks installing a too-unified conception of subjectivity and social
identity. I want to argue instead that the regulative ideal of mutual understanding must be enlarged and recast so as to embrace
both the concreteness of otherness and the indeterminacy of social identities and relations. For it is precisely the indeterminate
nature of social relations that keeps ever before us the possibility
of political transformation. Such transformations do not occur
automatically, as implied in the mechanistic models of systemically
guaranteed resistances and subversions, but rather through processes of mutual understanding and dialogue. By way of conclusion, I want to place Habermas in relation to Ernesto Laclau and
Chantal Mouffe, two of his most trenchant critics, with the aim of
opening up but also justifying his theory.[24]

In *Hegemony and Socialist Strategy: Towards a Radical Democratic
Politics*, Laclau and Mouffe aim to redress what they identify in
classical Marxism as the reduction of the concrete to the abstract
on the level of social as well as historical understanding. Classical
Marxism reduces divergent subject-positions to a single (class)
position; likewise, any historical moment, including the present,
is apprehended only as a point within a trajectory determined a
priori. Reading from within the more open-ended and versa-
tile concept of *hegemony*, they apprehend the subject and the
social through a concept of textual polysemy: "the category of
the subject is penetrated by the same ambiguous, incomplete,
and polysemical character which overdetermination assigns to
every discursive entity" (121). We must recognize and trace
overdeterminations rather than perceive subjects as unitary or
fixed; this is the first step toward enabling "the possibility
of the deepening of a pluralist and democratic conception"
(166).

The problem Laclau and Mouffe set for themselves is to avoid an absolutized dispersion or atomism while still assiduously renouncing any regressive appeal to a transcendental subject. Crucial to their reconception is the principle of "antagonism," a category of social interaction defined not positively but rather *against* a notion of "opposition" which regressively conceives identities that face off as a priori fixities. Antagonism—unstable, ever-shifting—reflects the partial and precarious nature of all identification. Laclau and Mouffe bring before us the force of such precariousness precisely through the evocation of an encounter: "the presence of the 'Other' prevents me from being totally myself":

> Insofar as there is an antagonism, I cannot be a full presence for myself. But nor is the force that antagonizes such a presence: its objective being is a symbol of my non-being, and, in this way, it is overflowed by a plurality of meanings which prevent its being fixed as full positivity. Real opposition is an *objective* relation—that is, determinable, definable—among things; contradiction is an equally definable relation among concepts; antagonism constitutes the limits of every objectivity, which is revealed as a partial and precarious *objectification*. (125)

For Laclau and Mouffe, antagonism is a function of the radical contingency of the social; but rather than serving to render politics impossible, it serves as the precondition for transformation, and precisely at the level of social alliances. The radical nonfixity of identity gives us the freedom collectively to construct new hegemonies which will emerge through mutually transforming encounters between variously constituted groups. Such social processes are vital to progressive social transformation: "For there to be a 'democratic equivalence' we need the construction of a new 'common sense' which changes the identity of the different groups in such a way that demands are articulated equivalentially with those of the others" (183). In this conception no form of fixed identity can be said to constitute the groups whose identity is produced and transformed through their various encounters and struggles with one another: "equivalence is always hegemonic insofar as it does not simply establish an 'alliance' between given

interests, but modifies the identity of the forces engaging in that
alliance" (183–84).

Laclau and Mouffe's "radical relationalism of social identities" derives from a post-structuralist linguistic model and hence
might seem, in this respect, to elaborate the ambiguities and in-
stabilities of identity from a systems-perspective. Yet we must
keep in mind the primacy of intersubjective "antagonism," which
is not elaborated from such a perspective. Indeterminacy becomes
simply the condition of our irreducibly social identities that enables us endlessly to renegotiate and re-create our relations to
others, as both individuals and members of nonreified collectives.
That is, indeterminacy serves as the precondition but not the
guarantee of political transformation. Only in and through the
relations between subjects and groups are identities constituted
and transformed; so in an important sense, and quite self-consciously, Laclau and Mouffe avoid the objectivism that inhabits
post-structuralist systems theory while still forwarding a general
theoretical account of the social.

An important question remains, however: does the concept
of antagonism as constitutive of the social entirely foreclose or
undermine any conception of communicative reason? In their
more recent work, these thinkers have stressed the importance of
the situated social agent through a reconstructed conception of
Gadamerian phronesis (detached from its traditionalist resonances and reconceived more along the lines of the Wittgenstein-
ian language game).[25] Although Laclau and Mouffe themselves
see Habermas as engaged in the deluded project of attempting to
guarantee the political efficacy of Enlightenment ideals, I want to
suggest that there are tacit similarities between Habermas's conception of communicative action as the site of emancipatory potential and Laclau's developing account of hegemonic struggle. In
an article that extends many of the claims in *Hegemony and Socialist
Strategy*, Laclau elaborates in further detail how antifoundation-
alism can serve as the ground for a profound political optimism.
He does so precisely by specifying a communicative model of
social praxis, arguing that society should be "understood as a vast
argumentative texture through which people construct their own
reality." This then produces a further claim: "Inasmuch as argument and discourse constitute the social, their open-ended char-

acter becomes the source of a greater activism and a more radical libertarianism" ("Politics" 79).

But if Laclau is to justify a transformative praxis through a conception of society as fundamentally discursive, he must presuppose communicative norms, even in the face of the radical disruptions of antagonism. In order to appropriate the radically open and transformable character of social identities for a new hegemony—in order to articulate a common sense—we must presuppose some form of communicative understanding, unless we are to imagine that such articulations take place behind the backs of social subjects/It seems to me that the turn to phronesis is itself an attempt to render more explicit those communicative and reconstructive processes involved in mutually transforming intersubjective alliances. Yet it also seems that an unacknowledged intersubjective ideal underlies the whole concept of a new common sense. We may acknowledge that power is constitutive of all interactions, and that identity is indeterminate, and still aim to foster regulative ideals of equality and reciprocal respect. Otherwise, what meaning does "democracy" or "the left" have? In other words, if the Habermasian account must be revised to give prominence to social indeterminacy and concrete social positions, then the idea of "equivalences" and "common sense" must be deepened through an acknowledgment of the intersubjective ideals that underlie them. Insofar as it serves merely as the foundation of a procedural model, there is no need for communicative reason to be yoked to essentializing conceptions of identity, whether individual or social. A regulative ideal of mutual understanding does not render identity determinate, it merely renders politics possible.

Laclau and Mouffe generate an entirely promising vision of communicative politics in their thoroughgoing reconceptualization of rights. According to them, a radical democratic politics would be based on a demand for rights constituted through variable contexts and not determined a priori:

> The idea of 'natural' rights prior to society—and indeed, the
> whole of the false dichotomy individual/society—should be
> abandoned, and replaced by another manner of posing the
> problem of rights. It is never possible for individual rights to

> be defined in isolation, but only in the context of social rela-
> tions which define determinate subject positions. As a conse-
> quence, it will always be a question of rights which involve
> other subjects who participate in the same social relation.
> (184).

Given the multiplicity of subject-positions, as well as the fundamental unevenness of the social, any demand for rights must thus
take into account the rights claims of other groups: a reconstructed principle of equality must thus be balanced by a reconstructed principle of liberty, which recognizes differences and
hence leads to the notion of plurality. This is similar to Benhabib,
who wishes to balance the category of the general other (which
would correspond to the struggle for equality) with the category
of the concrete other (which enables and ensures a *plural* democracy). More importantly to the argument I have been making in
this essay, Laclau and Mouffe's different manner of posing the
problem of rights, their emphasis on social contexts and indeterminacy, still relies, if only implicitly, on a fundamental appeal to
the forms of mutual recognition upon which rights rest. Hence I
find peculiar their refusal to recognize the importance of the
theory of communicative action.

Mutually transforming reciprocal recognition, a condition of
any democratic and emancipatory practice, is an experience fundamentally foreclosed in those post-structuralisms that allow a
systems-perspective to dominate their account of the social world.
As I have tried to show throughout this essay, such accounts fail
to express the fundamentally intersubjective, participatory, and
open-ended nature of the social world. More significantly, the
systems-dominated post-structuralist paradigms do not adequately theorize their normative commitments. The project of
communicative ethics, on the other hand, allows us to do more
than describe and reinscribe the impasses of constructionism. In
place of social, political, and linguistic determinisms, it offers a
model of mutually constitutive agencies and antagonisms in which
our theories of intersubjectivity—and our intersubjective practices—may fairly be founded.

Notes

1. For an example of the pragmatic stance, see Fraser and Nicholson, "Social Criticism without Philosophy"; for examples of the admission of complicity, see Miller, *The Novel and the Police*, and Armstrong, *Desire and Domestic Fiction*.

2. In "Paul de Man: Resistance and Collaboration," Morrison shows how the claim of inherent subversiveness animates Derrida's defense of de Man. The politically inflected claim for the destabilizing effects of the unconscious is exemplified in the work of Rose (*Sexuality in the Field of Vision*).

3. As I will discuss later, Spivak has reconsidered her earlier position on strategic essentialism.

4. See Foucault, *The History of Sexuality, Volume I*, 101. Foucault's formulations in this text, however, tend to move back and forth between a version of the first approach, whereby resistance is itself a function of systemic power, and a dual approach that shifts between the local and the systemic (see especially 92–102). Some Foucauldians who privilege the systems-view subscribe to a cynical version of the first approach: in this case resistance is a function of the system, yet it fundamentally perpetuates rather than destabilizes or transforms that system. For example, see Miller, *The Novel and the Police*.

5. This discussion does not and cannot hope to cover the entire field of post-structuralist politics and ethics. I am interested here in analyzing some prominent approaches within the field of cultural criticism. For a useful survey that extends beyond the scope of this essay, see Jay, "The Morals of Genealogy."

6. See Benhabib, *Critique, Norm, and Utopia*; Bernstein, *Beyond Objectivism and Relativism*; and Cornell, "Toward a Modern/Postmodern Reconstruction of Ethics." Also see Brantlinger, *Crusoe's Footprints*, for a survey of the field of cultural studies which traces a recurring emphasis on a kind of communicative action among its practitioners; interestingly, he concludes his account with a call for a more explicit endorsement of Habermas's emphasis on communicative reason. See Habermas, *Theory*.

7. I borrow the word *cryptonormative* from Habermas, who uses it to characterize Foucault's failure to maintain a merely neutral stance toward the positivity of power (*Philosophical Discourse* 294).

8. See Spivak, "Criticism, Feminism, and the Institution," "Strategy, Identity, Writing," and "Subaltern Studies."

9. For endorsements and elaborations of reconsidered understandings of essentialism, some of them explicitly endorsing a double gesture similar to Spivak's, see Fuss, *Essentially Speaking*; Snitow, "A Gender Diary"; de Lauretis, *Technologies of Gender* 26, and "Upping the Anti (sic) in Feminist Theory"; Smith, *Discerning the Subject*; Martin, "Feminism, Criticism, and Foucault"; Braidotti, "The Politics of Ontological Difference"; Whitford, *Luce Irigaray*.

10. Moi reelaborates and further complicates this position in "Feminism, Postmodernism, and Style," arguing that we must "live out" the contradictions of not a double but a treble feminism, one that simultaneously affirms equality, difference, and deconstruction.

11. Her indication at one point that this strategy is "partially unwitting" (207) highlights rather than resolves this issue.

12. De Lauretis has made the most encompassing feminist reinscription of essentialism to date in "Upping the Anti (sic) in Feminist Theory." She argues, invoking Locke, that the essence appealed to in the writings of many so-called essentialists is a nominal and not a real essence; it is, in other words, a constructed essence. "It is a totality of qualities, properties, and attributes that such feminists define, envisage, or enact for themselves. . . .This is more a project, then, than a description of existent reality; it is an admittedly feminist project of 're-vision,' where the specifications *feminist* and *re*-vision already signal its historical location, even as the (re)vision projects itself outward geographically and temporally (universally) to recover the past and claim the future" (257). De Lauretis thus overcomes the tension between essentialism and constructionism by recasting the former as a version of the latter. Such an argument, however, involves a rather drastic reduction of cultural and radical feminisms, and ultimately has the effect of projecting a false unity upon the diverse and contested field of feminism.

13. Again, as should be clear from the reinvocation of Spivak, more than one version of strategic essentialism can appear within a single argument.

14. Snitow is here citing—and criticizing—Linda Alcoff's attempt to transcend the paradox in "Cultural Feminism Versus Post-Structuralism."

15. Also see *Discerning the Subject*, in which Paul Smith forwards a theoretical argument precisely featuring and privileging feminism's elaboration of doubled strategies.

16. Snitow is actually careful elsewhere not to generate an opposition like this; it is interesting that it emerges within her section on post-structuralism.

17. Other critics have avoided strategic essentialist arguments by endorsing a model of coalition based on a shared opposition to dominant power matrices. See Duggan, "Making It Perfectly Queer," and Mohanty, "Cartographies of Struggle." These approaches importantly argue that we can articulate political practices that integrate constructionist critique.

18. This emphasis exists in some tension with her arguments in favor of strategic essentialism.

19. Foucault's concept of reverse discourses would be a cogent counterexample, since these are waged by, and on behalf of, discursive *groups* (101).

20. Allowing the systemic perspective to "meaningfully inform" the intersubjective relation is not the same as asking that it *define* that relation, as in the case of Spivak's "shared positionality," a concept I criticized earler.

21. See de Lauretis, *Alice Doesn't* and *Technologies of Gender*; Martin and Mohanty, "Feminist Politics"; Alcoff, "Cultural Feminism Versus Post-Structuralism"; Martin, "Lesbian Identity and Autobiographical Difference[s]"; Mohanty, "Cartographies of Struggle."

22. Also see Benhabib, "The Generalized and the Concrete Other."

23. See Cornell, "Toward a Modern/Postmodern Reconstruction of Ethics" (299), for an eloquent argument on behalf of a conception of subjectivity as intersubjectively decentered.

24. In *New Reflections on the Revolution of Our Time* Laclau begins by defining his project in opposition to Habermas's, yet never really directly engages his theories. However, he does append to the volume an essay by Slavoj Žižek that casts the ideal speech situation as a fetish. See also Mouffe, "Radical Democracy," 31–32.

25. See Mouffe, "Radical Democracy," and Laclau, "Politics."

Works Cited

Alcoff, Linda. "Cultural Feminism Versus Post-Structuralism: The Identity Crisis in Feminist Theory." *Signs* 13.3 (1988): 405–36.

Armstrong, Nancy. *Desire and Domestic Fiction: A Political History of the Novel.* Oxford: Oxford UP, 1987.

Benhabib, Seyla. *Critique, Norm, and Utopia: A Study of the Foundations of Critical Theory.* New York: Columbia UP, 1986.

——. "The Generalized and the Concrete Other: The Kohlberg-Gilligan Controversy and Feminist Theory." *Feminism as Critique: On the Politics of Gender.* Ed. Seyla Benhabib and Drucilla Cornell. Minneapolis: U of Minnesota P, 1987. 77–95.

Bernstein, Richard J. *Beyond Objectivism and Relativism: Science, Hermeneutics, and Praxis.* Philadelphia: U of Pennsylvania P, 1983.

Braidotti, Rosa. "The Politics of Ontological Difference." *Between Feminism and Psychoanalysis.* Ed. Teresa Brennan. New York and London: Routledge, 1989. 89–105.

Brantlinger, Patrick. *Crusoe's Footprints: Cultural Studies in Britain and America.* New York and London: Routledge, 1990.

Butler, Judith. *Gender Trouble: Feminism and the Subversion of Identity.* New York and London: Routledge, 1990.

Cornell, Drucilla. "Toward a Modern/Postmodern Reconstruction of Ethics." *University of Pennsylvania Law Review* 133 (1985): 291–380.

de Lauretis, Teresa. *Alice Doesn't: Feminism, Semiotics, Cinema.* Bloomington: Indiana UP, 1984.

——. *Technologies of Gender: Essays on Theory, Film, and Fiction.* Bloomington: Indiana UP, 1987.

——. "Upping the Anti (sic) in Feminist Theory." *Conflicts in Feminism.* Ed. Marianne Hirsch and Evelyn Fox Keller. New York and London: Routledge, 1990. 255–70.

Dews, Peter. *Logics of Disintegration: Post-Structuralist Thought and the Claims of Critical Theory.* London: Verso, 1987.

Duggan, Lisa. "Making It Perfectly Queer: Theory, Politics, and Paradox in the 90s." *Socialist Review* (forthcoming).

Foucault, Michel. *The History of Sexuality, Volume I.* Trans. Robert Hurley. New York: Random, 1978.

Fraser, Nancy, and Linda J. Nicholson. "Social Criticism without Philosophy: An Encounter between Feminism and Postmodernism." *Feminism/Postmodernism.* Ed. Linda J. Nicholson. New York and London: Routledge, 1990. 19–38.

Fuss, Diana. *Essentially Speaking: Feminism, Nature, and Difference.* New York and London: Routledge, 1989.

Habermas, Jürgen. "Justice and Solidarity: On the Discussion Concerning 'Stage 6.'" Trans. Shierry Weber Nicholsen. *The Philosophical Forum* 21 (1989–90): 32–52.

——. *Moral Consciousness and Communicative Action.* Trans. Christian Lenhardt and Shierry Weber Nicholsen. Cambridge: MIT P, 1990.

——. *The Philosophical Discourse of Modernity.* Trans. Frederick Lawrence. Cambridge: MIT P, 1987.

_____. *The Theory of Communicative Action.* Trans. Thomas McCarthy. 2 vols. Boston: Beacon, 1984–87.

Heath, Stephen. "Difference." *Screen* 19.3 (1978): 50–112.

Jay, Martin. "The Morals of Genealogy: Or Is There a Post-Structuralist Ethics?" *The Cambridge Review* 110 (1989): 70–74.

Johnson, Richard. "What Is Cultural Studies Anyway?" *Social Text* 6.1 (1987): 38–80.

Laclau, Ernesto. *New Reflections on the Revolution of Our Time.* London: Verso, 1990.

_____. "Politics and the Limits of Modernity." *Universal Abandon? The Politics of Postmodernism.* Ed. Andrew Ross. Minneapolis: U of Minnesota P, 1988. 63–82.

Laclau, Ernesto, and Chantal Mouffe. *Hegemony and Socialist Strategy: Towards a Radical Democratic Politics.* London: Verso, 1985.

Martin, Biddy. "Feminism, Criticism, and Foucault." *Feminism and Foucault: Reflections on Resistance.* Ed. Irene Diamond and Lee Quinby. Boston: Northeastern UP, 1985. 3–18.

_____. "Lesbian Identity and Autobiographical Difference[s]." *Life/Lines: Theorizing Women's Autobiography.* Ed. Bella Brodzki and Celeste Schenck. Ithaca: Cornell UP, 1988. 77–103.

Martin, Biddy, and Chandra Talpade Mohanty. "Feminist Politics: What's Home Got to Do with It?" *Feminist Studies/Critical Studies.* Ed. Teresa de Lauretis. Bloomington: Indiana UP, 1986. 191–212.

Miller, D. A. *The Novel and the Police.* Berkeley: U of California P, 1988.

Mohanty, Chandra Talpade. "Cartographies of Struggle: Third World Women and the Politics of Feminism." *Third World Women and the Politics of Feminism.* Ed. Chandra Talpade Mohanty, Ann Russo, and Lourdes Torres. Bloomington: Indiana UP, 1991. 1–47.

Moi, Toril. "Feminism, Postmodernism, and Style: Recent Feminist Criticism in the United States." *Cultural Critique* 9 (1988): 3–22.

_____. *Sexual/Textual Politics: Feminist Literary Theory.* New York: Methuen, 1985.

Morrison, Paul. "Paul de Man: Resistance and Collaboration." *Representations* 32 (1990): 50–74.

Mouffe, Chantal. "Radical Democracy: Modern or Postmodern?" *Universal Abandon? The Politics of Postmodernism.* Ed. Andrew Ross. Minneapolis: U of Minnesota P, 1988. 31–45.

Riley, Denise. *"Am I That Name?": Feminism and the Category of "Women" in History.* Minneapolis: U of Minnesota P, 1988.

Rose, Jacqueline. *Sexuality in the Field of Vision.* London: Verso, 1986.

Smith, Paul. *Discerning the Subject.* Minneapolis: U of Minnesota P, 1988.

Snitow, Ann. "A Gender Diary." *Conflicts in Feminism.* Ed. Marianne Hirsch and Evelyn Fox Keller. New York: Routledge, 1990. 9–43.

Spivak, Gayatri Chakravorty. "Criticism, Feminism, and the Institution." Interview with Elizabeth Grosz (1984). *The Post-Colonial Critic.* Ed. Sarah Harasym. New York: Routledge, 1990. 1–16.

_____. "In a Word." Interview with Ellen Rooney (1988). *Differences* 1 (1989): 124–56.

_____. "Strategy, Identity, Writing." Interview (1986). *The Post-Colonial Critic.* New York: Routledge, 1990. 35–49.

——. "Subaltern Studies: Deconstructing Historiography." *In Other Worlds:* *Essays in Cultural Politics.* New York: Routledge, 1988. 197–221.

Whitford, Margaret. *Luce Irigaray: Philosophy in the Feminine.* London: Routledge, 1991.

Žižek, Slavoj. Appendix: "Beyond Discourse Analysis." *New Reflections on the Revolution of Our Time.* By Ernesto Laclau. London: Verso, 1990. 249–60.

Exteriority and Appropriation: Foucault, Derrida, and the Discipline of Literary Criticism

Jeffrey T. Nealon

In the past decade, Michel Foucault's thought has been gaining increasing currency in literature departments in the United States. If one were to plot schematically the rise and fall of theories in literature departments, one could easily tie the rise of Foucault's genealogical discourse to the fall of another contemporary French discourse, Jacques Derrida's deconstruction; in fact, Foucault's thought first comes on the American literary critical scene thematized as a socially and institutionally engaged alternative to what many politically oriented critics saw as the paralyzing textualism of Derrida and his disciples at Yale. Raman Selden gives a representative account of the debate in *A Reader's Guide to Contemporary Literary Theory*:

> There is another strand in post-structuralist thought which believes the world is more than a galaxy of texts, and that some theories of textuality ignore the fact that discourse is involved in power. . . . [For Foucault] it is evident that real power is exercised through discourse, and that this power has real effects. (98)

© 1992 by *Cultural Critique*. 0882-4371 (Spring 1992). All rights reserved.

Thus, Foucault is brought to bear on deconstruction in order to re-orient literary criticism to the real world, to the workings of "real power" in discourse and history. In fact, a whole school of criticism has sprouted up around Foucault's texts, "new historicism," which takes from a reading of Foucault its ground notion that "discourse is like everything else in our society: the object of a struggle for power" (Harari 43).

In this essay, I would like to take issue with the terms of this debate—specifically with the notion that Foucault is somehow a champion of historical *praxis* over Derrida's purely textual *theoria*. But I would like to do so not in order presumptuously to expose misreadings of either Foucault or Derrida in the service of a better understanding of their relationship to literary criticism, but, rather, in order to say some things about the discipline of literary criticism itself. In other words, I am interested less in exposing supposed "misreadings" of either thinker's work within this secondhand debate than I am in examining the institutional and disciplinary imperatives which make these misreadings possible—in fact, I will argue that a certain economy of misreading is even *necessary* if literary criticism is to "use" either Foucault or Derrida at all.

And attempt to *use* them it does. The discipline of literary criticism is hungry for paradigms—hungry for new readings and new methods. The theory explosion of the 1970s brought with it an entire "theory industry" within and around literature departments; the backbone of this industry is the theoretical guidebook: there are evaluative studies like the aforementioned *Reader's Guide*, Terry Eagleton's *Literary Theory: An Introduction*, much of Jonathan Culler's early work, or Frank Lentricchia's *After the New Criticism*; and there are essay collections like Donald Keesey's *Contexts For Criticism*, Josué Harari's *Textual Strategies: Perspectives in Poststructuralist Criticism*, or H. Aram Veeser's *The New Historicism*. Books such as these are a major source of "theory" for many literary critics, and they present to the profession various methods or strategies for reading texts, for producing critical analyses.[1] As Harari writes in his collection *Textual Strategies*, "method has become a strategy" (72), and for Harari, the future of literary criticism is to be a struggle among these critical strategies, these truth strategies:

I have presented the various critical struggles at play among contemporary theorists. It remains to inscribe these strategies in a more global framework, to put them in the ring of criticism as it were, and to determine how the rounds are to be scored. (69)

Harari here invokes a perhaps all-too-familiar picture of the literature department—indeed of "pluralistic" society on the whole—as engaged in a violent struggle for the truth, for truth as strategic "victory," for truth as appropriation.[2] Such a conception, unfortunately, seems to replicate rather than displace the violent will-to-truth that is in question in many of the theoretical discussions he presents. Also, Harari's notion of truth as critical struggle rather problematically recuperates thinking such as Foucault's or Derrida's within an institution—it names and preserves the interior, protected space of the university as the nexus of discourse's truth, the "ring" where various truth strategies will be tested and a winner declared.

The notion of a "ring of criticism" is particularly apt here because the space of interiority suggested by the image of a ring is precisely what literary criticism has to secure for itself in order to isolate its object and to perform its work. If a truth about a text is to be revealed and preserved in criticism, then there must be a protected interior space where this truth can lie: the structure of the work, the biography of the author and its relation to his or her other works, the relation of the work to its historical circumstances, and so on. But any such notion of interiority—a place protected from the play of a larger network, a place where meaning can rest unmolested—is precisely one of the things in question in many of these "critical strategies," in thinking like Foucault's or Derrida's.[3] For example, in "What Is an Author?," an essay anthologized (I am tempted to say canonized) in Harari's collection, Foucault calls for a writing about literature that is not based on the accepted interior unities of the author or the book; rather, he speaks of the possibility of a topology of discourse based on statements, positivities that "cannot be constructed solely from the grammatical features, formal structures, and objects of discourse" (157). Statements cannot be expected, contra Harari's hope, to stay in one place and fight it out in the ring of criticism because, as Gilles Deleuze notes, "each statement is itself a multiplicity, not a structure or a system" (6)—each statement is exterior, diffused, overflowing the totality of interiority.

It is precisely here, with the exteriority of the statement, that Foucault poses his most dangerous question to literary criticism; he writes in *The Archaeology of Knowledge*: "Language, in its appearance as a mode of being, is the statement [*l'énoncé*]: as such, it belongs to a description that is neither transcendental nor anthropological" (113/148).[4] He goes on to explain:

> . . . the analysis of statements treats them in the systematic form of exteriority. Usually, the historical description of things said is shot through with [*tout entière traversée par*] the opposition of interior and exterior; and wholly directed by [*tout entière commandée par*] a move from the exterior—which may be no more than contingency or mere material necessity, a visible body or uncertain translation—towards the essential nucleus of interiority. (120–21/158–59)

This formulation of the "historical description of things said" also holds, I think, for the literary critical description of things said: literary criticism moves from the exterior (the other, the untranslatable, the unthematized) to the interior (the same, the translation, the theme). Foucault challenges the (possibility of such a) totalizing impulse in the human sciences and outlines a thinking whose task is "to describe a group of statements not with reference to the interiority of an intention, a thought, or a subject, but in accordance with the dispersion of an exteriority" (125/164).

Notions such as dispersion and exteriority pose serious problems for literary criticism, whose traditional field enables it to explain what is *inside* a text by putting to work certain notions from *outside* a text, from a constructed place of critical privilege such as the author, reader, structure, or historical circumstances of the text. Paradoxically then, in the literary critical model, "outside" the text becomes another name *not* for an exteriority which would disperse the text's meanings, but rather for another—perhaps more pernicious—*interiority* which can protect and preserve the text's meanings; in other words, for criticism, the "outside" of the text is simply another name for an interior space—a space which can maintain its purity because it is beyond the play of the textual network. For example, in "What Is an Author?" Foucault takes up the problem of the text's relation to the author—"the manner in which the text points to this 'figure' that, at least in appearance, is outside it and antecedes it" (141)—and argues that the author is one such privileged space of interiority that is outside the text:

> [The author] is a certain functional principle by which, in our culture, one limits, excludes, and chooses; in short, by which one impedes the free circulation, the free manipulation, the free composition, decomposition, and recomposition of fiction. (159)

Foucault here points out that criticism employs the notion of the author to preserve a space of meaning, an interiority which can arrest the exterior hazards of signification. But it is problematic—if not impossible—to locate and maintain such spaces of interiority because, as Foucault notes,

> the margins of a book are never clear-cut: beyond the title, the first lines, and the last full stop, beyond its internal configuration and its autonomous form, it is caught up in a system of references [un système de renvois] to other books, other texts, other sentences: it is a node within a network. (Archaeology 23/34, translation modified)

For Foucault, the book exists in an exterior network of statements where the interiority of totality is always dispersed; hence, there is no protected interior space within this network which could rule the entire network. Likewise, there is no place above or below the surface of discourse—no "outside," no pure interior space beyond the reach of the exterior network's effects—which could explain discourse, which could force discourse to render up a secret truth. This is what he calls the flattening of discourse: all discourse is on a flat surface; therefore no instance of discourse can claim to rule from outside—above, below, or from a protected interior space upon—the surface, can explain or ground the entire chain or preserve an instance of determinate meaning within the network. He writes, "There is no sub-text [Il n'y a pas de texte d'en dessous].

And therefore no plethora. The enunciative level is identical with its own surface" (*Archaeology* 119/157).

At this point, we may have to circle back to where we started, with literary criticism's recent romancing of Foucault at the expense of Derrida—to Raman Selden, who goes on to write in his *Reader's Guide*: "Like other post-structuralists, Foucault regards discourse as a central human activity, but not as a universal, 'general text,' a vast sea of signification" (98). This would seem to be the party line on the huge difference between Foucault's thought and Derrida's: Foucault's thought is interested in active power and history, Derrida's in passive thought and textuality.[5] But I would like to step back and try to read Derrida and Foucault together. Strangely enough, I would like to read them together at the point where they seem farthest apart, at that "place" in Derrida's text that a whole host of his critics (including Foucault) have pointed to as the metaphysical Achilles' heel of deconstruction: Derrida's notion of "general text," which Selden glosses as a totalizing "universal" that denies the world and history in favor of a "vast sea of signification."[6]

Derrida has been dealing with this reading of his texts for years, and it will, I think, be instructive to look at exactly *how* he deals with the charge that he transforms the world into a place of rampant, undecidable textualization. First, Derrida emphasizes that the text or general text is not what we think of as a text—a book—but rather

> a differential network, a fabric of traces referring endlessly to something other than itself, to other differential traces. Thus the text overruns all the limits assigned to it so far (not submerging or drowning them in an undifferentiated homogeneity, but rather making them more complex, dividing and multiplying strokes and lines). ("Living On" 84)

With his notion of general text, Derrida is not attempting to cast the text and the world in what Foucault calls "the gray light of neutralization" ("Author" 145), but rather to complicate notions of exterior and interior—not attempting "to extend the reassuring notion of the text to a whole extra-textual realm and to transform the world into a library by doing away with all boundaries,

all framework, all sharp edges," but rather "to work out the theoretical and practical system of these margins, these borders, once
more, from the ground up" ("Living On" 84). Derrida's notion of
text, then, seems to have at least this much in common with
Foucault's notion of the exteriority of a network of statements:
both posit a discursive field or network in which no term can rule
from a privileged place of interiority,[7] and both share what
Foucault calls a "*limit-attitude*" ("Enlightenment" 45), an interest
in re-working thought's borders in the wake of the Enlightenment.

But it is at this limit that the dominant literary critical–political reading of Foucault triumphs over Derrida; Foucault, given
this reading, is interested in "reference and reality," with the
"world of institutions and action" (Arac 250, 243),[8] while Derrida
reinscribes everything within the rigid limit of the prison house of
language. Again, I think this is an inadequate reading of both
thinkers. Derrida sums up the relation between text and limit or
context like this:

> I set down here as an axiom and as that which is to be proved
> that the reconstitution cannot be finished. This is my starting
> point: no meaning can be determined out of context, but no
> context permits saturation. What I am referring to here is not
> richness of substance, semantic fertility, but rather structure:
> the structure of the remnant or of iteration; ("Living On" 81)

while Foucault writes,

> A statement always has borders [*marges*] peopled by other
> statements. These borders are not what is usually meant by
> 'context'—real or verbal—that is, all the situational or linguis-
> tic elements, taken together, that motivate a formulation and
> determine its meaning. They are distinct from such a 'context'
> precisely in so far as they make it possible. (*Archaeology* 97–
> 98/128–29)

Here again it seems that we see Foucault and Derrida in general
agreement against traditional and critical notions of context: one
cannot appeal to (historical or extra-textual) context to rein in the
significations of a statement or a text; a space of interior privilege

cannot be maintained "outside the text." In fact, both Derrida and Foucault seem to agree that context cannot rule text—a place of interiority cannot be maintained in an exterior field—precisely because context is not really "outside" the text at all. Quite the contrary: both text and context are engendered or made possible in the same field, under the same conditions—for Foucault this field is the "flat" network of statements, for Derrida it is the "structure of the remnant or of iteration."[9] Both notions serve to make it impossible for literary criticism to preserve a space of interiority by which it could construct a critical system—a saturated critical context above, below, or outside the text—to reveal and protect meaning.

This, it seems to me, is precisely why many literary critics simply *have* to read Derrida and Foucault as they do—Derrida as the last in a transcendentalist philosophical line and Foucault as the last in a materialist historicist line, as the founders of a "textual" deconstructive criticism and a "worldly" new historicism. Such readings are necessary if literary criticism is to continue as an autonomous discipline, because if literary criticism accepts a notion of exteriority, it not only has to face the problem of doing something other than revealing a meaning in the text, it has the much more pervasive problem of actually isolating its object, of separating inside- from outside-text, *texte* from *hors-texte*. Hence we see the institutional imperative for literary critics to read Derrida's famous phrase "*il n'y a pas de hors-texte*" as "there is nothing outside of the text": if everything can be found within texts or textuality, and critics read texts for a living, then obviously the place or role of criticism is secured. However, if one translates this phrase as "there is no extra-text [literally, out-text]," it brings out a much different reading: a network of exteriority (here named "text") is given—has no determinable origin or telos—and no one term or discourse can claim privilege over another within this field; no space can be protected from the play of the network. Obviously, while the latter reading is positively disastrous for literary criticism's project, the former interpretation allows a continued central role for criticism: it allows critics to produce a deconstructive methodology and apply it to the whole of their field—revealing that, indeed, there is a nothing outside the determinate text precisely by applying a deconstructive methodology from this ultra-privileged site of the outside.[10]

This easy methodologizing is one of Foucault's central critiques of Derrida's thought; Foucault argues that certain notions of the intransitivity of literature, distilled from the texts of Barthes and Blanchot, "are quickly taken up in the interior of an institution . . . : the institution of the university" (*Live* 114). But, as we have seen, it is only given a certain (rather suspect) reading of Derrida's thought that it can be taken up for such institutional imperatives—and, as is becoming clear in the movement or methodology called new historicism, Foucault's is no less prone to hypostatization. One might profitably object here that Foucault's work has no essential relation to new historicism—as Rodolphe Gasché has argued concerning Derrida's relation to deconstructive criticism[11]—but there is no denying the *perceived* influence of Foucault's work, both in the texts of new historicists and critics of new historicism alike. Foucault's perceived link to new historicism is so strong, for example, that Frank Lentricchia's essay in *The New Historicism*, "Foucault's Legacy: A New Historicism?" does not quote *one word of Foucault's text*; granted, the original printing of Lentricchia's essay places it after his long and involved discussion of Foucault in *Ariel and the Police*, but when Lentricchia turns specifically to discuss new historicism, he mentions Stephen Greenblatt throughout in the same breath as Foucault, reinforcing the widespread belief that new historicism is simply a translation of Foucault—that because "Foucault's key obsessions and terms shape Greenblatt's argument" ("Foucault's Legacy" 242n), the relation between Foucault's texts and new historicism is an unproblematic one.[12] This claim, in fact, could be said to comprise the "dominant" reading of new historicism—it supposedly takes directly from Foucault its ground notion, its "key obsession": a discontinuous power that moves through everything. For example, Carolyn Porter reads Greenblatt's assertion that "theatricality . . . is not set over against power but is one of its essential modes" as a translation of Foucault's claim that power "induces pleasure, forms knowledge, produces discourse" (262). In a crowning irony, one can now find Foucault being referred to as a practitioner of Berkeley new historicism,[13] just as Derrida was or is thought of as a Yale critic.

Insofar as Foucault (infamously) criticizes Derrida's thinking as "a historically well-determined little pedagogy" ("My Body" 27), all of this institutional attention creates something of a problem for him, though it seems fairly easy to locate the beginning of a Foucauldian response to his own methodization: power produces, an institutional discipline produces, and it consistently needs new processes by which to produce new objects of study or new thematizations; in short, a discipline like literary criticism needs determinate—and determin*ing*—methodologies. New historicism, then, takes Foucault's exterior notions of power and discontinuity in historical analysis and turns them into usable, interior, ontological notions: new historicism often analyzes texts by studying the slippery relations of power in texts and in history. This historicism is "new" in that it takes into account the discontinuity of history, but it can quickly become "old" again when it takes up a notion of discontinuity as a simple, declarable discontinuity: studies are produced which tell us that while we used to think history was continuous, it was in fact *dis*continuous. For example, in *Habits of Thought in the English Renaissance* (Volume 13 of Greenblatt's New Historicism series), Debora K. Shuger takes up "[t]he new historicist critique of traditional formulations of Renaissance thought" (1); she writes:

> Investigation of these habits of thought in the dominant culture of the English Renaissance yields surprising results. Despite their general agreement on doctrinal matters, the figures studied present an unexpected and sometimes drastic ideological pluralism. *Instead of a monologic world view, one uncovers complex and divergent assumptions.* . . . The [Renaissance] impulse to define and distinguish . . . results from a *prior sense of confusion and lack of demarcation.* (9–10, my emphases)

For Shuger, new historicism uncovers the "complex and divergent assumptions" that underlie a supposedly or traditionally "monologic world view"; in fact, she seems to argue that behind any historical or intellectual order(ing) there is "a prior sense of confusion and lack of demarcation." She concludes her introduction with what seems to be an apt formulation of the new historicist critique: "Renaissance works noticeably lack a systematic coherence, *their discontinuities instead exposing the struggle for meaning that fissures the last premodern generation*" (16, my emphasis). If this is the case, then the place or value of Foucault in new historicism is his discovery or *exposure* of the disorder which lies under or behind the supposed order of history—that behind what seems to be a historical continuity, one can always and everywhere find or uncover discontinuity.

We have, however, already seen Foucault problematizing this language of depth and his skepticism about "exposing" hidden origins (whether they be origins of order or disorder); likewise, such a reading of Foucault precisely allows the easy methodological institutionalization that he criticizes Derrida for promoting— allows discontinuity to lie behind every continuity, and allows for the exposure of this discontinuity as/in the end of a discipline or method. Foucault responds to such a fetishizing of discontinuity:

> My problem was not at all to say, '*Voilà*, long live discontinuity, we are in the discontinuous and a good thing too,' but to pose the question, 'How is it that at certain moments and in certain orders of knowledge, there are these sudden take-offs, these hastenings of evolution, these transformations which fail to correspond to the calm, continuist image that is normally accredited?' (*Power/Knowledge* 112)

For Foucault, it is not a matter of offering a choppy, discontinuist image of history to combat the "normally accredited" image of calm continuity, but rather a matter of attending to the disruptions themselves. Discontinuity, as a declarable historical or philosophical principle, can and does lead back to a totalizing image or picture of the historical "orders of knowledge"—is part and parcel of a very continuous institutional and methodological project. As Foucault writes about historical discourse at the end of the eighteenth century: "the regular historians were revealing continuities, while the historians of ideas were liberating discontinuities. But I believe that they are two symmetrical and inverse effects of the same methodological renewal of history in general" (*Live* 47).

The methodological problematic that Foucault outlines here, no doubt, doubles my own: I do not wish simply or primarily to offer a "symmetrical and inverse picture" of Foucault and Derrida—to say, '*Voilà*, literary criticism misreads Foucault and Derrida, and here is the correct way to read them'—but to try to ask how or why it is, in some sense, *inevitable* that they will be misread by a discipline, and to ask if there is a mechanism in either thinker's text for explaining this appropriation—perhaps also complicating it—and to locate difference(s) through this operation. I am, to reiterate, less interested in "exposing" poor readings and misappropriations (though there is obviously a necessarily critical or polemical tone to parts of my text) than I am in tracing the institutional and systematic imperatives of these appropriations. The question at hand becomes, then, can Foucault or Derrida provide a rationale for their own appropriation by the discipline of literary criticism—can their thinking of the reflexive moment of exteriority explain its own, for lack of a better word, re-interiorization within an institution or a method, within "new historicism" or "deconstructive criticism"?[14] Perhaps tracing out possible answers to this question will help bring out important differences which, so far at least, I have been at great pains to collapse.

As I argue above, Foucault's explanation for his own appropriation would revolve around the problematics of power, and the way in which instances of power tend to move the exterior toward the interior—that even institutional studies which liberate in some way also create a new object or topic for discourse or study, a new subject(ification). Foucault puts it quite succinctly in "La folie, l'absence d'oeuvre," an appendix to the second edition of *Histoire de la folie*:

> [Someday,] everything that we experience today in the form of a limit or as foreign or insupportable, will have taken on the serene characteristics of what is positive. And what for us today designates this Exterior risks one day designating us. (Trans. and cited in Carroll 76)

Later in his career, Foucault criticizes *Madness and Civilization* for its naive notions of power (*Power/Knowledge* 118–19) and of "experience" (*Archaeology* 16/27),[15] but this "early" quotation seems to be consistent with "late" Foucauldian interest in "a form of power which makes individuals subjects . . . a form of power which subjugates and makes subject to" ("Subject" 212). Every liberation (of a cause, a discourse, a group, especially of an "individual" like the madman liberated from his madness) can and will transform into a type of subjugation—into a subject for definition—and subsequently into the conditions of emergence for later definitions, later designations.[16] The exterior does not remain exterior; it "risks one day designating us." Through this formulation, Foucault names the logic by which his thought is brought into an institution. He offers no "counter-formulation" precisely because he does not want to play into the hands of this logic by designating alternative conditions of possibility; his texts do not attempt to theorize or "ground" an outside precisely as a buffer against a totalizing logic which could then subsume or sublate it. He refuses to play the game on the terms of transcendental/dialectical philosophy, on Hegel's terms.

Indeed, Hegel is the thinker who poses the greatest question to thinking in our "postmodern" epoch (insofar as he is the thinker of the completion or totalization of the modern): how does one think against a Hegelian system that is fueled by negation, which diffuses contradiction or opposition by consuming it as merely a higher form of the system's own truth? As Derrida summarizes Hegelian sublation in his essay on Bataille, "The Hegelian *Aufhebung* is produced entirely within discourse, from within the system or the work of signification. A determination is negated and conserved in another determination which reveals the truth of the former" ("From Restricted" 275). All critical discourse, then, risks playing directly into Hegel's hands, "risks agreeing to the reasonableness of reason, of philosophy, of Hegel, who is always right, as soon as one opens one's mouth in order to articulate meaning" ("From Restricted" 263). For Foucault, this question of Hegel is perhaps the most important question for postmodern thought:

[T]ruly to escape Hegel involves an exact appreciation of the price we have to pay to detach ourselves from him. It assumes that we are aware of [*suppose de savoir*] the extent to which Hegel, insidiously perhaps, is close to us; it implies a knowledge, in that which permits us to think against Hegel, of that which remains Hegelian. We have to determine the extent to which our anti-Hegelianism is possibly one of his tricks directed against us, at the end of which he stands, motionless, waiting for us. (*L'ordre* 74–75; *Archaeology* 235)

Here Foucault takes up the question that Hegel poses to contemporary thought: how to think against a structure that anticipates or negates such thinking, that in fact thrives on determinate negations? And it is precisely because of his suspicion of Hegelian sublation that it is difficult to read Foucault as ideology critique— as, for example, Habermas would like to read him.[17] Ideology critique depends on a moment of liberation through reason, on the demystification of ideology in order to unmask knowledge. As Louis Althusser writes, ideology critique moves in the service of "*scientific* knowledge, against all the mystifications of *ideological* 'knowledge.' Against the merely moral denunciation of myths and lies, for their rational and rigorous criticism" (11). But, for Foucault, "criticism"—as an attempt to stake out a more excellent reason or ground—guarantees that the winner has already been declared: Hegel in a unanimous decision; the dialectic continues undisrupted; reason is reassured. As Foucault writes, "'Dialectic' is a way of evading the always open and hazardous reality of conflict by reducing it to a Hegelian skeleton" (*Power/Knowledge* 114–15).

The overarching criticism of Foucault's work in literary critical circles revolves around his refusal to acknowledge a moment of liberation through reason. For example, Edward Said, while sympathetic to components of Foucault's work, refuses to accept the notion that there is no space or end of liberation in criticism, or that a discipline like literary criticism necessarily creates a kind of subjugation as it studies phenomena; he writes,

> criticism must think of itself as life-enhancing and constitutively opposed to every form of tyranny, domination, and abuse; its social goals are noncoercive knowledge produced in the interests of human freedom. (29)[18]

While these certainly are reassuring sentiments, for Foucault reassurance is precisely the problem here: a "belief in noncoercive human community" (Said 246) is a claim for the self-evidence of the critical project—is ultimately a justification that cannot be examined or questioned, just as the ideological justifications for the political powers Said would wish to demystify ultimately protect themselves from examination. Likewise, it seems that the most traditional critic could see his or her project in Said's formulation: "noncoercive knowledge" seems precisely a translation of "disinterested knowledge," and as such serves to protect the institutional interests of criticism all the more strongly.[19] For Foucault, there is no simple "liberation" through knowledge; as he writes, "knowledge is not made for understanding; it is made for cutting" ("Nietzsche" 88). The "knowledge" produced by the human sciences cannot move away from its origins as/in a kind of violence—and literary criticism (in both its institutional and systematic functions) is implicated in the movement of "liberation" through the subjugation of knowing: a discipline makes a new object to be studied out of the liberation itself, thereby reasserting reason's control. Liberation is confronted at its end by the smiling figure of Hegel, who has been there all along.

But this does not lead Foucault to a kind of stagnation or silence. The absence of a determinate methodology in his work and his denial of liberation within a discourse—so frustrating and ultimately paralyzing to some—have certainly not curtailed his production of important studies: studies of the madhouse, the prison, the clinic, sexuality. But, one might profitably ask, why does Foucault produce studies if they do not lead to the Enlightenment goals of heightened understanding or liberating knowledge? Why go on? As he takes a chair at the Collège de France, he discusses his "projects":

> [T]he analyses I intend to undertake fall into two groups. On the one hand, the 'critical' group which sets the reversal-principle to work. I shall attempt to distinguish forms of exclusion, limitation and appropriation. . . . I shall try to show how they are formed, in answer to which needs, how they are modified and displaced, which constraints they have effectively exercised, to what extent they have been worked on. On the other hand, the 'genealogical' group, which brings the other three principles [chance, discontinuity, and materiality] into play: how series of discourse are formed, through, in spite of, or with the aid of these systems of constraint: what were the specific forms for each, and what were their conditions of

> appearance, growth, and variation. (*L'ordre* 61–62; *Archaeology* 231–32)

Foucault's answer is necessarily double, thinking necessarily both inside and outside a system that is to be interrogated. For Foucault, like Derrida, analysis begins with an indispensable "critical" or polemical phase of reversal, a phase which attempts "to distinguish forms of exclusion, limitation and appropriation." But, and this is the crucial point, Foucault's *analysis does not stop here* with an overturning; if it does, it cannot truly escape Hegel—it is doomed to repeat the exclusions it uncovers.[20] The overturning or uncovering itself must be subjected to an examination, but one which brings a sort of indeterminacy to bear on the overturning, on its emergence among various possibilities, chances, and discontinuities. Contra many of his critics, Foucault certainly does recognize a kind of "progress" in or through disciplines and the human sciences,[21] but it is necessarily a progress that leads to other—though, admittedly, often more humane or palatable—forms of exclusion and subjugation, *not* to a space of unproblematic, reassuring freedom. The progress of knowledge is itself a Hegelian ruse, and for Foucault, it is only if one takes into account a certain exteriority in the conditions of emergence for a discourse—thereby refusing an alternative, determinate ground or higher knowledge—that one has the chance of denying Hegel his otherwise predetermined victory. One can "beat" Hegel only by refusing to play the game of knowledge on his terms.

This is perhaps where we see the major point of conflict between Foucault and Derrida: Derrida, rather than refusing to play on Hegel's terms, attempts to beat Hegel at his own game; he encounters transcendental/dialectical philosophy and tries to disrupt it by theorizing *its* conditions of possibility—which must, he argues, be partially nontranscendental, impure. This gives us a way of offering what might be Derrida's answer to the question of his appropriation by criticism: a transcendental or critical discourse will, to be sure, expel the otherness within it—the dialectic will totalize, will bring becoming into being—but for Derrida, an otherness still remains. He writes,

> There is no choosing here: each time a discourse *contra* the transcendental is held, a matrix—the (con)striction itself—constrains the discourse to place the nontranscendental, the

outside of the transcendental field, the excluded, in a structuring position. The matrix in question constitutes the excluded as transcendental of the transcendental, as imitation
transcendental, transcendental contra-band. The contra-
band is *not yet* dialectical contradiction. To be sure, the contra-
band necessarily becomes that, but its not-yet is not-yet the
teleological anticipation, which results in it never becoming
dialectical contradiction. The contra-band *remains* something
other than what, necessarily, it is to become.

Such would be the (nondialectical) law of the (dialectical)
stricture, of the bond, of the ligature, of the garrote, of the
desmos in general when it comes to clench tightly in order to
make be. Lock of the dialectical. (*Glas* 244a)

Derrida offers a logic of his own appropriation which is at once
very similar to Foucault's and at the same time radically different.
Derrida's text can explain its interiorization in terms of the violence of dialectical thinking: the violence of the dialectical stricture "when it comes to clench tightly in order to make be"; the
need within dialectical thinking (which is also critical thinking) for
definition, synthesis; critical thinking's necessary interiorizing of
an outside in order to cover up the structuring (literally *transcendental*) position of an outside within that thinking. Derrida attempts to disrupt this movement of making be by thinking the
"transcendental of the transcendental," the structuring principle
of the transcendental which the transcendental itself cannot
think—that is, if it is to do the work of a traditional transcendental.

So perhaps we have come to the point where Derrida's thinking and Foucault's most radically part company: for Foucault, the
"transcendentalist" emphasis of Derrida's work is simply unac-
ceptable, too prone to become a new orthodoxy. For all the similar
effects and attributes of a Foucauldian network of statements and
Derridean general text, perhaps the overriding difference is that
"for statements it is not a condition of possibility but a law of
coexistence" (*Archaeology* 116/153).[22] For Foucault, Derrida's involvement with a transcendental vocabulary allows the possibility
that a transcendental space of interiority

can be purified in the problematic of trace, which, prior to all
speech, is the opening of inscription and the difference of

deferred time [*écart du temps différé*]; it is always the historico-transcendental theme that is reinvested. (*Archaeology* 121/159, translation modified)

Such a potential for reification, according to Foucault, plays into the hands of institutional, status quo thinking. But it seems, in the wake of Hegel, that these are the risks of thinking itself—the risks of thinking or speaking at all.[23] Foucault's disruptive materialist discourse is no less difficult to take up for institutional uses than Derrida's disruptive transcendental discourse. And Derrida, for his part, is acutely aware of the institutionalization of undecidability or unreadability as a reading method in American literary criticism; Derrida writes his essay in *Deconstruction and Criticism*, one of the first of the theory anthology books, with this caveat concerning Blanchot's *L'arrêt de mort*:

> The readability of unreadability is as improbable as an *arrêt de mort*. No law of (normal) reading can guarantee its *legitimacy*. By normal reading I mean every reading that insures knowledge transmittable in its own language, in a language, in a school or academy, knowledge constructed and insured in institutional constructions, in accordance with *laws* made so as to resist (precisely because they are weaker) the ambiguous threats with which the *arrêt de mort* troubles so many conceptual oppositions, boundaries, borders. The *arrêt de mort* brings about the *arrêt* of the law. ("Living On" 171)

This *arrêt*, this interruption, this gap, this falling out of (the dialectical movement of) work, lives on and remains un-institutionalizable, untranslatable, impossible to legitimate, precisely because it disrupts the laws by which it could be institutionalized, defined, or legitimated. Even after its seeming sublation, for Derrida the *arrêt* remains.

And perhaps it is here that Derrida and Foucault can be thought together again; they both attempt to bring about and attend to a certain disruption of work,[24] an *arrêt*, a break, a fissure, a discontinuity of/at/on/in the otherwise smooth, confident flow of dialectical thinking. Whether this break is located at a transcendental or emergent level seems, to me anyway, not as important as the insistence on the break or hesitation itself, the moment of exteriority that poses a very difficult question for critical thinking—including literary critical thinking: can this hesitation, this otherness, be attended to "critically," that is, thematically or in a revelatory discourse, one which attempts to uncover a determinate truth? Or does it require what Derrida calls a "thinking altogether differently" ("Sending" 326)? It very well may. Perhaps Foucault puts the question most succinctly—the question that both he and Derrida, in different ways, pose to literary criticism:

> There are times in life when the question of knowing if one can think differently than one thinks, and perceive differently than one sees, is absolutely necessary if one is to go on looking and reflecting at all. . . . [W]hat is philosophy today—philosophical activity, I mean—if it is not the critical work that thought brings to bear on itself? In what does it consist, if not in the endeavor to know how and to what extent it might be possible to think differently, instead of legitimating what is already known? (*Use of Pleasure* 8–9)[25]

Notes

1. These types of books are, of course, especially prevalent in—and, I hasten to add, important for—introductory courses in graduate curricula, where the traditional "Bibliography and Methods" course is quickly metamorphosing into a theory course.

2. In fact, Harari gleefully celebrates criticism as violent appropriation: "all criticism *is* strategic. To the question: how should the critic approach knowledge? I know of only one answer: *strategically*. The power and productivity, the gains and losses, the advances and retrenchments of criticism are inscribed in this term: strategy, reminding us of its obsolete—obsolete?—definition: 'A violent and bloody act.' In the game of knowledge, method has become a strategy: the 'violent and bloody' agent by which criticism *executes* the work and in so doing, paradoxically, canonizes it" (72, his emphasis).

3. Foucault and Derrida do, of course, perform "readings" of texts, philosophical and literary, but their readings are different from the majority of literary critical thematizations because of a certain exterior or reflexive moment in their readings: crudely put, there is the genealogical moment in Foucault, where the will to truth puts itself in question; and for Derrida, there is the second move of the double reading, which is a displacement and reinscription of the opposition uncovered in the first reading. Literary criticism attempts to reproduce these reflexive moments, but generally preserves an interiority of meaning through a valorization of the *reflexivity itself* as the meaning of all reading, all texts.

4. Here and throughout, I cite the translation page number first.

5. Foucault is, of course, more than partially responsible for this thematization of his thought vis-à-vis Derrida's, but I am not considering in this essay his rather vitriolic—and, it seems to me, unfair—response to Derrida in "My Body, This Paper, This Fire." This may seem like an outrageous avoidance on my part, but I justify it on two counts: 1) Foucault's text consists almost entirely of a point-by-point refutation of Derrida's reading of Descartes on the dreamer and the madman, something which does not directly concern me here (Foucault's infamous remarks concerning the metaphysical and pedagogical danger of "there is nothing outside the text" are dealt with below); 2) Foucault himself later criticizes *Histoire de la folie*, as I also outline below, for its naive notions of the metaphysical "experience" of madness—a criticism which, to a great extent, actually *agrees with Derrida's*: "everything [in *Histoire de la folie*] transpires as if Foucault *knew* what 'madness' means. Everything transpires as if, in a continuous and underlying way, an assured and rigorous precomprehension of the concept of madness, or at least of its normal definition, were possible and acquired" ("Cogito" 41). For an excellent discussion of the conflict, see Geoff Bennington's "Cogito Incognito," a brief but insightful introduction to his translation of Foucault's essay.

6. The secondary sources for such a reading of Derrida are too numerous to mention—it has become critical commonplace; so, instead, let me cite a book concerning Derrida and criticism that *doesn't* contain such a reading of general text: Rodolphe Gasché's incomparable *The Tain of the Mirror*.

7. In fact, one could gloss Derrida on the undecidability of text by quoting Foucault on the network of statements: "there is no statement in general, no free, independent statement; but a statement always belongs to a series or a whole, always plays a role among other statements, deriving support from them and distinguishing itself from them: it is always part of a network of statements" (*Archaeology* 99/130).

8. Arac's "To Regress From the Rigor of Shelley," a review of Harari's *Textual Strategies* and Bloom et al.'s *Deconstruction and Criticism*, champions the essays in the Harari collection that have an overt historical or political agenda, but it does not question the institutional imperatives which might give rise to such collections; he seems, on the contrary, to toast these imperatives. He writes, building on an image from Shelley: "The 1970's have experienced critical fermentation, following the notable effervescence that began the decade" (242).

9. See Carolyn Porter's "History and Literature: 'After the New Historicism,'" in which she tries similarly to read Derrida and Foucault together: "to say that there is nothing outside the text because there is no transcendental signified is precisely to cancel depth in order to foreground a signifying process which operates in and constitutes a horizonless plane" (266).

10. See, for example, J. Hillis Miller, who gives this summary of the "deconstructive strategy of interpretation" (223) in *Deconstruction and Criticism*: "In attempting to expel that other than itself contained within itself, logocentric metaphysics deconstitutes itself, according to a regular law which can be demonstrated in the self-subversion of all the great texts of Western metaphysics from Plato onward" (228).

11. See his "Deconstruction as Criticism."

12. It should be noted that Greenblatt is scarcely responsible for such a reading. Greenblatt stubbornly refuses to offer a methodologization of Foucault—in fact, he cites Foucault quite sparsely, only twice in *Shakespearean Negotiations*—

and refuses to offer a ready-made method for his own project, defining cultural poetics rather open-endedly as the "study of the collective making of distinct cultural practices and inquiry into the relations among these practices" (5). Likewise, Greenblatt stresses the institutional focus of cultural poetics, especially in essays like "Shakespeare and the Exorcists."

13. See Richard Lehan's "The Theoretical Limits of the New Historicism," where, citing Hayden White, he attacks "the logic of new historicism, at least as practiced by Foucault" (540). Lehan goes on to name Foucault's thinking the dominant component of "a theory that has now fashionably emerged as the representation school" (540).

14. It is interesting to note here Gayatri C. Spivak's provocative comments on her position in the new historicism/deconstruction debate: she writes, citing Derrida, that "the conflict between New Historicism and deconstruction can now be narrowed down to a turf battle between Berkeley and Irvine, Berkeley and Los Angeles. . . . At any rate, since I see the *new* historicism as a sort of media hype mounted against deconstruction, I find it hard to position myself in its regard" (280).

15. Here the translation incorrectly renders *"expérience"* as "experiment." See Carroll's excellent discussion of this problem (53–67); I must credit him also with drawing my attention to the mistaken translation (57n).

16. Cf. Deleuze: "From *Madness and Civilization* on, Foucault analyzed the discourse of the 'philanthropist' who freed madmen from their chains, without concealing the more effective set of chains to which he destined them" (54).

17. Habermas's first lecture on Foucault in *The Philosophical Discourse of Modernity* is entitled "An *Unmasking* of the Human Sciences: Foucault," and he clearly sympathizes with the "critical" side of Foucauldian analyses, but cannot agree with his genealogical analyses in that they deny the moment of "liberating" knowledge that ideology critique seeks.

18. See also Jim Merod's *The Political Responsibility of the Critic*, where he writes, on the Chomsky/Foucault debate that Said (246) makes much of: "Chomsky stresses 'the normal creativity of everyday life' which prompts the emergence of language, culture, and both individual and societal practices that cannot be thought of as regulatory or repressive in any systematic way, but rather as life-giving and constructive, genuinely experimental" (168).

19. See Paul Bové's insightful discussion of Said and Foucault in *Intellectuals in Power*: "My objection . . . to Said's position is that it leaves this regime [the regime of truth] unchanged insofar as it validates the traditional role played by the leading intellectual who, above all, will not call into question his or her own interests in exploiting the ability to imagine and promote 'alternatives' continually in order to maintain or achieve authority and identity in society" (234).

20. Likewise for Derrida: "Deconstruction cannot limit itself or proceed immediately to a neutralization: it must, by means of a double gesture, a double science, a double writing, practice an *overturning* of the classical opposition *and* a general *displacement* of the system. It is only on this condition that deconstruction will provide itself the means with which to *intervene* in the field of oppositions that it criticizes, which is also a field of non-discursive forces" (*Margins* 329).

21. Cf. Richard Rorty's critique in "Foucault/Dewey/Nietzsche": "We liberals in the USA wish that Foucault could have managed, just once, what . . . he always resisted: 'some positive evaluation of the liberal state.' . . . You would never guess, from Foucault's account of the changes in European social institutions

during the last three hundred years, that during that period suffering had decreased considerably, nor that people's chances of choosing their own styles of life increased considerably" (3). Foucault, I think, would be very suspicious of Rorty's notion of progress as increasing lifestyle choices for Western "liberals."

22. See Dreyfus and Rabinow, who make much of this distinction (52–58).

23. See Derrida's "The Principle of Reason": "'thought' risks in its turn (but I believe this risk is unavoidable—it is the risk of the future itself) being reappropriated by socio-political forces that could find it in their interest in certain situations. Such a 'thought' indeed cannot be produced outside of certain historical, techno-economic, politico-institutional and linguistic conditions. A strategic analysis that is to be as vigilant as possible must thus with its eyes wide open attempt to ward off such reappropriations" (17).

24. For the dilemma this worklessness creates in literary criticism, see Stanley Fish, who writes that literary critical "theories always work and they will always produce exactly the results they predict. . . . Indeed, the trick would be to find a theory that *didn't* work" (68).

25. One of the happier tasks of disciplinary work is the acknowledgment of friends. I owe special thanks here to Paul Davies, whose remarkable reading of Foucault first prompted this project. Thanks also to Sherry Brennan for countless insightful comments that have substantially improved this work.

Works Cited

Althusser, Louis. *Lenin and Philosophy and Other Essays.* Trans. Ben Brewster. New York: Monthly Review, 1971.

Arac, Jonathan. "To Regress From the Rigor of Shelley: Figures of History in American Deconstructive Criticism." *boundary 2* 8.3 (1980): 241–57.

Bennington, Geoff. "Cogito Incognito." *Oxford Literary Review* 4.1 1979: 5–8.

Bloom, Harold, et al., eds. *Deconstruction and Criticism.* New York: Seabury, 1979.

Bové, Paul. *Intellectuals in Power: A Genealogy of Critical Humanism.* New York: Columbia UP, 1986.

Carroll, David. *Paraesthetics: Foucault, Lyotard, Derrida.* New York: Methuen, 1987.

Deleuze, Gilles. *Foucault.* Trans. and ed. Seán Hand. Minneapolis: U of Minnesota P, 1988.

Derrida, Jacques. "Cogito and the History of Madness." *Writing and Difference.* Trans. Alan Bass. Chicago: U of Chicago P, 1978. 31–65.

———. "From Restricted to General Economy: A Hegelianism Without Reserve." *Writing and Difference.* 251–77.

———. *Glas.* Trans. John P. Leavey, Jr., and Richard Rand. Lincoln and London: U of Nebraska P, 1986.

———. "Living On—Border Lines." Trans. James Hulbert. Bloom 75–176.

———. *Margins of Philosophy.* Trans. Alan Bass. Chicago: U of Chicago P, 1982.

———. "The Principle of Reason: The University in the Eyes of its Pupils." Trans. Catherine Porter and Edward P. Morris. *Diacritics* 12.3 (1983): 3–20.

———. "Sending: On Representation." Trans. Peter and Mary Ann Caws. *Social Research* 49 (1982): 295–326.

Dreyfus, Herbert, and Paul Rabinow. *Michel Foucault: Beyond Structuralism and Hermeneutics.* Chicago: U of Chicago P, 1982.

Eagleton, Terry. *Literary Theory: An Introduction*. Minneapolis: U of Minnesota P, 1983.

Fish, Stanley. *Is There a Text in This Class?: The Authority of Interpretive Communities*. Cambridge: Harvard UP, 1980.

Foucault, Michel. *The Archaeology of Knowledge* and *The Discourse on Language*. Trans. A. M. Sheridan Smith. New York: Pantheon, 1972. *L'archéologie du savoir*. Paris: Gallimard, 1969. *L'ordre du discours*. Paris: Gallimard, 1971.

——. *Foucault Live*. Trans. John Johnston. Ed. Sylvère Lotringer. New York: Semiotext(e), 1989.

——. *The Foucault Reader*. Ed. Paul Rabinow. New York: Pantheon, 1984.

——. "My Body, This Paper, This Fire." Trans. Geoff Bennington. *Oxford Literary Review* 4.1 (1979): 9–28.

——. "Nietzsche, Genealogy, History." Trans. Donald Bouchard and Sherry Simon. *The Foucault Reader* 76–100.

——. *Power/Knowledge: Selected Interviews and Other Writings, 1972–1977*. Trans. Colin Gordon et al. Ed. Colin Gordon. New York: Pantheon, 1980.

——. "The Subject and Power." Dreyfus and Rabinow 208–26.

——. *The Use of Pleasure*. Trans. Robert Hurley. New York: Vintage, 1986.

——. "What Is an Author?" Trans. Josué Harari. Harari 141–60.

——. "What Is Enlightenment?" Trans. Paul Rabinow. *The Foucault Reader* 32–50.

Gasché, Rodolphe. "Deconstruction as Criticism." *Glyph* 6 (1979): 177–215.

——. *The Tain of the Mirror: Derrida and the Philosophy of Reflection*. Cambridge: Harvard UP, 1986.

Greenblatt, Stephen. *Shakespearean Negotiations: The Circulation of Social Energy in Renaissance England*. Berkeley: U of California P, 1988.

Habermas, Jürgen. *The Philosophical Discourse of Modernity: Twelve Lectures*. Trans. Fredrick G. Lawrence. Cambridge: MIT P, 1990.

Harari, Josué, ed. *Textual Strategies: Perspectives in Poststructuralist Criticism*. Ithaca: Cornell UP, 1979.

Lehan, Richard. "The Theoretical Limits of the New Historicism." *New Literary History* 21.3 (1990): 533–54.

Lentricchia, Frank. *After the New Criticism*. U of Chicago P, 1980.

——. *Ariel and the Police: Michel Foucault, William James, Wallace Stevens*. Madison: U of Wisconsin P, 1988.

——. "Foucault's Legacy: A New Historicism?" Veeser 231–42.

Merod, Jim. *The Political Responsibility of the Critic*. Ithaca: Cornell UP, 1987.

Miller, J. Hillis. "The Critic as Host." Bloom 217–53.

Porter, Carolyn. "History and Literature: 'After the New Historicism.'" *New Literary History* 21.2 (1990): 253–70.

Rorty, Richard. "Foucault/Dewey/Nietzsche." *Raritan* 14.4 (1990): 1–8.

Said, Edward W. *The World, the Text, the Critic*. Cambridge: Harvard UP, 1983.

Selden, Raman. *A Reader's Guide to Contemporary Literary Theory*. Lexington: U of Kentucky P, 1985.

Shuger, Debora K. *Habits of Thought in the English Renaissance*. Berkeley: U of California P, 1990.

Spivak, Gayatri Chakravorty. "New Historicism: Political Commitment and the Postmodern Critic." Veeser 277–92.

Veeser, H. Aram, ed. *The New Historicism*. New York and London: Routledge, 1989.

Between Apocalypse and Redemption:
John Singleton's *Boyz N the Hood*

Michael Eric Dyson

By now the dramatic decline in black male life has become an unmistakable feature of our cultural landscape—though of course the causes behind the desperate condition of black men date much further back than its recent popular discovery. Every few months, new reports and conferences attempt to explain the poverty, disease, despair, and death that shove black men toward social apocalypse.

If these words appear too severe or hyperbolic, the statistics testify to the trauma. For black men between the ages of 18 and 29, suicide is the leading cause of death. Between 1950 and 1984, the life expectancy for white males increased from 63 to 74.6 years, but only from 59 to 65 years for black males. Between 1973 and 1986, the real earnings of black males between the ages of 18 and 29 fell 31 percent as the percentage of young black males in the work force plummeted 20 percent. The number of black men who dropped out of the work force altogether doubled from 13 to 25 percent.

By 1989, almost 32 percent of black men between 16 and 19

were unemployed, compared to 16 percent of white men. And while blacks compose only 12 percent of the nation's population, they make up 48 percent of the prison population, with men accounting for 89 percent of the black prison population. Only 14 percent of the white males who live in large metropolitan areas have been arrested, but the percentage for black males is 51 percent. And while 3 percent of white men have served time in prison, 18 percent of black men have been behind bars.[1]

Most chillingly, black-on-black homicide is the leading cause of death for black males between the ages of 15 and 34. Or to put it another way: "One out of every 21 black American males will be murdered in their lifetime. Most will die at the hands of another black male." These words appear in stark white print on the dark screen that opens John Singleton's masterful film, *Boyz N the Hood*. These words are both summary and opening salvo in Singleton's battle to reinterpret and redeem the black male experience. With *Boyz N the Hood* we have the most brilliantly executed and fully realized portrait of the coming-of-age odyssey that black boys must undertake in the suffocating conditions of urban decay and civic chaos.

Singleton adds color and depth to Michael Schultz's groundbreaking *Cooley High*, extends the narrative scope of the Hudlin brothers' important and humorous *House Party*, and creates a stunning complement to Gordon Parks's pioneering *Learning Tree*, which traced the painful pilgrimage to maturity of a rural black male. Singleton's treatment of the various elements of contemporary black urban experience—gang violence, drug addiction, black male–female relationships, domestic joys and pains, and friendships—is subtle and complex. He layers narrative textures over gritty and compelling visual slices of black culture that show us what it means to come to maturity, or to die trying, as a black male.

We have only begun to understand the pitfalls that attend the path of the black male. Social theory has only recently fixed its gaze on the specific predicament of black men in relation to the crisis of American capital, positing how their lives are shaped by structural changes in the political economy, for instance, rather than viewing them as the latest examples of black cultural pathology.[2] And social psychology has barely explored the deeply ingrained and culturally reinforced self-loathing and chronic lack of self-esteem that characterize black males across age group, income bracket, and social location.

Even less have we understood the crisis of black males as rooted in childhood and adolescent obstacles to socioeconomic stability, and in moral, psychological, and emotional development. We have just begun to pay attention to specific rites of passage, stages of personality growth, and milestones of psycho-emotional evolution that measure personal response to racial injustice, social disintegration, and class oppression.

James P. Comer and Alvin F. Poussaint's *Black Child Care*, Marian Wright Edelman's *Families in Peril*, and Darlene and Derek Hopson's foundational *Different and Wonderful* are among the exceptions which address the specific needs of black childhood and adolescence. *Young, Black and Male in America: An Endangered Species*, edited by Jewelle Taylor Gibbs, has recently begun to fill a gaping void in social-scientific research on the crisis of the black male.

In the last decade, however, alternative presses have vigorously probed the crisis of the black male. Like their black independent film peers, authors of volumes published by black independent presses often rely on lower budgets for advertising, marketing and distribution. Nevertheless, word-of-mouth discussion of several books has sparked intense debate. Nathan and Julia Hare's *Bringing the Black Boy to Manhood: The Passage*, Jawanza Kunjufu's trilogy *The Conspiracy to Destroy Black Boys*, Amos N. Wilson's *The Developmental Psychology of the Black Child*, Baba Zak A. Kondo's *For Homeboys Only: Arming and Strengthening Young Brothers for Black Manhood*, and Haki Madhubuti's *Black Men: Obsolete, Single, Dangerous?* have had an important impact on significant subsections of literate black culture, most of whom share an Afrocentric perspective.

Such works remind us that we have too infrequently understood the black male crisis through coming-of-age narratives, and a set of shared social values that ritualize the process of the black adolescent's passage into adulthood. Such narratives and rites serve a dual function: they lend meaning to childhood experience, and they preserve and transmit black cultural values across the generations. Yet such narratives evoke a state of maturity—

rooted in a vital community—that young black men are finding elusive or, all too often, impossible to reach. The conditions of extreme social neglect that besiege urban black communities—in every realm from health care to education to poverty and joblessness—make the black male's passage into adulthood treacherous at best.

One of the most tragic symptoms of the young black man's troubled path to maturity is the skewed and strained state of gender relations within the black community. With alarming frequency, black men turn to black women as scapegoats for their oppression, lashing out—often with physical violence—at those closest to them. It is the singular achievement of Singleton's film to redeem the power of the coming-of-age narrative while also adapting it to probe many of the very tensions that evade the foundations of the coming-of-age experience in the black community.

While mainstream American culture has only barely begun to register awareness of the true proportions of the crisis, young black males have responded in the last decade primarily in a rapidly flourishing independent popular culture, dominated by two genres: rap music and black film. The rap music of Run D.M.C., Public Enemy, Boogie Down Productions, Kool Moe Dee, N.W.A., Ice Cube, and Ice T., and the films of Spike Lee, Robert Townsend, and now Matty Rich and Mario Van Peebles, have afforded young black males a medium to visualize and verbalize their perspectives on a range of social, personal, and cultural issues, to tell their stories about themselves and each other while the rest of America consumes and eavesdrops.

John Singleton's film makes a powerful contribution to this enterprise. Singleton filters his brilliant insights, critical comments, and compelling portraits of young black male culture through a film that reflects the sensibilities, styles, and attitudes of rap culture.[3] Singleton's shrewd casting of rapper Ice Cube as a central character allows him to seize symbolic capital from a real-life rap icon, while tailoring the violent excesses of Ice Cube's rap persona into a jarring visual reminder of the cost paid by black males for survival in American society. Singleton skillfully integrates the suggestive fragments of critical reflections on the black male predicament in several media and presents a stunning vision of black male pain and possibility in a catastrophic environment: South Central Los Angeles.

Of course, South Central Los Angeles is an already storied geography in the American social imagination. It has been given cursory—though melodramatic—treatment by news anchor Tom Brokaw's glimpse of gangs in a highly publicized 1988 TV special, and was mythologized in Dennis Hopper's film about gang warfare, *Colors*. Hopper, who perceptively and provocatively helped probe the rough edges of anomie and rebellion for a whole generation of outsiders in 1969's *Easy Rider*, less successfully traces the genealogy of social despair, postmodern urban absurdity, and longing for belonging that provides the context for understanding gang violence. Singleton's task in part, therefore, is a filmic demythologization of the reigning tropes, images, and metaphors that have expressed the experience of life in South Central Los Angeles. While gangs are a central part of the urban landscape, they are not its exclusive reality. And though gang warfare occupies a looming periphery in Singleton's film, it is not its defining center.

Boyz N the Hood is a painful and powerful look at the lives of black people, mostly male, who live in a lower-middle-class neighborhood in South Central Los Angeles. It is a story of relationships—of kin, friendship, community—of love, rejection, contempt, and fear. At the story's heart are three important relationships: a triangular relationship between three boys, whose lives we track to mature adolescence; the relationship between one of the boys and his father; and the relationship between the other two boys and their mother.

Tre (Cuba Gooding, Jr.) is a young boy whose mother Reva Devereaux (Angela Bassett), in an effort to impose discipline upon him, sends him to live with his father across town. Tre has run afoul of his elementary school teacher for challenging both her authority and her Eurocentric curriculum. And Tre's life in his mother's neighborhood makes it clear why he is not accommodating well to school discipline. By the age of ten, he has already witnessed the yellow police tags that mark the scenes of crimes and viewed the blood of a murder victim. Fortunately for Tre, his mother and father love him more than they couldn't love each other.

Doughboy (former N.W.A. rapper Ice Cube, in a brilliant cinematic debut) and Ricky (Morris Chestnut) are half-brothers who live with their mother Brenda (Tyra Ferrell) across the street from Tre and his father. Brenda is a single black mother—a member of a much-maligned group that, depending on the amateurish social theory of the day, is vilified with charges of promiscuity, judged to be the source of all that is evil in the lives of black children, or, at best, is stereotyped as the helpless beneficiaries of the state. Singleton artfully avoids these caricatures by giving a complex portrait of Brenda, a woman plagued by her own set of demons, but who tries to provide the best living she can for her sons.

Even so, Brenda clearly favors Ricky over Doughboy—and this favoritism will bear fatal consequences for both boys. Indeed in Singleton's cinematic worldview both Ricky and Doughboy seem doomed to violent deaths because—unlike Tre—they have no male role models to guide them. This premise embodies one of the film's central tensions—and one of its central limitations. For even as he assigns black men a pivotal role of responsibility for the fate of black boys, Singleton also gives rather uncritical "precedence" to the impact of black men, even in their absence, over the efforts of present and loyal black women who more often prove to be at the head of strong black families.

While this foreshortened view of gender relations within the black community arguably distorts Singleton's cinematic vision, he is nonetheless remarkably perceptive in examining the subtle dynamics of the black family and neighborhood, tracking the differing effects that the boys' siblings, friends, and environment have on them. There is no bland nature-versus-nurture dichotomy here: Singleton is too smart to render life in terms of a Kierkegaardian either/or. His is an Afrocentric world of both/and.

This complex set of interactions—between mother and sons, between father and son, between boys who benefit from paternal wisdom or maternal ambitions, between brothers whose relationship is riven by primordial passions of envy and contempt, between environment and autonomy, between the larger social structure and the smaller but more immediate tensions of domestic life—defines the central shape of *Hood*. We see a vision of black life that transcends insular preoccupations with "positive" or "negative" images and instead presents at once the limitations and virtues of black culture.

As a result, Singleton's film offers a plausible perspective on how people make the choices they do—and on how choice itself is not a property of autonomous moral agents acting in an existential vacuum, but rather something that is created and exercised within the interaction of social, psychic, political, and economic forces of everyday experience. Personal temperament, domestic discipline, parental guidance (or its absence), all help shape our understanding of our past and future, help define how we respond to challenge and crisis, and help mold how we embrace success or seem destined for failure.

Tre's developing relationship with his father, Furious Styles (Larry Fishburne), is by turns troubled and disciplined, sympathetic and compassionate—finely displaying Singleton's open-ended evocation of the meaning of social choice as well as his strong sensitivity to cultural detail. Furious Styles's moniker vibrates with double meaning, a semiotic pairing that allows Singleton to signify in speech what Furious accomplishes in action: a wonderful amalgam of old-school black consciousness, elegance, style, and wit, linked to the hip-hop fetish of "dropping science" (spreading knowledge) and staying well informed about social issues.

Only seventeen years Tre's senior, Furious understands Tre's painful boyhood growth and identifies with his teen aspirations. But more than that, he possesses a sincere desire to shape Tre's life according to his own best lights. Furious is the strong presence and wise counselor who will guide Tre through the pitfalls of reaching personal maturity in the chaos of urban childhood—the very sort of presence denied to so many in *Hood*, and in countless black communities throughout the country.

Furious, in other words, embodies the promise of a different conception of black manhood. As a father he is disciplining but loving, firm but humorous, demanding but sympathetic. In him, the black male voice speaks with an authority so confidently possessed and equitably wielded that one might think it is strongly supported and valued in American culture, but of course that is not so. The black male voice is rarely heard without the inflections of race and class domination that distort its power in the home and community, mute its call for basic respect and common dignity, or amplify its ironic denial of the very principles of democracy and equality that it has publicly championed in pulpits and political organizations.

Among the most impressive achievements of Singleton's film is its portrayal of the neighborhood as a "community." In this vein Singleton implicitly sides with the communitarian critique of liberal moral autonomy and atomistic individualism.[4] In *Hood* people love and worry over one another, even if they express such sentiments roughly. For instance, when the older Tre crosses the street and sees a baby in the path of an oncoming car, he swoops her up, and takes her to her crack-addicted mother. Tre gruffly reproves her for neglecting her child and insists that she change the baby's diapers before the baby smells as bad as her mother. And when Tre goes to a barbecue for Doughboy, who is fresh from a jail sentence, Brenda beseeches him to talk to Doughboy, hoping that Tre's intangible magic will "rub off on him."

But Singleton understands that communities, besides embodying resistance to the anonymity of liberal society as conceived in Aristotle via MacIntyre, also reflect the despotic will of their fringe citizens who threaten the civic pieties by which communities are sustained. *Hood*'s community is fraught with mortal danger, its cords of love and friendship under the siege of gang violence, and by what sociologists Mike Davis and Sue Riddick call the political economy of crack.[5] Many inner-city communities live under what may be called a "juvenocracy": the economic rule and illegal tyranny exercised by young black men over significant territory in the black urban center. In the social geography of South Central L.A., neighborhoods are reconceived as spheres of expansion where urban space is carved up according to implicit agreements, explicit arrangements, or lethal conflicts between warring factions.

Thus, in addition to being isolated from the recognition and rewards of the dominant culture, inner-city communities are cut off from sources of moral authority and legitimate work, as underground political economies reward consenting children and teens with quick cash, faster cars, and, sometimes, still more rapid death.[6] Along with the reterritorialization of black communal space through gentrification, the hegemony of the suburban mall over the innercity and downtown shopping complex, and white flight and black track to the suburbs and exurbs, the inner city is continually devastated.

Such conditions rob the neighborhood of one of its basic social functions and defining characteristics: the cultivation of a self-determined privacy in which residents can establish and preserve their identities. Police helicopters constantly zoom overhead in *Hood*'s community, a mobile metaphor of the ominous surveillance and scrutiny to which so much of poor black life is increasingly subjected. The helicopter also signals another tragedy that *Hood* alludes to throughout its narrative: ghetto residents must often flip a coin to distinguish Los Angeles's police from its criminals. After all, this is Daryl Gates's L.A.P.D., and the Rodney King incident only underscores a long tradition of extreme measures that police have used to control crime and patrol neighborhoods.[7]

This insight is poignantly featured in a scene just after Tre comes to live with his father. One night, Furious hears a strange noise. As an unsuspecting young Tre rises to use the toilet, Furious eases his gun from the side of his bed, spies an intruder in the living room and blasts away, leaving two holes in the front door. After they investigate the holes and call the police, Furious and Tre sit on the front porch, waiting an hour for the police to arrive. Furious remarks that "somebody musta been prayin' for that fool 'cause I swear I aimed right for his head." When Tre says that Furious "shoulda blew it off," Furious censors his sentiment, saying that it would have simply been the senseless death of another black man.

After the interracial police team arrive, the black policeman expresses Tre's censored sentiment with considerably more venom. "[It would be] one less nigger out here in the streets we'd have to worry about." As they part, the policeman views Furious's scornful facial expression, and asks if something is wrong. "Yeah," Furious disdainfully responds, "but it's just too bad you don't know what it is—brother." The black policeman has internalized the myth of the black male animal, and has indiscriminately demonized young black males as thugs and dirt. As fate would have it, this same police team accosts seventeen-year-old Tre and Ricky after they have departed from a local hangout that was dispersed by a spray of bullets. The policeman puts a gun to Tre's neck, uttering vicious epithets and spewing words which mark his hatred of black males and, by reflection, a piteous self-hatred. It recalls the lyrics from an Ice Cube rap, *F—— tha Police*: "And don't let it be a black and a white one/ Cause they'll slam ya down to the street top/ Black police showin' out for the white cop."

Furious's efforts to raise his son in these conditions of closely surveilled social anarchy reveal the galaxy of ambivalence that surrounds a conscientious, community-minded brother who wants the best for his family, but who also understands the social realities that shape the lives of black men. Furious's urban cosmology is three-tiered: at the immediate level, the brute problems of survival are refracted through the lens of black manhood; at the abstract level, large social forces such as gentrification and the military's recruitment of black male talent undermine the black man's role in the community; at the intermediate level, police brutality contends with the ongoing terror of gang violence.

Amid these hostile conditions, Furious is still able to instruct Tre in the rules of personal conduct and to teach him respect for his community, even as he schools him in how to survive. Furious says to Tre, "I know you think I'm hard on you. I'm trying to teach you how to be responsible. Your friends across the street don't have anybody to show them how to do that. You gon' see how they end up, too." His comment, despite its implicit self-satisfaction and sexism (Ricky and Doughboy, after all, do have their mother Brenda), is meant to reveal the privilege of a young boy learning to face life under the shadow of fatherly love and discipline.

While Tre is being instructed by Furious, Ricky and Doughboy receive varying degrees of support and affirmation from Brenda. Ricky and Doughboy have different fathers, both of whom are conspicuously absent. In Doughboy's case, however, his father is symbolically present in that peculiar way that damns the offspring for their resemblance in spirit or body to the despised, departed father. The child becomes the vicarious sacrifice for the absent father, though he can never atone for the father's sins. Doughboy learns to see himself through his mother's eyes, her words ironically re-creating Doughboy in the image of his invisible father. "You ain't shit," she says. "You just like yo' Daddy. You don't do shit, and you never gonna amount to shit."

Brenda is caught in a paradox of parenthood, made dizzy and stunned by a vicious cycle of parental love reinforcing attractive qualities in the "good" and obedient child, while the frustration with the "bad" child reinforces his behavior. Brenda chooses to save one child by sacrificing the other—lending her action a Styronian tenor, Sophie's choice in the ghetto. She fusses *over* Ricky; she fusses *at* Doughboy. When a scout for USC's football team visits Ricky, Brenda can barely conceal her pride. When the scout leaves, she tells Ricky, "I always knew you would amount to something."

In light of Doughboy's later disposition toward women, we see the developing deformations of misogyny. Here Singleton is on tough and touchy ground, linking the origins of Doughboy's misogyny to maternal mistreatment and neglect. Doughboy's misogyny is clearly the elaboration of a brooding and extended ressentiment, a deeply festering wound to his pride that infects his relationships with every woman he encounters.

For instance, at the party to celebrate his homecoming from his recent incarceration, Brenda announces that the food is ready. All of the males rush to the table, but immediately before they begin to eat, Tre, sensing that it will be to his advantage, reproves the guys for not acting gentlemanly and allowing the women first place in line. Doughboy chimes in, saying, "Let the ladies eat; 'ho's gotta eat too," which draws laughter, both from the audience with which I viewed the film, and the backyard male crowd. The last line is a sly sample of Robert Townsend's classic comedic send up of fast-food establishments in *Hollywood Shuffle*. When his girlfriend (Meta King) protests, saying she isn't a "'ho,'" Doughboy responds, "Oops, I'm sorry, bitch," which draws even more laughter. In another revealing exchange with his girlfriend, Doughboy is challenged to explain why he refers to women exclusively as "bitch, or 'ho', or hootchie." In trying to reply, Doughboy is reduced to the inarticulate hostility (feebly masquerading as humor) that characterizes misogyny in general: "'cause that's what you are."

"Bitch" and "'ho'," along with "skeezer" and "slut," have by now become the standard linguistic currency that young black males often use to demonstrate their authentic machismo. "Bitch" and equally offensive epithets compress womanhood into one indistinguishable whole, so that all women are the negative female, the seductress, temptress, and femme fatale all rolled into one. Hawthorne's scarlet A is demoted one letter and darkened; now an imaginary black B is emblazoned on the forehead of every female. Though Singleton's female characters do not have center stage, by no means do they suffer male effrontery in silent complicity. When Furious and Reva meet at a trendy restaurant to discuss the possibility of Tre returning to live with his mother, Furious says, "I know you wanna play the mommy and all that, but it's time to let go." He reminds her that Tre is old enough to make his own decisions, that he is no longer a little boy because "that time has passed, sweetheart, you missed it." Furious then gets up to fetch a pack of cigarettes as if to punctuate his self-satisfied and triumphant speech, but Tre's mother demands that he sit down.

As the camera draws close to her face, she subtly choreographs a black woman's grab-you-by-the-collar-and-set-you-straight demeanor with just the right facial gestures, and completes one of the most honest, mature, and poignant exchanges between black men and women in film history.

> It's my turn to talk. Of course you took in your son, my son, our son and you taught him what he needed to be a man, I'll give you that, because most men ain't man enough to do what you did. But that gives you no reason, do you hear me, no reason to tell me that I can't be a mother to my son. What you did is no different from what mothers have been doing from the beginning of time. It's just too bad more brothers won't do the same. But don't think you're special. Maybe cute, but not special. Drink your cafe au lait. It's on me.

Singleton says that his next film will be about black women coming of age, a subject left virtually unexplored in film. In the meantime, within its self-limited scope, *Hood* displays a diverse array of black women, taking care not to render them as either mawkish or cartoonish: a crack addict who sacrifices home, dignity, and children for her habit; a single mother struggling to raise her sons; black girlfriends hanging with the homeboys but demanding as much respect as they can get; Brandi (Nia Long), Tre's girlfriend, a Catholic who wants to hold on to her virginity until she's sure it's the right time; Tre's mother, who strikes a Solomonic compromise and gives her son up rather than see him sacrificed to the brutal conditions of his surroundings.

But while Singleton ably avoids flat stereotypical portraits of his female characters, he is less successful in challenging the logic that at least implicitly blames single black women for the plight of black children.[8] In Singleton's film vision, it is not institutions like the church that save Tre, but a heroic individual—his father Furious. But this leaves out far too much of the picture.

What about the high rates of black female joblessness, the sexist job market which continues to pay women at a rate that is seventy percent of the male wage for comparable work, the further devaluation of the "pink collar" by lower rates of medical insurance and other work-related benefits, all of which severely compromise the ability of single black mothers to effectively rear their children?[9] It is the absence of much more than a male role model and the strength he symbolizes that makes the life of a growing boy difficult and treacherous in communities such as South Central L.A.

The film's focus on Furious's heroic individualism fails, moreover, to fully account for the social and cultural forces that prevent more black men from being present in the home in the first place. Singleton's powerful message, that more black men must be responsible and present in the home to teach their sons how to become men, must not be reduced to the notion that those families devoid of black men are necessarily deficient and ineffective. Neither should Singleton's critical insights into the way that many black men are denied the privilege to rear their sons be collapsed into the idea that all black men who are present in their families will necessarily produce healthy, well-adjusted black males. So many clarifications and conditions must be added to the premise that *only* black men can rear healthy black males that it dies the death of a thousand qualifications.

In reality, Singleton's film works off the propulsive energies that fuel deep, and often insufficiently understood, tensions between black men and black women. A good deal of pain infuses relations between black men and women, recently dramatized with the publication of Shahrazad Ali's infamous and controversial underground best-seller, *The Blackman's Guide to Understanding the Blackwoman*. The book, which counseled black women to be submissive to black men, and which endorsed black male violence toward women under specific circumstances, touched off a furious debate that drew forth the many unresolved personal, social, and domestic tensions between black men and women.[10]

This pain follows a weary pattern of gender relations that has privileged concerns defined by black men over feminist or womanist issues. Thus, during the civil rights movement, feminist and womanist questions were perennially deferred, so that precious attention would not be diverted from racial oppression and the achievement of liberation.[11] But this deference to issues of racial freedom is a permanent pattern in black male-female relations; womanist and feminist movements continue to exist on the fringe of black communities.[12] And even in the Afrocentric worldview that Singleton advocates, the role of black women is often subordinate to the black patriarch.

Equally as unfortunate, many contemporary approaches to the black male crisis have established a rank hierarchy that suggests that the plight of black men is infinitely more lethal, and hence more important, than the conditions of black women. The necessary and urgent focus on the plight of black men, however, must not come at the expense of understanding its relationship to the circumstances of black women.

At times, Singleton is able to subtly embody a healthy and redemptive vision of black male-female relations. For instance, after Tre has been verbally abused and physically threatened by police brutality, he seeks sanctuary at Brandi's house, choreographing his rage at life in South Central by angrily swinging at empty space. As Tre breaks down in tears, he and Brandi finally achieve an authentic moment of spiritual and physical consummation previously denied them by the complications of peer pressure and religious restraint. After Tre is assured that Brandi is really ready, they make love, achieving a fugitive moment of true erotic and spiritual union.

Brandi is able to express an unfettered and spontaneous affection that is not a simplistic "sex-as-proof-of-love" that reigns in the thinking of many teen worldviews. Brandi's mature intimacy is both the expression of her evolving womanhood and a vindication of the wisdom of her previous restraint. Tre is able at once to act out his male rage and demonstrate his vulnerability to Brandi, thereby arguably achieving a synthesis of male and female responses, and humanizing the crisis of the black male in a way that none of his other relationships—even his relationship with his father—are able to do. It is a pivotal moment in the development of a politics of alternative black masculinity that prizes the strength of surrender and cherishes the embrace of a healing tenderness.

As the boys mature into young men, their respective strengths are enhanced, and their weaknesses are exposed. The deepening tensions between Ricky and Doughboy break out into violence when a petty argument over who will run an errand for Ricky's girlfriend provokes a fistfight. After Tre tries unsuccessfully to stop the fight, Brenda runs out of the house, divides the two boys, slaps Doughboy in the face, and checks Ricky's condition. "What you slap me for?" Doughboy repeatedly asks her after Ricky and Tre go off to the store. She doesn't answer, but her choice, again, is clear. Its effect on Doughboy is clearer still.

Such everyday variations on the question of choice are, again, central to the world Singleton depicts in *Hood*. Singleton obviously understands that people are lodged between social structure and personal fortune, between luck and ambition. He brings a nuanced understanding of choice to each character's large and small acts of valor, courage, and integrity that reveal what contemporary moral philosophers call virtue.[13] But they often miss what Singleton understands: character is not only structured by the choices we make, but by the range of choices we have to choose from—choices for which individuals alone are not responsible.

Singleton focuses his lens on the devastating results of the choices made by *Hood*'s characters, for themselves and for others. *Hood* presents a chain of choices, a community defined in part by the labyrinthine array of choices made and the consequences borne, to which others must then choose to respond. But Singleton does not portray a blind fatalism or a mechanistic determinism; instead he displays a sturdy realism that shows how communities affect their own lives, and how their lives are shaped by personal and impersonal forces.

Brenda's choice to favor Ricky may not have been completely her own—all the messages of society say that the good, obedient child, especially in the ghetto, is the one to nurture and help—but it resulted in Doughboy's envy of Ricky, and contributed to Doughboy's anger, alienation, and gradual drift into gang violence. Ironically and tragically, this constellation of choices may have contributed to Ricky's violent death when he is shot by members of a rival gang as he and Tre return from the neighborhood store.

Ricky's death, in turn, sets in motion a chain of choices and consequences. Doughboy feels he has no choice but to pursue his brother's killers, becoming a more vigilant keeper to his brother in Ricky's death than he could be while Ricky lived. Tre, too, chooses to join Doughboy, thereby repudiating everything his father has taught, and forswearing every virtue he has been trained to observe. When he grabs his father's gun, but is met at the door by Furious, the collision between training and instinct is dramatized on Tre's face, wrenched in anguish and tears.

Though Furious convinces him to relinquish the gun, Furious's victory is only temporary. The meaning of Tre's manhood is at stake; it is the most severe test he has faced, and he chooses to sneak out of the house to join Doughboy. All Furious can do is tensely exercise his hands with two silver ben-wa balls, which in this context are an unavoidable metaphor for how black men view their fate through their testicles—they are constantly up for grabs, attack, or destruction. Then sometime during the night, Tre's impassioned choice finally rings false, a product of the logic of vengeance he has desperately avoided all these years; he insists that he be let out of Doughboy's car before they find Ricky's killers.

Following the code of male honor, Doughboy kills his brother's killers. But the next morning, in a conversation with Tre, he is not so sure of violence's mastering logic anymore, and says that he understands Tre's choice to forsake Doughboy's vigilante mission, even as he silently understands that he is in too deep to be able to learn any other language of survival.

Across this chasm of violence and anguish, the two surviving friends are able to extend a final gesture of understanding. As

Doughboy laments the loss of his brother, Tre offers him the bittersweet consolation that "you got one more brother left." Their final embrace in the film's closing moment is a sign of a deep love that binds brothers, a love that, however, too often will not save brothers.

The film's epilogue tells us that Doughboy is murdered two weeks later, presumably to avenge the deaths of Ricky's killers. The epilogue also tells us that Tre and Brandi manage to escape South Central as Tre pursues an education at Morehouse College, with Brandi at neighboring Spelman College. It is testimony to the power of Singleton's vision that Tre's escape is no callow Hollywood paean to the triumph of the human spirit (or, as some reviewers have somewhat perversely described the film, "life-affirming"). The viewer is not permitted to forget for a moment the absurd and vicious predictability of the loss of life in South Central Los Angeles, a hurt so colossal that even Doughboy must ask: "If there was a God, why he let motherfuckers get smoked every night?" Theodicy in gangface.

Singleton is not about to provide a slick or easy answer. But he does powerfully juxtapose such questions alongside the sources of hope, sustained in the heroic sacrifice of everyday people who want their children's lives to be better. The work of John Singleton embodies such hope by reminding us that South Central Los Angeles, by the sheer power of discipline and love, sends children to college, even as its self-destructive rage sends them to the grave.

Notes

1. These statistics, as well as an examination of the social, economic, political, medical, and educational conditions of young black men, and public policy recommendations for the social amelioration of their desperate circumstances, are found in a collection of essays edited by Jewelle Taylor Gibbs, *Young, Black, and Male in America.*

2. In *The Truly Disadvantaged*, William Julius Wilson has detailed the shift in the American political economy from manufacturing to service employment, and its impact upon the inner city and the ghetto poor, particularly upon black males who suffer high rates of joblessness (which he sees as the source of many problems in the black family). For an analysis of the specific problems of black males in relation to labor force participation, see Gerald David Jaynes and Robin M. Williams, Jr., eds., *A Common Destiny*, 301, 308–12.

3. I have explored the cultural expressions, material conditions, creative limits, and social problems associated with rap in "Rap, Race and Reality," "The Culture of Hip-Hop," "2 Live Crew's Rap: Sex, Race and Class," "As Complex as They Wanna Be: 2 Live Crew," "Tapping Into Rap," "Performance, Protest and Prophecy in the Culture of Hip-Hop," and "Taking Rap Seriously."

4. I have in mind here the criticism of liberal society, and the forms of moral agency it both affords and prevents, that has been gathered under the rubric of communitarianism, ranging from MacIntyre's *After Virtue* to Bellah et al.'s *Habits of the Heart.*

5. See Mike Davis and Sue Riddick's brilliant analysis of the drug culture in "Los Angeles: Civil Liberties between the Hammer and the Rock."

6. For an insightful discussion of the relationship between the underground or illegitimate economy and people exercising agency in resisting the worse injustices and effects of the legitimate economy, see Don Nonini, "Everyday Forms of Popular Resistance."

7. For a recent exploration of the dynamics of social interaction between police as agents and symbols of mainstream communal efforts to regulate the behavior and social place of black men, and black men in a local community, see Elijah Anderson, *Streetwise.*

8. According to this logic, as expressed in a familiar saying in many black communities, black women "love their sons and raise their daughters." For a valiant, though flawed, attempt to get beyond a theoretical framework that implicitly blames black women for the condition of black men, see Clement Cottingham, "Gender Shift in Black Communities." Cottingham attempts to distance himself from arguments about a black matriarchy that stifles black male social initiative and moral responsibility. Instead he examines the gender shifts in black communities fueled by black female educational mobility and the marginalization of lower-class black males. But his attempt is weakened, ironically, by a prominently placed quotation by James Baldwin, which serves as a backdrop to his subsequent discussions of mother/son relationships, black male/female relationships, and black female assertiveness. Cottingham writes:

> Drawing on Southern black folk culture, James Baldwin, in his last published work, alluded to black lower-class social patterns which, when set against the urban upheaval among the black poor from the 1960s onward, seem to encourage this gender shift. He characterizes these lower-class social patterns as "a disease peculiar to the Black community called 'sorriness.' It is," Baldwin observes, "a disease that attacks black males. It is transmitted by Mama, whose instinct is to protect the Black male from the devastation that threatens him from the moment he declares himself a man."
>
> Apart from its protectiveness toward male children, Baldwin notes another dimension of "sorriness." "Mama," he writes, "lays this burden on Sister from whom she expects (or indicates she expects) far more than she expects from Brother; but one of the results of this all too comprehensible dynamic is that Brother may never grow up—in which case the community has become an accomplice to the Republic." Perceptively, Baldwin concludes that the differences in the socialization of boys and girls eventually erode the father's commitment to family life. (522)

When such allusive but isolated ethnographic comments are not placed in an analytical framework that tracks the social, political, economic, religious, and historical forces that shape black (female) rearing practices and circumscribe black male-female relations, they are more often than not employed to blame black women for the social failure of black children, especially boys. The point here is not to suggest that black women have no responsibility for the plight of black families. But most social theory has failed to grapple with the complex set of forces that define and delimit black female existence by too easily relying upon anecdotal tales of black female behavior that prevents black males from flourishing, and by not examining the shifts in the political economy, the demise of low-skilled, high-waged work, the deterioration of the general moral infrastructure of many poor black communities, the ravaging of black communities by legal forces of gentrification and illegal forces associated with crime and drugs, etc. These forces, and not black women, are the real villains.

9. For a perceptive analysis of the economic conditions which shape the lives of black women, see Julianne Malveaux, "The Political Economy of Black Women."

10. The peculiar pain that plagues the relationships between black men and black women across age, income, and communal strata was on bold and menacing display in the confrontation between Clarence Thomas and Anita Hill during Senate hearings to explore claims by Hill that Thomas sexually harassed her while she worked for him at two governmental agencies. Their confrontation was facilitated and constructed by the televisual medium, a ready metaphor for the technological intervention into contemporary relations between significant segments of the citizenry. Television also serves as the major mediator between various bodies of public officials and the increasingly narrow publics at whose behest they perform, thus blurring the distinctions between public good and private interest. The Hill/Thomas hearings also helped expose the wide degree to which the relations between black men and black women are shaped by a powerful white male gaze. In this case, the relevant criteria for assessing the truth of claims about sexual harassment and gender oppression were determined by white senatorial surveillance.

11. Thus, it was unexceptional during the civil rights movement for strong, articulate black women to be marginalized, or excluded altogether, from the intellectual work of the struggle. Furthermore, concerns about feminist liberation were generally overlooked, and many talented, courageous women were often denied a strong or distinct institutional voice about women's liberation in the racial liberation movement. For a typical instance of such sexism within civil rights organizations, see Clayborne Carson's discussion of black female dissent within SNCC, (In Struggle 147–48).

12. For insightful claims and descriptions of the marginal status of black feminist and womanist concerns in black communities, and for helpful explorations of the complex problems faced by black feminists and womanists, see Bell Hooks's Ain't I a Woman, Michele Wallace's Invisibility Blues, Audre Lorde's Sister/Outsider, and Alice Walker's In Search of Our Mother's Garden.

13. Of course, many traditional conceptions of virtue display a theoretical blindness to structural factors that circumscribe and influence the acquisition of traditional moral skills, habits, and dispositions, and the development of alternative and non-mainstream moral skills. What I mean here is that the development of virtues, and the attendant skills that must be deployed in order to

practice them effectively, are contingent upon several factors: where and when one is born, the conditions under which one must live, the social and communal forces that limit and define one's life, etc. These factors color the character of moral skills that will be acquired, shape the way in which these skills will be appropriated, and even determine the list of skills required to live the good life in different communities. Furthermore, these virtues reflect the radically different norms, obligations, commitments, and socioethical visions of particular communities. For a compelling critique of MacIntyre's contextualist universalist claim for the prevalence of the virtues of justice, truthfulness, and courage in all cultures, and the implications of such a critique for moral theory, see Alessandro Ferrara's essay "Universalisms." For an eloquent argument that calls for the authors of the communitarian social vision articulated in *Habits of the Heart* to pay attention to the life, thought, and contributions of people of color, see Vincent Harding, "Toward a Darkly Radiant Vision of America's Truth: A Letter of Concern, an Invitation to Re-Creation."

Works Cited

Ali, Shahrazad. *The Blackman's Guide to Understanding the Blackwoman.* Philadelphia: Civilized Pubns., 1990.

Anderson, Elijah. *Streetwise.* Chicago: U of Chicago P, 1991.

Bellah, Robert N., Richard Madsen, William N. Sullivan, Ann Swidler, and Steven M. Tipton. *Habits of the Heart: Individualism and Commitment in American Life.* Berkeley: U of California P, 1985.

Carson, Clayborne. *In Struggle: SNCC and the Black Awakening of the 1960s.* Cambridge: Harvard UP, 1981.

Comer James P. and Alvin F. Poussaint. *Black Child Care: How to Bring up a Healthy Black Child in America.* New York: Simon and Schuster, 1975.

Cottingham, Clement. "Gender Shift in Black Communities." *Dissent* (Fall 1989): 521–25.

Davis, Mike, and Sue Riddick. "Los Angeles: Civil Liberties between the Hammer and the Rock." *New Left Review* (July–Aug. 1988): 37–60.

Dyson, Michael Eric. "As Complex as They Wanna Be: 2 Live Crew." *Z Magazine* (Jan. 1991): 76–78.

———. "The Culture of Hip-Hop." *Zeta Magazine* (June 1989): 44–50.

———. "Performance, Protest and Prophecy in the Culture of Hip-Hop." *The Emergency of Black and the Emergence of Rap.* Ed. Jon Michael Spencer. Durham: Duke UP, 1991. 12–24.

———. "Rap, Race and Reality." *Christianity and Crisis* 16 Mar. 1987: 98–100.

———. "Taking Rap Seriously: Theomusicologist Michael Eric Dyson on the New Urban Griots and Peripatetic Preachers (An Interview)." By Jim Gardner. *Artvu* (Spring 1991): 20–23

———. "Tapping Into Rap." *New World Outlook* (May–June 1991): 32–35.

———. "2 Live Crew's Rap: Sex, Race and Class." *Christian Century* 2–9 Jan. 1991: 7–8.

Edelman, Marian Wright. *Families in Peril: An Agenda for Social Change.* Cambridge: Harvard UP, 1987.

Ferrara, Alessandro. "Universalisms: Procedural, Contextual and Prudential."

Universalism vs. Communitarianism: Contemporary Debates in Ethics. Ed. David Rasmussen. Cambridge: MIT P, 1990. 11–38.

Gibbs, Jewelle Taylor, ed. *Young, Black, Male in America: An Endangered Species.* Dover: Auburn, 1988.

Harding, Vincent. "Toward a Darkly Radiant Vision of America's Truth: A Letter of Concern, an Invitation to Re-Creation." *Community in America: The Challenge of* Habits of the Heart. Ed. Charles H. Reynolds and Ralph V. Norman. Berkeley: U of California P, 1988. 67–83.

Hare, Nathan and Julia Hare, *Bringing the Black Boy to Manhood: The Passage.* San Francisco: Black Think Tank, 1987.

Hooks, Bell. *Ain't I a Woman: Black Women and Feminism.* Boston: South End, 1981.

Hopson, Darlene Powell and Derek S. Hopson. *Different and Wonderful: Raising Black Children in a Race-Conscious Society.* New York: Prentice Hall, 1990.

Jaynes, Gerald David, and Robin M. Williams, Jr., eds. *A Common Destiny: Blacks and American Society.* Washington: Nat. Acad., 1989.

Kondo, Baba Zak A. *For Homeboys Only: Arming and Strengthening Young Brothers for Black Manhood.* Washington, DC: Nubia Press, 1991.

Kunjufu, Jawanza. *Countering the Conspiracy to Destroy Black Boys.* 3 vols. Chicago: African American Images, 1985–90.

Lorde, Audre. *Sister/Outsider.* Freedom: Crossing, 1984.

MacIntyre, Alisdair. *After Virtue.* Notre Dame: U of Notre Dame P. 1981.

Madhubuti, Haki R. *Black Men: Obsolete, Single, Dangerous?: Afrikan American Families in Transition: Essays in Discovery, Solution, and Hope.* Chicago: Third World P, 1990.

Malveaux, Julianne. "The Political Economy of Black Women." *The Year Left 2—Toward a Rainbow Socialism: Essays on Race, Ethnicity, Class and Gender.* Ed. Mike Davis, Manning Marable, Fred Pfeil, and Michael Sprinker. London: Verso, 1987. 52–72.

Nonini, Don. "Everyday Forms of Popular Resistance." *Monthly Review* (Nov. 1988): 25–36.

Walker, Alice. *In Search of Our Mother's Garden.* New York: Harcourt, 1983.

Wallace, Michele. *Invisibility Blues: From Pop to Theory.* London: Verso, 1990.

Wilson, Amos N. *The Developmental Psychology of the Black Boy.* New York: Africana Research Publications, 1978.

Wilson, William Julius. *The Truly Disadvantaged: The Inner City, the Underclass, and Public Policy.* Chicago: U of Chicago P, 1987.

Voyeurism and Class Consciousness:
James Agee and Walker Evans,
Let Us Now Praise Famous Men

Paula Rabinowitz

> [T]he age of Photography corresponds precisely to the explo-
> sion of the private into the public, or rather into the creation
> of a new social value, which is the publicity of the private: the
> private is consumed as such, publicly. . . .
> —Roland Barthes, *Camera Lucida*

> [P]hotography is dumb.
> —Martha Rosler, *Three Works*

If one takes Barthes at his word, then all the comfortable categories by which we have theorized gender, history, and representation—such as the capitalist separation of the spheres of production and reproduction, the public and domestic, masculine
and feminine, disappear at the very moment of their inception.
By bringing the images of daily life and ordinary people into
public view, photography remakes vision and in so doing produces (or reproduces) new forms of (class) consciousness.

I am fascinated by the photographic image, by what I can see of the world, its people and their objects, but also by what those images let me see of myself. Looking at photographs is both a transgressive and comfortable act—difference is domesticated, brought home for inspection, open to critique, but the everyday is also glaringly made strange remarking on one's own position even as another's life is revealed. This essay is an attempt to explore the interrelationship between looking and power, or more technically, between voyeurism and class consciousness, and the implications this link has for radical intellectuals like myself who inhabit yet challenge bourgeois culture. I believe the history of photography—which argues about the photograph's imprecise status between art and document—mirrors the troubling relationship of leftist intellectual and her objects of knowledge—often cultures and classes different from her own. The photograph, because it distinguishes observer from observed, yet brings the two into intimate contact, embodies this contradiction yet seems unable to enter the realm of political effectivity. Is this also true of the radical intellectual?

As histories of bourgeois subjectivity, photographic documents, and personal narratives are intimately linked—each indicating middle-class normalcy through absence. The photo, revealing the lack of material objects in the lives of the poor, affirms by contrast the abundance of its viewer; the case study, revealing the lack of coherence in the neurotic's story, affirms by contrast the health of the well-plotted life.[1] Composed of photographs and narrative, *Let Us Now Praise Famous Men*, James Agee and Walker Evans's Depression-era reportage of "the daily living" of three southern tenant families, transforms their documentary project "to recognize the stature of a portion of unimagined existence" into an uncanny history of middle-class perception and its relationship to the powers and pleasures of looking at others. The complicity between readers and authors in the construction of a social order that can find no place for "an appallingly damaged group of people" except "a soft place in their hearts" produces a text that challenges us to refuse its authority and break our expectations (Agee xiv); yet its post-1960s emergence as a "genuine American classic" according to the cover blurb demands that we reread it to discover what else we observe of ourselves and others in it. Agee's "printed words" and Evans's "motionless camera" produce the power of the gaze as a sexual and class practice. *Let Us Now Praise Famous Men* links the construction of the gaze—as a relationship of bourgeois subject to its object—and the mobilization of class consciousness—as the resistance of that reified object to its history. In so doing, Agee and Evans express and critique their awkward relationship to each other and to their objects of knowledge, shedding light on the connections between the psychosexual desires and political effectiveness of people like myself.

In order to make my argument, an argument that crosses a number of boundaries—between print and photography, reportage and theory—that the scene of class domination is the same as the scene of voyeurism, both depending on an (unspoken) power of the objects of the bourgeois subject's knowledge repossessing her power as difference, I bring together a curious array of characters. They inhabit the nineteenth and twentieth centuries, British and American cultures, Marxist and Freudian theories, and literary and art histories. I set up an imaginary conversation among Walter Benjamin, Georg Lukács, and Sigmund Freud on classed vision. Arthur Munby, James Agee, and Louise Gudger talk about the female subject, marginalized by childhood and poverty. In much the same way that Carolyn Steedman juxtaposes Dora's case history with the story of the watercress girl in *Landscape for a Good Woman*, by defying geographical, temporal and class boundaries, these "conversations" enable each voice to speak over and against those already speaking for and about the other. Trinh T. Minh-ha suggests that the "conversation of man with man" is always a "conversation of 'us' with 'us' about 'them'" (65). Agee and Evans's text bears this out, but it also indicates the moments of resistance when their objects defy them, challenge them and reverse the gaze to produce another form of consciousness.

My essay picks up Freud's discussions of scopophilia to discover in them class(ed) consciousness. I look at Lukács's theory of class consciousness and find in his outline of bourgeois perception an analysis of documentary photography which parallels that of Walter Benjamin. I am drawn back to nineteenth-century Britain where the diaries and photographs Arthur Munby kept to remember his encounters with poor and working-class women and girls historicize the tensions Agee and Evans express as committed artists in twentieth-century America. Munby's comments about Ellen Grounds's large "size" and Rat Man's "curiosity" about his governesses' undergarments tell us much about why Louise Gudger's "paralyzing eyes" so disturb Agee. The bulk of this essay lies in a reading of Agee and Evans's text, which stands as a paradigmatic instance of the problems intellectuals face when they search out and describe their social others.

I

". . . both the subject and object of its proper knowledge . . ."
—Lukács, *History and Class Consciousness*

That the invention of photography coincides with the rise of commodity culture and serves as evidence of it, Walter Benjamin, the most astute theorist of photography, has made clear. Like the commodity itself, and the woman within commodity culture, photography's contribution to fabricating a society of the spectacle is dual—photographs are themselves objects of the gaze as well as purveyors of images. The relations of looking and being looked at while deeply implicated in the construction of sexual and gender positions always reveal class markers on bodies; moreover the visual manifestations of class position also depict bourgeois constructions of sexuality. The photographic image reinforces bourgeois culture even when it seeks to expose its damaging effects as in the case of documentary photographs that reveal "How the Other Half Lives." Yet these objects—the classed, sexed and gendered bodies of visual imagery—have the power to hold the gaze of their viewers; they are produced by *and* produce the "political unconscious" of middle-class culture.

Drawing connections between visual culture and bourgeois subjectivity, Georg Lukács's 1921 adumbration of Marx's theories of commodity fetishism, "Reification and the Consciousness of the Proletariat," published in *History and Class Consciousness*, whose title furnishes the basis for mine, articulates the processes of class differentiation. For Lukács, class consciousness within the proletariat is dependent upon the working class's ability to *see* itself as object and subject simultaneously. Reification produces a "doubling of personality . . . splitting up of men into an element of the movement of commodities and an (objective and impotent) *observer* of that movement" (*History* 164–66, emphasis added).[2] Bourgeois culture is fundamentally a specular culture—a culture of "the [passive] observer of society" whose "contemplative" stance is incapable of overcoming the "antinomies" of reification through the "practical" (*History* 100, 122).

For Lukács, the only resource the proletariat has in the face of bourgeois hegemony of "knowledge, culture and routine" is its "ability to *see* the social totality . . . ; to *see* the reified forms as processes between men; to *see* the immanent meaning of history . . . raise it to consciousness and put it into practice" (*History* 197). The proletariat must "adopt its own point of view" based on its "place in society" vis-à-vis the "perceiving subject" of bourgeois culture.[3] As a class that embodies the subject and object simultaneously, its coming into consciousness marks a potential break with the culture of spectatorship, producing revolutionary praxis, according to Lukács's hopeful predictions. But Lukács's attention to the culture of the specular reveals the limits of class-conscious vision as outlined in Marxist theory. What we come to understand as class consciousness from Lukács is not how it develops, but rather how it gets expressed within commodity culture.[4] Like the failure of the camera to produce a social critique because "it can only re-present the visible . . . it cannot show, but only refer to, social forces," the commodity cannot disclose its own emergence (Rosler 82). The learning process of class consciousness comes from the proletariat's own understanding of itself as a commodity and producer of commodities simultaneously. But where does that leave those outside the process of commodity production—women, children, or the tenant farmers Agee and Evans document?

Without a theory of the transmission of class consciousness from one generation to the next, from one gender to the other, Lukács's visualized proletariat enters fully formed into the structures of social processes as adult and male through commodity production. But there is more to the working class than that. For instance, vision as a psychosocial process also structures both sexual and gender relations and it does so within the child so that the awareness of difference is arranged through an awareness of generational difference. The consciousness of the proletariat then is little more than the rearticulation of bourgeois culture, the first instance of which already takes place as every (middle-class) child passes through early childhood.

Thus at this point we might turn to Freud to understand how Lukács's theory of class consciousness entangles seeing and knowing in ways similar to those suggested by Freud's linkage of scopophilia to epistemophilia and as such participates in the consolidation of bourgeois ideologies of class. Freud argued that the constituent ego instincts—scopophilia, the pleasure in looking, and epistemophilia, the pleasure in knowing—were linked to the "cruelty instinct" which is expressed actively as sadism—the desire to master. Scopophilia, epistemophilia, and the desire to master as ego instincts depend upon social relations—I look *at* some object or that object looks *at* me—and produce narratives—my looking, knowing and mastering suggest a development of my ego.

Freud's discussions of voyeurism, the "perverse" form of scopophilia, are most fully elaborated in his case study of an obsessional neurosis, otherwise known as the Rat Man case. The Rat Man's story begins as he recounts his earliest "sexual life" characterized as a "scene" in which he "[crept] under [the] skirt" of his governess and fingered her genitals. "After this," he says, "I was left with a burning and tormenting curiosity to see the female body." Each time his governess took him and his sisters to the baths, he would await the moment when she undressed to "appease my curiosity" (10: 160). In his discussion of the analysis of the Rat Man, Freud observes that "the histories of obsessional patients almost invariably reveal an early development and premature repression of the sexual instinct of looking and knowing . . ." (10: 245). While Freud fails to register the significance of just what the Rat Man is looking at—his servants' bodies—he does link the Rat Man's obsessive behavior after his father's death to his ambivalence about his father's wealth and his premarital sexual interest in a woman of "humble means" as well as his own sexual desire for his father. In addition to the homoerotic component of looking, Freud intuited the class-based significance of the scopophilic instinct and its perverse manifestation, voyeurism, late in his writings. He cryptically notes that it is not only "in proletarian families that it is perfectly possible for a child . . . to be a witness of the sexual act between his parents" (16: 369). But, he stresses, usually among his middle-class patients the memory of parental intercourse is coded in such a way as to reveal its origin in fantasy and in the passive form of scopophilia, the desire to be looked at. The presumption here seems to indicate that among the poor and working classes it is quite common for the child to actually see sexual intercourse because children sleep in the same room, even the same bed, as their parents.

I think this single sentence opens up Freud's theories about voyeurism to a class analysis. For the Rat Man, whose "curiosity" begins as he looks up his governess's skirts, sexuality depends as much upon class as anatomical differences. Perhaps, then, economic circumstances produce a different experience of seeing and knowing (for) the child of poverty. This difference becomes crucial to James Agee as he documents the lives of the three tenant families.

Active and passive looking implicitly reveal masculine and feminine subject positions in Freud's analysis. Yet they also suggest other differential relations, particularly those coded in class differences, as, I believe Freud's gesture towards class awareness indicates.[5] In other words, Freud's theories of sexuality, because they represent a classed sexuality, are also a theory of class. Lukács's depiction of proletarian consciousness as one that "serves and observes" commodities (including itself as a commodity) connects the simultaneity of the subject/object position to that of the photographic image.[6] As such, it also undermines its own intuition about potential for working-class revolution.

Admittedly, I am making much of the fragmentary inferences in Freud's nod to a class-based sexuality and Lukács's glimpse of a specularly-based class consciousness. But these nods and glimpses provide the background for my look at voyeurism through James Agee's prose and Evans's photos in *Let Us Now Praise Famous Men*. Their text, which celebrates, exposes, perpetuates and challenges the gendered, classed, and (at points) racial disparities organizing not only vision and narrative, but political and economic relations in Depression America, attempts to circumvent generic boundaries separating text from image, fiction from documentary, the "people" from the self. Their attempts to write other stories, encode other images, than those of either sadism or revolution indicate their discomfort (and mine) with their subjectivity as they try to open up a space in which the objects of their political desire resist their inscription.[7] Like me, Agee constructs his position as a voyeur—a "spy," a "bodyless eye," an "alien"—and those he looks at look back at him. The voyeur, like the radical intellectual, needs its objects *and* their resistance, and it is in this double knowledge, as Lukács noted, that the other holds the potential to revise the terms of power. But, before I turn to *Let Us Now Praise Famous Men*, I want to begin—as all discussions of middle-class consciousness must—in nineteenth-century Britain with the diary and photo collection of Arthur J. Munby. Munby's catalogue of the clothing and work habits, speech patterns and countenances of the working women he spied crossing London Bridge or walking the lanes of Wigan are tinged with nostalgia, desire and transference. His position as a middle-class man afforded him access to approach and inspect these women. His "curiosity" is driven by sexual and class differences—seeing them he must know them, knowing them he must own them, in the form of their images and stories which he keeps in his collection and diary. Following the conventions of nineteenth-century domesticity, Munby's desires are kept secret; they represent the private arrangement he constructs with members of the working class. His diary and collection speak to and serve personal desire even as they endorse and encode political and economic power. The writings and images from the 1930s, however, moved literary and visual expression into the public realm as they attempted to document, record and, ultimately, change the world.

Nevertheless, Munby's observations of working women in London, Wigan and throughout the continent served as documentary evidence for labor reformers eager to curtail women's work. His search for young working women, as well as his curious relationship with Hannah Cullwick—his servant and wife—who often posed for photographers dressed in the garb of a variety of working men and women—however, served his own desire to seek a "completeness of relief . . . after London life" in a "new world chatting with rough hearty men, rough hearty wenches;

treated by all as an equal, hearing their broad salient speech and speaking it too as far as I can do so . . ." (Hiley 72).

Social reformers like Henry Mayhew in Britain or Lewis Hine in the United States explored the dark caverns of working-class quarters ostensibly to expose and better their conditions. However Munby's work, like Agee's after him, comes out of a personal connection with his subjects. He went to Wigan to live among the "pit broo wenches," he posed with them and posed them for his collection of photographs and *cartes de visite* picked up in his travels across Britain. On 10 September 1873 he writes:

> I reached Wigan . . . and walked up Scholes, the main street of the collier's quarter of Wigan, to call on Ellen Grounds, the nearest of my friends, and learn from her the news of the pits. . . . Then we talked about being 'drawed aht.' Ellen said she had been 'drawed aht' twice 'i' my pit claes', and has seen her own picture hanging up for sale. It is not good however. . . . So Ellen promised to come tomorrow in her pit clothes to Wigan marketplace. . . . The only question was, whether she should come with a black face or a clean one. She observed that one often looks just as well with a black face and I left the point to her discretion; but asked to see her working dress. . . . Ellen went upstairs and came down again with her trousers over her arm. . . : a pair of trousers made up of various colors, but toned down by coaldust to blackish brown. They were warmly lined and wadded, especially at the knees, to protect them when kneeling among coals or crawling up the shoot; a garment well fitted to keep warm the legs of a woman doing outside work. And (which spoke well for the fair wearer) the *inside* of the trousers was clean. . . . (Hiley 91–92)

Munby's interest in Ellen's clothes may have a more prurient sound to it than Agee's almost religious ecstasy at the Cézanne blues of the overalls worn by the tenant farmers (or Evans's art historical quotation of Van Gogh's *Les Soulieres*), but at least Munby asked to inspect the articles. Agee's illicit inspection of the Gudgers' possessions, which he likens to masturbating in his grandfather's house, leaves him unable to look them in the eye. But Munby proudly poses with Ellen, he says, to "show how nearly she approached me in size."

In conventional Left iconography—for instance John Sloan's *Masses* prints—it is the bourgeois woman who controls the bodies of working-class women through her gaze. The bourgeoisie as "passive observer" is represented as female, whose position of moral superiority is bought with her access to social and economic power while the proletariat by virtue of this logic is of necessity male. The structural position of the worker within commodity culture is feminized; but the Left's metaphors of gender insist on his virility. This masculinized worker can overcome the "antinomies" of reification. In this configuration, the working-class woman can appear only as a prostitute (as sex worker) and the bourgeois male drops from sight. Innocent of the violence of the gaze, his eyes are elsewhere.

Thus Munby's collection of *cartes de visite* presents a catalogue of the curious—the phenomenon of the working woman in an era when bourgeois femininity demanded that women shrink from performing heavy labor. What makes these working women so interesting to Munby aside from their masculine dress is their obvious pleasure in their strength, in their bodies, in their occupations. He records a conversation with a "trotter scraper," and marvels that mucking around in offal has not affected her desirability. Munby's fantasmatic of virile femininity and his ability to control its depiction surely represent one of the most excessive examples of the collusion between the visual dimension of class difference and voyeurism as its sexualized expression. What I want to argue, and why I have enlisted Munby in my argument, is that this slippage between class power and sexual knowledge operates again and again in the documentaries using image and text to reveal "the other half."

II

"[P]articipation and observation are socially inevitable lines of conduct . . ."
　　　　　　　—Lukács, "Idea and Form in Literature"

According to Lionel Trilling, 1930s cultural expressions in the United States were marked by a "social consciousness" that often was "without fiber and contradiction," because it drew its energy "too much from the drawing room" and its sentiment from "a pity which wonderfully served the needs of the pitier" (99–100). In his 1942 review of *Let Us Now Praise Famous Men*, Trilling was distinguishing the recently published "photo-textual documentary book," as John Puckett calls it, from most of the reportage of the 1930s.[8] However, by 1941, the year it and Richard Wright's *12 Million Black Voices* were published (and the United States entered WWII), this form, and more importantly the concerns it embraced, no longer held the liberal imagination. Both the form and its concerns depended upon the extraordinary achievements of Roy Stryker's Historical Section of the Farm Security Administration. This agency sent photographers across America (but primarily to the South and Midwest) to document the devastation wreaked on those in rural America by the economic and climatological disasters of the 1930s in order to persuade Congress to implement many of the New Deal's agricultural programs. However, in 1930s America, documentary photography, which was institutionalized by the federal government, effaced its politics. At most, Roy Stryker's "shooting scripts" asked Dorothea Lange in 1936 for "some good slum pictures in the San Francisco area. . . . Do not forget that we need some of the rural slum type of thing, as well as the urban," and by 1940 demanded of Jack Delano "autumn pictures . . . cornfields, pumpkins. . . . Emphasize the idea of abundance—the "horn of plenty"—and pour maple syrup over it—you know mix well with white clouds and put on a sky-blue platter" (Hurley 70).

Despite, or because of, this, Evans insisted that his work could build a "record" but with "NO POLITICS whatever" (112). Evans seems to be resisting the bureaucratic maneuverings of New Dealism, but also safe-keeping his status as artist. Nevertheless, the project to record initiated by the FSA *was* political and instrumental; it sought social change. Stryker's team needed to provide evidence of the brutalizing conditions of rural poverty to insure that the programs instituted by the New Deal would continue; but they also needed to create striking images, icons that could enter and alter cultural memory.[9] Of course, the history of photography is fraught with the tensions animating the various takes on documentary that emerged in the 1930s—tensions between photography as art and as record, between posed vs. candid images, of public vs. private ownership—precisely because the photograph represented a commodified and reproducible form (Benjamin, "A Short History" 69–76).

These tensions represent some of the same ones animating Left discussions of the newly emerging genre of reportage. As a form that sought to overcome the divisions between literature and history, private thought and public action, subjectivity and objectivity, reportage appeared to overcome the contradictions literary radicals felt between their position as intellectuals and their allegiance to the working class. American Marxist criticism of the 1930s unproblematically celebrated reportage as *the* genre best suited to reproduce the proletarian realism first advocated by Michael Gold.[10] Reportage seemed to provide the seamless melding of culture and politics, intellectual and proletarian, observer and participant, art and ideology, called for in much of the criticism.[11] Through its first person narrative the reader was placed in the middle of unfolding events, seeing them through the eyes of the narrator as directly as possible.

Typically, reportage foregrounds a rather ecstatic voice of the "I" who proclaims a presence, a self, an identity that is directly connected to "the people." This "I" generally gives way, toward the end of the piece, to the more utopian and less conventional pronoun "we" drawing the reader into direct contact through the narrator with the masses. Richard Wright's *12 Million Black Voices* however employs the "we" throughout. The story of black migration north is of course also his story, one that becomes subsumed within that of the masses. But in a more typical piece, journalist and revolutionary Agnes Smedley begins "The People of China," simply: "I rode from the village and town through Fan Chang district." First Smedley conveys her authenticity as an observer through statements such as "I saw many thousands of children growing into manhood and womanhood during the war in mental darkness." She saw; but moreover, she interpreted what she saw. Then she recounts her increasing participation in the struggle through her own suffering as she lives under constant artillery fire and contracts malaria. Finally, the eye of the journalist and the I of the revolutionary merge with her subject so that Smedley becomes part of the masses when "we ate bitterness" (Smedley

211).[12] This movement from the eye/I to we coded quite neatly the ideal transition from middle-class intellectual to class-conscious historical actor needed to create the revolution in writing and in practice. Presumably, if one read enough of these accounts one would be moved off the couch and into the streets as well. However, as Trilling noted in his review of *Let Us Now Praise Famous Men*, guilt, pity and sentimentality were more often the result.

In 1932, Georg Lukács had condemned proletarian literature in general because the mechanical fetishization of the fact served as a petit-bourgeois compensatory gesture towards objectivity but was really just another form of the overly subjective psychological novel.[13] Lukács's analysis might have formed the core of Trilling's review ten years later. For both critics what seems most appalling about the literature of social consciousness was its embarrassingly self-serving disclosures, its desire to appease the guilt of the left-wing intellectual in the face of depression, fascism and working-class militance. For Lukács, genuine reportage never "simply depicts" the facts, but "always presents a connection, discloses causes and proposes consequences." Reportage caught a moment, fixed a particular case, and drew from its typicality an analysis of the larger social relations containing it. The realist novel, by contrast, "portrayed" totality in its sweeping dialectical movement between subject and object, form and content. Lukács opposed a mechanically objective fiction, what he called "the reportage novel," because of its "fetishistic dismemberment of reality . . . [its] inability to see relations between people (class relations) in the 'things' of social life," i.e., its complicity with commodity culture. ("Reportage" 49).

Walter Benjamin also denounced the work produced by the New Objectivity writers and photographers for their "New Matter of Factness." According to Benjamin's reading, this genre commodified class struggle and so "has made the struggle against poverty an object of consumption" for its mostly bourgeois audience ("Author as Producer" 96). For all of these critics, reportage could never overcome its conditions of production because even when it was conscious of its class alignment, it still "fail[ed] to alienate the productive apparatus from the ruling class" ("Author as Producer" 94). Eventually Robert Warshow would complain that reportage, in fact virtually the entire Left culture of the 1930s, tended "to distort and eventually destroy the emotional and moral content of experience, putting in its place a system of convention-alized 'responses'" (38). The anti-Stalinist Warshow glimpses a horror not so much at the contamination of genres (as was Lukács more correctly Stalinist response) nor at the contamination of intellectuals (as was Benjamin's less correctly Stalinist response), but at the debasement and contamination of authentic experience itself (as if paradoxically 1930s literary radicalism was in fact the first instance of the postmodern condition).[14]

III

"... an appallingly damaged group of people ..."
—James Agee, *Let Us Now Praise Famous Men*

In many ways, Agee and Evans's *Let Us Now Praise Famous Men* strives to produce that "authenticity" so lacking in report-age.[15] Appearing as a quintessentially postmodern text—mixing genres, forms and discourses, circling back obsessively on its grammar, empowering yet resisting language and image,[16] this "classic of the thirties' documentary genre . . . epitomizes the rhetoric in which it was made, and explodes it, surpasses it, shows it up," according to the book's most enthusiastic critic, William Stott (266). Agee continually reminds us of his position as out-sider. Listing himself and Evans as spy and counterspy respec-tively in "Persons and Places", he wonders what his intrusive pres-ence looks like to the people whose "living" he has come "to reproduce and communicate as nearly exactly as possible" (232). His attempts to see himself through their eyes even as he scruti-nizes them mean "the centers of my subject are shifty" (10). Yet his narrative remains intact, drawing on the powerful generic conventions, not only of the documentary or its hybrid reportage, but of the spiritual autobiography—the conversion narrative that looks for signs amid the ordinary for proof of one's righteous-ness.[17]

For Agee, the signs are best discovered through photography: "the camera seems to me, next to unassisted and weaponless consciousness, the central instrument of our time" (11). Words cannot embody, their meanings are arbitrary; but the camera can "perceive simply the cruel radiance of what is" (11). In addition to being many other things, the entire book is a paean to the power of vision. Most important of course are Evans's photographs, which constitute the prelude to Agee's prose and establish looking as a prevailing practice. Even in a passage not concerned with recording images, toward the end of the book when Agee recounts his first night spent with the Gudgers without Evans, he uses cinematic and photographic metaphors: "But from where I say, 'The shutters are opened,' I must give this up, and must speak in some other way, for I am no longer able to speak as I was doing, or rather no longer able to bear to. Things which were then at least immediate in my senses, I now know only as at some great and untouchable distance; distinctly, yet coldly as through reversed field-glasses, and with no warmth or traction or faith in words: so that at best I can hope only to 'describe' what I would like to 'describe,' as at a second remove, and even that poorly" (403). As a "bodyless eye," Agee hopes to look as deeply as a camera: "one reason I so deeply care for the camera is just this: so far as it goes . . . and handled cleanly and literally in its own terms, as an ice-cold, some ways limited, some ways more capable, eye, it is . . . incapable of recording anything but absolute, dry truth" (234). However, Agee's medium is "not a still or moving camera, but is words" (235), and it is the insufficiencies of language that propel his narrative on and on. The stubborn linearity of print and its tendency to metaphorize make language suspicious. "'Description,'" writes Agee echoing Lukács, "is a word to suspect," because "words cannot embody, they can only describe" (238), but the eye can locate sounds in space, grasp simultaneity and depth, enact the "globular" through its compression of space (111). The endlessly meandering prose, circling back on itself, repeating incantationally the names of objects hidden in drawers, displayed on walls, is an attempt to encode this globular vision of the camera and eye and to proclaim his authority through spectatorship. He declares imperially, "If I were not here; and I am alien; a bodyless eye; this would never have existence in human perception" (187); but his musings are interrupted by a violin wasp who "is not unwelcome here: he is a builder; a tenant. He does not notice; he is no reader of signs" (188).

The three vignettes that begin the text, "Late Sunday Morning," "At the Forks" and "Near a Church," highlight, through intensely visual interactions between Agee and others—black tenants singing for their white landlord, starving and almost demented white croppers, and a young black couple—the discordant relations among black and white, rich and poor, in rural Alabama. They display the twisted pose Agee and Evans must assume within the cotton culture when they set out to produce "this record and analysis [as] exhaustive, with no detail, however trivial it may seem, left untouched, no relevancy avoided" (xiv–xv). In each case, Agee tries to dislodge the meaning and power of his class and race and gender, desperately trying to communicate through looks and slight gestures that he is not like the white southern male landowners who represent power and authority for the poor white and black tenants; however, he shows these attempts at camaraderie as futile and even as destructive and dangerous for each group of people. He *must* act the part assigned him by the landlords and ask the men to sing another song, then another, and then flick them fifty cents. He *must* offend the porch sitters by attempting to speak to them at all, by seeing their failure. He *must* frighten the young black couple as he runs after them, leaving the woman trembling with fear for herself and her husband at his approach. Because of his position, he can't help himself and his awkward moves towards reciprocity will always backfire, further alienating and embarrassing those he seeks to comfort. And when Agee rails against his complacent readers and strikes a pose of humility before the tenants (but arrogance before his audience), he implicates us in his predicament as well.

The ability to see, to read signs, is power; and this is nowhere more clear than in the passages about Louise Gudger during which he and she are locked in an intensely symbiotic gaze. He stares at her as she poses for her family portrait the first day he and Evans meet the three families: ". . . and it is while I am watching you here, Louise, that suddenly yet very quietly I realize a little more clearly that I am probably going to be in love with you: while I am watching you in this precious imposture of a dress, standing up the strength of your father and looking so soberly and so straight into the plexus of the lens through those paralyzing eyes of yours . . ." (369). In this scene ten-year-old Louise's paralyzing eyes seem to hold the same power over him as the camera holds. He appears subject to her visual control; yet she is the spectacle trapped by the power of the camera to capture her as her father wants her to look.

Later, when he returns without Evans to the Gudgers' house, she fixes her gaze onto his plexus, becoming in a sense the camera that had earlier fixed her. This interchange of looks between Louise, Agee and the imaginary camera is charged with sexual energy put into play through the gaze: ". . . something very important to me is happening, and this is between me and Louise. She sits squarely and upright in her chair . . . watching me, without smiling, whether in her mouth or her eyes: and I come soon to realize that she has not taken her eyes off me since we entered the room: so that my own are drawn back more and more uncontrollably toward them and into them. From the first they have run chills through me, a sort of beating and ticklish vacuum at the solar plexus, and though I already have frequently met them I cannot look into them long at a time . . ." (400). Again, Agee empowers the ten-year-old girl because her gaze functions as the camera's—implacable, central, invariable—and able to (trans)fix him with its power. This girl looks differently.

The photo session which inaugurates the relationship between the families and Agee and Evans has revealed a number of differences among and between the families. Agee describes the painful embarrassment of Sadie Ricketts before the camera as she attempts to resist her husband's insistence that her family be photographed. Her disheveled children are brought into stark contrast when George Gudger arrives with his family in their Sunday clothes, which Agee discerns to be the cheapest imitation of middle-class attire. Minute class distinctions among the tenants point up the larger class differences dividing the families from Agee and Evans, and the gender hierarchy prevailing means Sadie is subject to the desires of both her husband and the strange men. Agee is not unaware of the visual exchanges that pass among the members of the families, in fact he enters into them with Sadie and Louise; yet he insists he is powerless to overcome their shame before the lens and once again speaks silently by looking into "the unforgiving face, the eyes, of Mrs Ricketts" and then telling us of his pain at causing her pain: "I know I have lost whatever shameful little I had gained for her, and it is now hard for me to meet her eyes at all, the whole thing has become so complicated and so shameful. (It occurs to me now as I write that I was as helpless as she; but I must confess I don't want to make anything of it . . .)" (370).

Agee's dilemma about his relationship to his subjects becomes an anxiety about the form of the book—its lack of a center—and incidentally resembles Lukács's distress over the blurred generic boundaries of the reportage novel. The decision to narrate or describe that differentiates realist from naturalist fiction for Lukács is connected to the distinction between knowing and seeing that marks bourgeois culture. The naturalist writer, like the journalist whom Agee deplores, can only see details packed up tightly, but the realist novelist can reveal totality—can know the social relations embedded within the objects of the world.

Agee's denunciations of journalism declare his separation from the reified vision of the bourgeoisie. The globular vision he desires could begin to "embody" totality in a form that differs from realist fiction; yet it too begins with the details of a man's life and expands to include family, work, environment, and on and on. But like peeling back layers of onion skin to reveal some essence only to be foiled in one's pursuit, the "center" shifts. This shifting becomes the structuring device for Agee's twin perspectives—documentary and autobiography—description and narration. Reportage sought to realign this tension by incorporating the eye/I and its other to produce the we, but Agee knows he cannot bridge this gap. Yet he searches over and over for a way, and in one of several endings, seems to locate it in the bodies of two children. Declaring that "the last words of this book have been spoken," he leaves us with "descriptions of two images" (441). The first is of Squinchy Gudger, relaxing into sleep while nursing, whose face is "beatific" against his mother's breast and who is "the Madonna's son, human divinity sunken from the cross at rest against his mother, and more beside, for at the heart and leverage of that young body, gently, taken in all the pulse of his being, the penis is partly erect." Once again, Agee has re-presented the scene for us through references to high bourgeois culture—a classic image from Renaissance painting in this case. Then he discovers an even more "universal" figure:

> And Ellen where she rests, in the gigantic light: she, too, is completely at peace . . . her knees are flexed upward a little and fallen apart, the soles of the feet facing: her blown belly swimming its navel, white as flour; and blown full broad with slumbering blood into a circle: so white all the outward flesh, it glows of blue; so dark, the deep hole, a dark red shadow of life blood: the center and source, for which we have never contrived any worthy name, is as if it were breathing, flowering, soundlessly, a snoring silence of flame; it is as if flame were breathed forth from it and subtly played about it: and here in this breathing and play of flame, a thing so strong, so valiant, so unvanquishable, it is without effort, without emotion, it shall at length outshine the sun. (442)

Agee's text refuses a "center"; yet it obsessively seeks one in all the usual places—here we are strangely back to the Rat Man whose "desire to see the female body" initiated his obsessive "curiosity" to peer beneath surfaces. This ecstatic vision of the "center and source," twenty-month-old Ellen's "flaming" navel, returns to another conventional image of "uncanny" power. Unlike the Rat Man, whose illicit peerings up his governesses' skirts sparked his "curiosity," Agee is an active inscriber of anatomical difference. Its representation here recenters *his* "curious" text by reinstating sexual difference as an "ordering" (Rose 51). If the objects Agee has presented to us throughout the book resist "ordering" within the norms of bourgeois culture—although he has certainly sought to establish them there by likening them to icons familiar from art, music and literary histories—his "images" of sexual difference reposition these things within the seemingly stable representations of sexual difference that order bourgeois culture.[18] The sight of these children asleep and open to inspection, described with these words which are "not words," concludes the record of the tenant farmers' lives. Their "unimagined existence" has been reordered into a more legible story and image, as class difference becomes "embodied" by sexual difference.

When Agee finally concludes the book with the third "On the Porch" section, the movement from the documentary image of the tenants to the narrative of his own subjectivity is complete, and with it, the movement from visual to descriptive, from the people to the self. So the final mood of the book is the quiet eroticism of Evans and Agee listening together to the foxes baying while the two men curl up for the night on the porch, talking and finally falling asleep. Ultimately, the narrative closure of the two asleep repeats the closure of the documentary vision Agee presented with the two sleeping children. Just as the Rat Man's curiosity betrayed his desire for his father, the desire to see and to know the tenants that has propelled the two men leads them to each other.[19]

Voyeurism and its attendant sadism is at the heart of the documentary narrative that depends on the powers of the gaze to construct meanings for the writer and the reader of "the people." Furthermore, the two terms—documentary, narrative—remain at odds with each other. Insisting upon a particularity of vision and a polemic, yet requiring the conventions of plot and structure, reportage is a "bastard" genre.[20] Agee constantly reminds us of the painful embarrassment his position as a Harvard-educated, white, male writer creates for all of his subjects including himself among them. Agee may read himself into the tenants' lives with, according to Paul Goodman, "insufferable arrogance" (86), but, writes Ruth Lechlitner, "as readers of this book, we have moved in on Mr. Agee (even as he moved in on the cotton tenant families) and we learn possibly as much about him (and the things about ourselves which he represents) as we do about the sharecroppers. Perhaps this . . . is the book's chief social documentary value" (10). No matter what its political intentions, the documentary narrative invariably returns to the middle class, enlisting the reader in a process of self-recognition. We read ourselves into the people. What the middle-class man sees of the tenants in Alabama can only be read back through his vision as (uncanny) images. The "eye" and the "I" have become interchangeable for narrator and reader, and the "subject" of the work shifts from an examination of the families to a disclosure of the self.

This seems less clear when we look at Evans's photographs. They resist narrative insofar as they remain uncaptioned. They present an anachronism—a throwback to a "generation that was not obsessed with going down to posterity in photographs, rather shyly drawing back into their private space in the face of such proceedings . . . for that very reason allowed that space, the space where they lived, to get onto the plate with them" (Benjamin, "A Short History" 70–71). Evans's photos of the three families, their homes and environs, invite us to contemplate this lost era by refusing to name his subjects. But perhaps in so doing, or in ceding the work of captioning to Agee's prose, he suggests just how much the "caption become[s] the most important part of the photograph" (Benjamin, "A Short History" 75). When Walker Evans refuses captions and lets the images speak, he resists the movement "whereby photography turns all life's relationships into literature"; yet the sequencing of the photos tells its own kind of story and their silence still foregrounds another's vision especially after Agee's words reinvest the images with new narrative capital.[21] Agee's pose of self-indulgent sexual obsessive works because Evans's photos seem to withhold all sentimentality through their insistence that the object of the photo directly address him, the subject, and then us, the subject at a remove.[22] They proclaim, in the process, "This is Art!" despite Agee's plea "Above all else: in God's name don't think of it as Art" (15); they also, through Agee's text, become political, despite Evans's demand for "NO POLITICS, whatever." Evans's photographs as much as possible resist sensationalism. Still, his photos of bodies and beds and kitchens and stores, the images that frame Agee's text, participate in the same work that Munby's collection of working women in England did. Their collection reveals the ways differences can be organized and contained.

IV

"[H]ow is it we got caught?"
—Agee (as Annie Mae)

In the by-now-mythical tale, James Agee and Walker Evans set out in summer 1936 on assignment for *Fortune* magazine to document the lives of white tenant farmers in Alabama's cotton belt. Evans was on loan from Roy Stryker's Historical Section of the Farm Security Administration because Stryker wanted as broad exposure of the plight of rural poverty as possible and the slick mass-circulation magazines provided him easy access to a large audience. As the story goes, the 20,000 words, already far too long for the magazine, became 40,000, then more and more as Agee continued to write and revise. It was not until 1941 that Houghton Mifflin brought out a small edition of *Let Us Now Praise Famous Men* which despite many fine reviews (here the myth veers from reality) sold poorly and languished unread until its reissue in 1960 helped renew interest in Depression-era literature, photography and politics. In the ensuing decades Agee and Evans's work has assumed the status of a "masterpiece" of modernist or postmodernist realism.[23] By the 1980s, *Let Us Now Praise Famous Men* had spawned an eerie industry of rephotographic projects, as journalists, filmmakers and photographers tracked down the Tingles, Fieldses and Burroughses to rephotograph them and to get their impressions of the famous book.[24] In these works, Agee and Evans often have come under indictment as invaders: intellectuals who pried into the lives of innocent folk and revealed all the dirty secrets of poverty in America. According to these stories, some family members are still angry and bitter over the way they were portrayed and talk of suits and reparations to get some of the money Evans and Agee ostensibly made off their images. But others assure us that Agee's words and Evans's photographs were "true." In any case, a whole new generation of middle-class spectators is encouraged simultaneously to inspect the faces and stories of the southern rural poor—now living in trailers rather than pine shacks—as well as to castigate the two men who originally brought these faces and stories to us.

However, we are not asked to think of ourselves as coconspirators—as spy and counterspy, as Agee identified himself and Evans—but as moral guardians of propriety who need to question the voyeuristic exposé attendant on the first inspection—but never that of the return visit. *And Their Children After Them* attempts to historicize the families by describing the demise of cotton tenancy. This "sequel" to *Let Us Now Praise Famous Men* reproduces its format beginning with uncaptioned photographs and continuing with details of the families and their descendants. Yet it is prefaced by the sensational account of Maggie Louise Gudger's suicide by rat poison.[25] Ironically, Sherrie Levine's appropriations of Evans's images seem somehow purer in their very effort to demonstrate the impurity of photography. Coming "After Walker Evans," she at least refuses to invade the lives of the subjects of Evans's images, and instead takes over only the images themselves. Just as *Fortune* was a specious location from which to launch a critique of capitalism, so, too, the *New York Times* or PBS or *American Photographer* seem unpromising sites for a critique of liberalism.[26] So, I might add, is this volume of sophisticated theory.

The critique of capitalism implicitly and explicitly argued in these texts reveals yet another trope for the elaboration of a gendered bourgeois subjectivity. The power of narrative and image insure that "the people" are recontained within the frame of "the self." They remain unremarkable; nothing can be said, after all, of those who can best be seen as "photographs," "fragments," "bits," "lumps," and "pieces" (13) whose difference emanates from the "leverage" and "source" of anatomy (442).

The histories of bourgeois subjectivity, photography and psychoanalysis are intimately linked: Freud understood sexuality as a series of questions involving visual representations; subjectivity developed through a series of impartially understood scenes and psychoanalysis re-presented those scenes through the talking cure. A visual culture knows itself through words. Benjamin in "The Author as Producer" says that writers must become photographers and photographers must write the meanings of their images in the caption. Agee and Evans working (as collaborators) together apart recontextualize each other's texts, as images and words penetrate, contradict and illuminate each other. Agee's "honesty" (Stott), his "authenticity" (Orvell), his "guilt" (Trilling) about his position as "spy," contaminate Evans's "tact and respect" (Hersey) for his subjects' lives and the objects in their possession, while Evans's bestowal of "timeless dignity, beauty and pain of rounded lives" redeems Agee's self-indulgence. Still, in all Agee's 471 pages of "caption" (though he rejects that name), we are riveted by the camera, by the importance of looking into the eyes of an "appallingly damaged group of human beings" and of having them see him and us in turn. This is the meaning of "At the Forks," "Late Sunday Morning" and "Near a Church." This is the meaning of Louise's, Ivy's and Sadie's eyes; a meaning that is quite different from Ellen Wood's flaming center: the unknowable, but fully visible hole which marks her difference, and her invisibility.

Agee's honesty masks his complicity in erasing the different gazes of the tenants. He rails against the false merger with the working class that so infuriated Benjamin about most intellectuals' posturings. But Agee cannot escape the confessional narrative of bourgeois selfhood: the story that encodes the middle class as the subject and object of its own narcissistic and self-loathing gaze. The story that seeks to "know" through what it can "see" of the other finds, not the other, but itself. Still, despite all his looking around, Agee opens himself, like a woman in the text, to "the wide open eyes" of Louise and the other women; thus it is Evans's masculine pose, as detached observer of surfaces, that overcomes the gender and genre confusions of the book, returning it to the visual and narrative conventions of bourgeois culture.

Because genre depends upon the representations of repressive "orderings" like sexual difference, its power to recontain any transgressions, to reestablish conventions, is also that which produces gender, sexual, class and racial hierarchies in bourgeois culture. Looking across classes at the underclass requires looking underneath their skirts, inspecting their pants, because the middle class knows itself as a spy whose desire is somehow "curious." Louise's "stolid" stare feels to Agee like another kind of looking, even another kind of knowing, but it ends up telling a familiar story: her resistance as a girl who openly looks is supplanted by Ellen's "to-be-looked-at-ness." Without a radical break from the regimes of vision and narrative we will only see and write with the eyes and hands of those who have already looked us over and described what they've seen (of) themselves.

Notes

Thanks to Alan Wald, T. V. Reed, Steve Vogel, Dick Ohmann, Gary Spears, Henry Abelove, Patricia Hill, Ann DuCille, Con Samaras, Laura Wexler, Ed Griffin, Carol Mason, Carolyn Porter, and Nancy Armstrong for comments and criticisms. All of their insights have helped this essay; any faults are mine entirely.

1. For more on this see Carolyn Kay Steedman, *Landscape for a Good Woman.* Her readings of the stories provided by the watercress girl in Mayhew's *London Labour and the London Poor* and of Freud's Dora (128–39) point to the differences

and similarities between "documents" and "case studies" and what this means for class and gender relations.

2. Lukács is referring to Marx's "Fetishism of Commodities and the Secrets Therein" in which he indicates the relationship between commodities is shrouded in the "mist-enveloped region" that obscures the social relations among men into that of a relationship between things, in a manner wholly unlike that of vision, which entails a connection between the subjective experience of light exciting the optic nerve and the objective properties of the object emitting its light (*Capital* 1: 83).

3. A few years later, the German Worker's Photography movement launched the first inexpensive mass magazine of photos and text to promote a "proletarian eye" with which to counter bourgeois control of representation in both "art" and "industrial" photography. Their journal "proclaim[ed] proletarian reality in all its disgusting ugliness, with its indictment of society and its demand for revenge." Yet, editor Edwin Hoernle acknowledged that few workers could see in any other way than through the lenses of bourgeois perception.

4. See Steedman, 12–15, for more on Lukács's (and Marx's) failure to register class consciousness as a psychological process that begins in childhood.

5. We might also think about his discussion of "Family Romances" (9: 236–41). Here, the desire on the part of the older child to reinstate the exalted parental figures of early childhood takes the form of debasing the parents—particularly the father—and in boys entails imagining a new father of higher economic and political status who was the mother's lover and thus is secretly the father.

6. See Rachel Bowlby, *Just Looking*, chapter two, for more on this connection.

7. Laura Mulvey's now classic declaration: "Sadism demands a story" has been revised by Teresa de Lauretis to read ". . . and a story demands sadism." Each theory of narrative argues that the desire mobilized in narrative (cinema) is always at the expense of someone. See Mulvey, "Visual Pleasure and Narrative Cinema," and de Lauretis, "Desire in Narrative," in *Alice Doesn't*.

8. See his *Five Photo-Textual Documentaries from the Great Depression*. (The photo-textual form was indebted to the popularity of *Life* magazine, which following its 1936 inauguration spawned numerous imitators.)

9. See Maren Stange, *Symbols of Ideal Life*, especially chapters three and four (89–148), for a persuasive analysis of this process.

10. See, for instance, Newton Arvin, "A Letter on Proletarian Literature," and E. A. Schachner, "Revolutionary Literature in the United States Today."

11. Barbara Foley has made this point effectively in a paper presented at the MMLA Convention 1988 entitled "Marxist Critics of the 1930s and Bourgeois Aesthetic Theory."

12. For more detail, see Charlotte Nekola, "Worlds Unseen," in *Writing Red* (189—98).

13. See Georg Lukács, "Reportage or Portrayal?" 49.

14. See chapter one of Andrew Ross, *No Respect*, for more on this.

15. See the final chapter of Miles Orvell, *The Real Thing*.

16. For a remarkably insightful explanation of the "postmodernist realism" of Evans and Agee's project, see T. V. Reed, "Unimagined Existence and the Fiction of the Real."

17. For an elaboration on the gendered implications of the dread of mixing genres, see Jacques Derrida, "The Law of Genre."

18. "The fixing of language and the fixing of sexual identity go hand in hand; they rely on each other and share the same forms of instability and risk" (Rose 228).

19. Agee was not unaware of the homoerotic elements in either his life or his text. While completing the manuscript, he and his second wife Alma Mailman, the working-class Jewish protégée of his ex-father-in-law, conceived a child. Agee instigated a "romantic liaison" between Alma and Walker Evans eventually leading to a sexual encounter which Agee insisted on watching, after which he wrote to Evans that he was "sorry and contemptuous of myself. However much . . . you happen to like each other, good: I am enough of an infant homosexual or postdostoevskian to be glad. However much you don't, that's all right too: I am enough of a 'man' not to care to think particularly whether I care or not" (Bergreen, *James Agee* 239). It would appear that all the elements Freud discerned in the Rat Man's case—anxiety over his homoerotic desire for his father and for his father's liaison with a woman of lower class status, resulting in the desire to visually penetrate the mystery of sexual difference, were put into play here by Agee. For a theoretical and textual analysis of the homoerotics of male collaboration, see Wayne Koestenbaum, *Double Talk*.

20. See Susan R. Suleiman, *Authoritarian Fictions*, on the dual pulls of "ideological fiction" which are akin to documentary reportage.

21. See John Berger and Jean Mohr, *Another Way of Telling*, for a contemporary meditation on the problem of disclosing the lives of peasant communities through images composed by (sympathetic) intellectuals: "A photograph quotes from appearances, but in quoting simplifies them" (119).

22. For an elaboration of this idea see Charles Wolfe, "Direct Address and the Social Documentary Photograph."

23. See John Hersey, "Introduction," vii. Also see two recent examples— Miles Orvell, *The Real Thing*, which argues that *Let Us Now Praise Famous Men* culminates a modernist search for authenticity, and T. V. Reed, "Unimagined Existence and the Fiction of the Real," which argues that Agee and Evans commence a postmodernist search for a political form of narrative.

24. See Howell Raines, "Let Us Now Revisit Famous Folk," Scott Osbourne, "A Walker Evans Heroine Remembers," and "Let Us Now Praise Famous Men— Revisited, *The American Experience 109.*

25. See Dale Maharidge and Michael Williamson, *And Their Children After Them: The Legacy of Let Us Now Praise Famous Men, James Agee, Walker Evans, and the Rise and Fall of Cotton in the South.*

26. See Rosler for an extensive unpacking of the issues involved in exposing documentary to a political critique.

Works Cited

Agee, James, and Walker Evans. *Let Us Now Praise Famous Men*. Boston: Houghton, 1960.

Arvin, Newton. "A Letter on Proletarian Literature." *Partisan Review* 3 (1936): 12–14.

Benjamin, Walter. "The Author as Producer." *Understanding Brecht*. Ed. Peter Demetz. London: Verso, 1983.

———. "A Short History of Photography." *Germany: The New Photography, 1927–33*. Ed. David Mellor. London: Arts Council of Great Britain, 1978. 69–76.

Berger, John, and Jean Mohr. *Another Way of Telling*. New York: Pantheon, 1982.

Bergreen, Laurence. *James Agee: A Life*. New York: Dutton, 1984.

Bowlby, Rachel. *Just Looking: Consumer Culture in Dreiser, Gissing and Zola*. New York: Routledge, 1985.

de Lauretis, Teresa. "Desire in Narrative." *Alice Doesn't*. Bloomington: Indiana UP, 1984. 103–57.

Derrida, Jacques. "The Law of Genre," *Glyph* 7 (1982): 202–32.

Evans, Walker. Handwritten draft memorandum to Roy Stryker, 1935. *Walker Evans at Work*. New York: Harper, 1982.

Foley, Barbara. "Marxist Critics of the 1930s and Bourgeois Aesthetic Theory." MMLA Convention. St. Louis. Nov. 1988.

Freud, Sigmund. *The Standard Edition of the Complete Psychological Works*. 24 vols. Trans. and Ed. James Strachey. London: Hogarth, 1955.

Goodman, Paul. Rev. of *Let Us Now Praise Famous Men*. *Partisan Review* IX.1 (1942): 62.

Hersey, John. "Introduction: Agee." *Let Us Now Praise Famous Men*. By James Agee and Walker Evans. Rev. ed. Boston: Houghton, 1991.

Hiley, Michael. *Victorian Working Women: Portraits from Life*. Boston: Godine, 1979.

Hoernle, Edwin. "The Working Man's Eye." *Germany: The New Photography, 1927–33*. Ed. David Mellor. London: Arts Council of Great Britain, 1978. 48–49.

Hurley, F. Jack. *Portrait of a Decade: Roy Stryker and the Development of Documentary Photography in the Thirties*. Baton Rouge: Louisiana State UP, 1972.

Koestenbaum, Wayne. *Double Talk: The Erotics of Male Literary Collaboration*. New York: Routledge, 1989.

Lechlitner, Ruth. "Alabama Tenant Families." Rev. of *Let Us Now Praise Famous Men*. *New York Herald Tribune Books* 24 August, 1941: 10.

"Let Us Now Praise Famous Men—Revisited." *The American Experience 109*. Boston, WGBH Educational Foundation. 29 Nov. 1988.

Lukács, Georg. *History and Class Consciousness*. Trans. Rodney Livingstone. Cambridge: MIT P, 1968.

———. "Reportage or Portrayal?" *Essays on Realism*. Ed. Rodney Livingstone. Trans. David Feunback. Cambridge: MIT Press, 1981. 45–75.

Maharidge, Dale, and Michael Williamson. *And Their Children After Them: The Legacy of Let Us Now Praise Famous Men, James Agee, Walker Evans, and the Rise and Fall of Cotton in the South*. New York: Pantheon, 1989.

Marx, Karl. *Capital: A Critique of Political Economy, Vol. 1*. Trans. Ben Fowkes. New York: Vintage, 1977.

Minh-ha, Trinh T. *Woman, Native, Other: Writing Postcoloniality and Feminism*. Bloomington: Indiana UP, 1989.

Mulvey, Laura. "Visual Pleasure and Narrative Cinema." *Screen* 16 (1975): 3–16.

Nekola, Charlotte. "Worlds Unseen: Political Women Journalists and the 1930s." *Writing Red: An Anthology of American Women Writers, 1930–1940*. Ed. Charlotte Nekola and Paula Rabinowitz. New York: Feminist, 1987. 189–98.

Orvell, Miles. *The Real Thing*. Chapel Hill: U of North Carolina P, 1990.

Osbourne, Scott. "A Walker Evans Heroine Remembers." *American Photographer* Sept. 1979: 70–73.

Puckett, John Roger. *Five Photo-Textual Documentaries from the Great Depression.* Ann Arbor: UMI, 1984.

Raines, Howell. "Let Us Now Revisit Famous Folk." *New York Times Magazine* 25 May 1980: 31–46.

Reed, T. V. "Unimagined Existence and the Fiction of the Real: Postmodernist Realism in *Let Us Now Praise Famous Men.*" *Representations* 24 (1988): 156–76.

Rose, Jacqueline. *Sexuality in the Field of Vision.* London: Verso, 1986.

Rosler, Martha. "in, around and after thoughts (on documentary photography)." *Three Works.* Halifax: Nova Scotia College of Art and Design, 1981. 82.

Ross, Andrew. *No Respect: Intellectuals and Popular Culture.* New York: Routledge, 1989.

Schachner, E. A. "Revolutionary Literature in the United States Today." *Windsor Quarterly* 2 (1934): 27–64.

Smedley, Agnes. "The People of China." Rpt. in *Writing Red: An Anthology of American Women Writers, 1930–1940.* Ed. Charlotte Nekola and Paula Rabinowitz. New York: Feminist, 1987. 203–14.

Stange, Maren. *Symbols of Ideal Life: Social Documentary Photography in America, 1890–1950.* Cambridge: Cambridge UP, 1989.

Steedman, Carolyn Kay. *Landscape for a Good Woman: A Story of Two Lives.* New Brunswick: Rutgers UP, 1987.

Stott, William. *Documentary Expression and Thirties America.* Chicago, U of Chicago P, 1986.

Suleiman, Susan R. *Authoritarian Fictions.* New York: Columbia UP, 1983.

Trilling, Lionel. "Greatness with One Fault in It." *Kenyon Review* 4.1 (1942): 99–102.

Warshow, Robert. "The Legacy of the Thirties." *The Immediate Experience.* Garden City: Doubleday, 1962. 33–48.

Wolfe, Charles. "Direct Address and the Social Documentary Photograph: 'Annie Mae Gudger' as Negative Subject." *Wide Angle* 9 (1987): 59–70.

Primitive Subversions: Totalization and Resistance in Native Canadian Politics

Peter Kulchyski

> Consider the "hidden meaning" (*Kaona*) of the inscription above the entrance to the Honolulu Board of Water Supply: *Uwe ka lani, ola ka honua* / "The heavens weep, the earth lives." Unlikely that the *haole* ("white men") and Japanese who now dominate the Hawaiian bureaucracy are aware that this anodyne snippet of pastoral poesy refers to a primordial copulation.
>
> —Marshall Sahlins

Let us, for a moment, obey Sahlins's injunction to "consider the 'hidden meaning'" of this inscription. As Sahlins points out in *Islands of History* the original inhabitants of Hawaii had developed a social system organized around "a political economy of love" (19). Sex and beauty were coinage in the exchanges that constituted wealth and power.[1] The language and poetry of the islanders reflected (and reflected on) this: sexual puns were a favored exchange. Among their origin myths the islanders positioned a male heaven and a female earth whose progeny were the gods. As an aside to his discussion of these matters Sahlins makes reference to the "anodyne snippet of pastoral poesy" that graces the entrance to the Honolulu Board of Water Supply. In centering this aside I want to focus our attention on what remains implied in Sahlins's text. "The heavens weep, the earth lives" is a harmless comment on water supply that the board appropriates in order to make a passing reference to the early inhabitants of the islands. This inscription, however, remains open to multiple readings, one of which—as a reference to "primordial copulation"—calls up the whole network of transgressive sexual relations that colonialism actively suppressed. This latter reading invokes the whole deeply sexual culture of the early Hawaiians and thereby vitiates the vacuous harmlessness implied by the phrase's status as inscription.

This aside in Sahlins's text raises in condensed fashion the problems I want to discuss in this paper. As inscription, the phrase "the heavens weep, the earth lives" marks a grudging acknowledgment to the existence of the island's original inhabitants. The inscription attempts to assign a particular status to its referents as long gone, as harmless folklore. At the same time, the inscription implies a more active presence, a set of social and sexual relations that represent alternatives to the established order. Because this latter implication, as Sahlins suggests, is probably unknown to the representatives of colonial power its presence, I would argue, can be read as a subversive gesture. In attempting to name and therefore bury the past, the inscription calls up all of the practices it is a part of the process of suppressing.

In recent years a great deal of energy has gone into examining the ways in which subversive practice often acts as a ruse of power. For example, Stephen Greenblatt has argued, with reference to the new historicism:

> . . . new historicism, as I understand it, does not posit historical process as unalterable and inexorable, but it does tend to discover limits or constraints upon individual intervention. Actions that appear to be single are disclosed as multiple; the apparently isolated power of the individual genius turns out to be bound up with collective, social energy; *a gesture of dissent may be an element in a larger legitimation process*, while an attempt to stabilize the order of things may turn out to subvert it. (165, emphasis added)

In Greenblatt's theoretical scheme there is room for and even an emphasis on social agency, but this emphasis is undercut by the degree to which he focuses on the "limits or constraints" upon collective as well as individual "interventions." While we must be careful not to idealize historical agents or to underestimate the power of the dominant order, a "textual figure can be deployed as an insurgent, an intervention destabilizing the meaning of imperial totalization" (Emberley 50). Such deployment, such readings, themselves carry forward the project of subversion.

This paper attempts to examine from a theoretical point of view the struggle between the State and Native people in Canada over the assimilation of so-called "primitive peoples" (I will discuss my use of this deeply charged term in the conclusion) into capitalist society. Primarily it employs the concepts of totalization, in order to interpret the locus of domination in this politics, and subversion, in order to interpret an emancipatory strategy. For Jean-Paul Sartre it was "the complex play of praxis and totalisation" that made history (39). The theoretical importance of continually examining *both* domination and emancipation must be stressed, because a theory that focuses exclusively on the former falls prey to a reinscription of the very power it seeks to critique through a reification of that power. There is always room for some kind of resistance, struggle or praxis to totalization. Native people in Canada, for example, *have* resisted these processes with a good measure of success for a long time. One of the jobs of theory is to decode this struggle, to read the strategies of resistance to power with as much attention as we devote to reading the strategies of power.

Today, in widely dispersed locations around the world, the people who belong to what have been variously described as gatherer/hunter, primitive, paleolithic, nomadic, foraging or band, societies are engaged in a life and death struggle against dominant, late capitalist Western "civilization." This struggle can be understood as a struggle between different modes of production that coexist in a single social formation, following Nicos Poulantzas's distinction (*Political Power* 15). The dominant mode of production is capitalism. With reference to Poulantzas's distinction, Fredric Jameson has emphasized that a social formation would contain both "vestiges and survivals of older modes of production . . . as well as anticipatory tendencies which are potentially inconsistent with the existing system but have not yet generated an autonomous space of their own" (*Political Unconscious* 95).[2] While the Native way of life would be associated with the gatherer/hunter mode of production, I would stress that inasmuch as the latter is a form of what Marx and Engels called primitive communism it also contains and embodies "anticipatory tendencies": it points to social relations and practices that are not just different, not just outdated, but possibly emancipatory. Hence the special animosity directed at primitive peoples in thought and action. Hence also the deeply coded strategies of resistance offered up in response. There is more at stake here than the survival of an "exotic" way of life. At risk is an embodied emancipatory possibility. That, perhaps, is why Félix Guattari has argued that "nothing is less marginal than the problem of the marginal" (262).

Totalization and the Established Order

Let us wage a war on totality.
—Jean-François Lyotard

Coexistence of different modes of production does not necessarily imply active antipathy. In its early years capitalism adopted structures and practices associated with feudalism, for example. Gatherer/hunters often live in close proximity and relative harmony with pastoral peoples. The opposition of capitalist society to gatherer/hunters, of postmodernism to paleolithic, is a specific relation. It involves specific strategies of hegemony and resistance. As a totalizing force, of course, capitalism ultimately attacks all social forms that impede its progress and oppose or do not accord with its order. The process of totalization as a form of domination is most directly confronted, I would argue, by the dispossessed, by those whom capital has reduced to the status of being "free, unprotected and rightless" though not yet proletarian, to borrow Marx's phrase (*Capital* 876). Those who live in what, from the perspective of capital, could be called the most inaccessible regions of the world tend to be gatherer/hunters. The process of dispossessing them has been more recent, and as a result a specific dynamic of struggle between primitive and postmodern has developed. By paying close attention to the intelligibility of this struggle we may come to understand more general lessons about strategic resistance to the established order.

Under examination here is the subtle but powerful process central to the history of domination in Western society, a process that can be called totalization or the totalizing movement of capital and capitalist society. It is this process, the uncontrolled dynamic that must necessarily absorb and bring under its ultimate hegemony virtually all aspects of human reality, that, conversely, creates exclusion, marginality and dispossession itself. There is a two-sided movement to this domination. First, there is the creation of dispossession and the expelling or marginalization of difference that it implies. That is, the ruthless destruction of precapitalist social relations. Second, though, there is the intense and equally powerful attempt to absorb and assimilate the dispossessed, in order to establish the necessary pool of labor power, thereby effacing all traces of difference. Both marginalization and assimilation, exclusion and absorption, are strategies of totalizing power. Both strategies are also subject to intense resistance at every turn.

There are also at least two parallel but distinct totalizing forces at work in Western society. There is the totalizing movement of capital itself, a process whose central dynamic has been described by Marx in the first part of *Capital*. This movement or process is related to another, equally powerful one, that of the capitalist State, which also acts in a totalizing fashion but in a different sphere and in a different way. Both forces play a role in dispossessing, marginalizing, silencing and excluding Native peoples. They also both attempt to manage, assimilate, absorb and subsume Native peoples.

Marx's texts continue to offer the most useful description of the totalizing dynamic that characterizes Western society. In the *Grundrisse*, for example, Marx argued that the bourgeois system's "development to its totality consists precisely in subordinating all elements of society to itself, or in creating out of it the organs which it still lacks" (278). Capitalism, in Marx's view, involved reshaping social relations so that producers took the form of workers, while owners of the means of production took the form of capitalists. Further, "capitalist production is not merely the reproduction of the relationship; it is its reproduction on a steadily increasing scale" (*Capital* 1062). That is, there is a *dynamic* to capital, a process that defines progress as the reproduction of the capitalist-worker social relation. Of course, this process has not been a one-sided one even in the Western world, and the specific form of the relationship remains a site of class confrontation.

Social relations in capitalism hinge upon the transformation of the direct producer to a worker: a seller of labor power. This in turns implies the commodification of the direct producer, and the process of commodification, the expansion of the commodity form examined by Marx in the first part of *Capital*, is the significant locus of totalization in our time. Capital totalizes by transforming objects, people, activities and symbols into commodities, into exchange values and use values. In this sense, capital continues to expand within the Western world because it continues to transform all aspects of the lives of westerners into the commodity form. Fredric Jameson's analysis of late-capitalist culture as postmodern can be understood, arguably, as a reading of the expansion of the commodity form in the sphere of culture and aesthetics.[3] In the margins, in those areas where social relations have not yet been transformed, totalization now works to transform social relations while simultaneously transforming culture.

This understanding of totalization as the expansion of the commodity form is relatively common. I rehearse it here as a reminder and to point again to Marx's contribution. What deserves more attention, in the present context, is the specific way in which the State acts as a totalizing force that is distinct from but related to capital. In *State, Power, Socialism* Nicos Poulantzas developed a sustained critique of the totalizing power of the late-capitalist State. Poulantzas argued that the State took control of regulating and imposing capitalist spatial and temporal "matrices" (99).[4] That is, the State attempts to construct, entrench and reproduce the modern nation by imposing capitalist space and time, territory and history, on a territorially defined social collectivity. Both space and time are organized along the same principle as the factory assembly line, that is, seriality.

Poulantzas's later analysis of the State stressed the manner in which Western, liberal-democratic states may be understood as "totalitarian," which he described as "separation and division in order to unify; parcelling out in order to structure; atomization in order to encompass; segmentation in order to totalize; closure in order to homogenize; and individualization in order to obliterate differences and otherness" (*State* 107). He made reference to the Bantustan, concentration camp and reservation in this context. He also saw genocide as a peculiarly modern phenomenon or at least one which has peculiarly modern features:

> Genocide is the elimination of what become 'foreign bodies' of the national history and territory: it expels them beyond space and time. The great confinement only comes to pass because it is at the same time the fragmentation and unification of serial and segmented time: concentration camps are a modern invention in the additional sense that the frontier-gates close on 'anti-nationals' for whom time and national historicity are *in suspense*. (*State* 114–15)

Totalization involves the imposition of serialized space and time, of individualization and homogenization. Those cultures and peoples that do not accord with the State-constructed nation are "foreign agents" in the national body and are therefore dispossessed. Dispossession today takes the form of spatial and temporal exclusion of "foreign bodies," systematic destruction of social relations and cultures that remain precapitalist or invoke postcapitalism, and finally, the reintegration and assimilation of the dispossessed.

Totalization is the expansion of the commodity form and the serialized organization of space and time that are presupposed by it. Capital itself and the capitalist State are totalizing forces. The analysis would perhaps be a bleak one were it not for the fact that the State and capital are not unopposed hegemonic forces. Totalization is resisted in different ways by different social groups. Marx's texts show more sensitivity to this than Poulantzas's. In the case of gatherer/hunters, resistance involves constructing enclaves of culture within the established order, of finding space in the interstices of power, of controlling the pace and nature of links with the dominant social organization and culture, of adapting Western technology to precapitalist social relations, of taking the tools offered by the State and capital and using them to strengthen rather than destroy primitive culture. These strategies of resistance have in common what I would call a subversive element because they involve working within totalizing structures and inverting the strategies employed by hegemonic power.

The Subversive Gesture: I

From the system's point of view, history always seems merely a series of accidental transgressions.
—V. N. Volosinov

Both totalization and resistance to it must be understood simultaneously in their synchronic, or structural, and diachronic, or historical, dimensions. Subversion as a specific form of resistance can only be understood in this twofold manner. The structural analysis of subversion leads to an awareness of its conditions of possibility, while the historical analysis reveals the context in which those possibilities may realize themselves. As a background to the theoretical discussion of subversion I would like to briefly illustrate where and how it takes place in the Canadian context. I have chosen two historical examples as exemplifications of the process. These historical examples—one dealing with the legal definition of Indian and the other the banning of specific indigenous cultural practices—point to the broad question of relations between Native people and the State and were significant moments in the development of their present structural relation.

During the mid and late nineteenth century the colonial (pre-Confederation) and Canadian states passed and consolidated legislation that attempted to achieve the "civilization" or "enfranchisement" of Native peoples. Two pieces of legislation were particularly important as foundations for the Indian Act. In 1857 the government of the United Canadas passed "an Act to encourage the gradual civilization of the Indians in this Province" or the "civilization act." Just over a decade later, in 1869, "An Act for the gradual enfranchisement of Indians" or "enfranchisement act" was passed. These acts attempted to consolidate earlier legislation and to establish a firm policy that would lead to the assimilation of Native peoples through "enfranchisement," a process whereby Native peoples surrendered their legal status as Indians in order to gain the franchise, the right to vote, and full status as Canadian citizens. The subsequent Indian Act of Canada functioned within the general framework of the "civilization act" until the major reconstruction of Indian legislation that took place in 1951. I would like to stress two related aspects of the early legislation: the definition of the Indian and the enfranchisement process.

Assimilation of Native people into non-Native society was the clear goal of Indian legislation from about 1815. For the first half of the nineteenth century "civilization" meant teaching Native people to cope with and live peacefully beside non-Natives. By the 1850s the meaning of civilization had shifted to mean assimilation: forcing and teaching Natives to *be* non-Natives.[5] Natives could legally become non-Natives by enfranchising. They could enfranchise themselves, or gain the rights of non-Natives, by meeting certain criteria: reading and writing English or French, being free of debt and of "good moral character." The 1869 act added a land allotment and agricultural activity as criteria. In order for this process to work, however, legislators had to define who a Native person, without the rights of other citizens, was.

The State had assumed the power to define Indians as early as 1850: in that year the government of Lower Canada had incorporated into its Indian legislation a broad definition that included, for example, non-Native people living with the band. The 1857 definition was somewhat more strict and had immediate consequences: non-Native people living with bands were no longer included, though gender discrimination—whereby Indian women who married non-Native men lost their Indian status—was not introduced until the 1869 enfranchisement act. As a whole, then, this legislation worked in a twofold way: it defined Indians and established criteria by which they could be enfranchised. The "paradox," as historian John L. Tobias argues, was that "the legislation to remove all legal distinctions between Indians and Euro-Canadians actually established them" (42).

What historians have not pointed to is the reason why this legal process became paradoxical. Legislators in the mid-nineteenth century had operated on the basis of a series of racist assumptions: they assumed, for example, that being an Indian was undesirable, that being unenfranchised involved a loss of the rights that would matter the most to Native people. The legal structure they inscribed was founded on those assumptions but did not do enough to activate or constitute them. In their practice and everyday lives Native people challenged the assumptions. For many Native people—certainly not all—surrendering their position or status as Indians was seen as more of a loss than a gain. And the definition of the Indian could be used to support arguments that Indians had specific rights that were distinct from but not inferior to the rights of non-Natives. A century later these rights would come to be known as aboriginal rights, a major legal/ political support for the Native's claim to have a special status in Canadian society.

Native people lost their status as Indians through the enfranchisement process even as late as the 1950s. Native women and their children lost status through marriage to non-Natives (and involuntary enfranchisement) up until a few years ago (1985).[6] The distinction between status and nonstatus Indians remains a significant one in Native politics and in the lives of Native people. However, over the course of the last century a struggle took place between an imposed, legal inscription embodying a Eurocentric value judgment on the one hand and the values, cultures and practices of Native peoples on the other hand. Faced with the choice of Native culture and way of life or enfranchisement, the vast majority of Native people struggled to retain and adapt their culture. Significantly, they were able to do so in part because the legislation that was developed to assimilate them had to define them in order to do so and the legal mark of difference could be ultimately reinterpreted as a support for their distinct subject position.

Native people effectively subverted a piece of legislation whose explicit intention was totalizing. In order to totalize, the State was forced to define and marginalize. The sign of difference, the legal demarcation of Indian status, was reinvested by Native people as having a positive value. Marginality became in part a position from which aboriginal culture could resist totalizing power. The State ended up providing Native people with a valuable tool in their struggle against it. This is not to suggest that all of the State's activities were open to such overturning, nor, in this particular context, that the Indian Act as a whole was not a repressive instrument of State power. But it suggests that the process was not as one-sided as it is normally portrayed and that we must be sensitive to the nuances of "the complex mobilities of the historical dialectic" (Jameson, *Late Marxism* 225). In order to illustrate the complexity of this process, we need only to turn to an examination of the repressive side of the Indian Act.

During the late nineteenth and early twentieth century through its assimilationist policies the State waged war with Native peoples on two fronts: the political organization of bands and the continued existence of Native cultures. On the first front, the State attempted to undermine traditional Native leaders by imposing non-Native political structures of representation on local bands. On the latter front, the State ruthlessly attacked Native culture both in assimilationist policies like those I pointed to earlier and in direct attacks on Native cultural practices like the potlatch and the sundance. These attacks point to the convergence of politics and culture in this specific political dynamic as well as to strategies of totalization and subversion.

Amendments to the Indian act passed in 1884 and in 1895 attacked the potlatch and the sundance. The earlier legislation simply named the activities and said that any Indians found participating in them would be liable to a misdemeanor (*Indian Acts* 52). The 1895 amendment was more general. It read:

> Every Indian or other person who engages in, or assists in celebrating or encourages either directly or indirectly another to celebrate, any Indian festival, dance or other ceremony of which the giving away or paying or giving back of money, goods or articles of any sort forms a part, or is a feature . . . and every Indian or other person who engages or assists in any celebration or dance of which the wounding or mutilation of the dead or living body of any human being or animal forms a part or is a feature, is guilty of indictable offense and is liable to imprisonment for a term not exceeding six months and not less than two months; but nothing in this section shall be construed to prevent the holding of any agricultural show or exhibition or the giving of prizes for exhibits thereat. (*Indian Acts* 95–96)

The State appealed to liberal and humanitarian sentiments so as to rationalize the banning of these practices. The potlatch, the giving of gifts, was attacked for creating economic problems; both potlatch and sundance were attacked as "barbaric" acts of violence and self-mutilation.

I am not here going to discuss the subversive struggle to maintain these cultural practices: rather, I want to focus on why they were seen by the State as dangerous, why they represented, for a totalizing State, "ideological crimes," to borrow Dominick LaCapra's evocative phrase.[7] Further, I am going to focus here on the sundance and by extension ceremonies and dances that involve "wounding or mutilation of dead or living persons or animals." This discussion, I believe, will point to the subversive aspect of Native culture itself and why the continued existence and viability of Native cultures poses a challenge to the State and the established order.

The banning of the sundance by the State fit comfortably with the dominant anthropological accounts of the dance. Diamond Jenness, a preeminent early-twentieth-century anthropologist in Canada, had this to say about the ceremony:

> When the Blackfoot and some other plains' tribes celebrated the sun-dance the most sensational incident, though actually an unessential one, was the voluntary torture endured by a few young warriors to excite the compassion and favour of the Great Spirit. These misguided devotees allowed their breasts or shoulders to be pierced with sharp skewers and attached by stout thongs to the sacred pole or to a heavy buffalo skull; and they strained at the pole, or dragged the skull, until they either broke loose or friends and relatives took pity on their sufferings and in some way or other secured their release. (316)[8]

This form of understanding, which appeared in Jenness's 1932 landmark text *The Indians of Canada*, is directly related to the justificatory ideology that supported banning the sundance. The chain of adjectives deserves our attention: Jenness refers to a "sensational" while at the same time "unessential" incident, the "voluntary torture" that is "endured" by "misguided devotees." His whole account of the sundance then is exhausted by his description of this "unessential" incident. The reason for the practice in Jenness's view is "to excite the compassion and favour of the Great Spirit." The closing moment of Jenness's account refers to "friends and relatives" whose compassion, unlike the Great Spirit's, is excited enough to take "pity" on the "sufferings" of the dancers and "release" them. The ending almost invokes the possibility of a kindly State that will spare everyone the trouble, take the place of "friends and relatives," and ban the self-torture outright.

Recent critical anthropology would question the series of presuppositions embodied in Jenness's account and in the State's practice. Let us begin with the assumption that the "sensational incident" may not be as "unessential" as Jenness would have us believe. Indeed, it is possible to understand the sundance wholly in terms of the practice of self-scarification. The work of Pierre Clastres deserves our attention in this context. Clastres understood these practices as "marking" and the marks as "the inscribed text of primitive law; in that sense they are a writing on the body" (187). Clastres argues that this writing on the body is best not seen as writing but rather as marking.[9] What is marked is, in a sense, the absence of writing itself as law. The scar and the pain that brings it mark the individual with the social. As Clastres understands it, the mark is a sign of a particular form of social being. The mark says "you are one of us. . . . None of you is less than us; none of you is more than us. And you will never be able to forget it. You will not cease to remember the same marks that we have left on your body" (186). This mark against writing is inscribed on the body and is therefore set against the writing that is separate from the body and represents the "distant, despotic law of the State" (188). Again, let me emphasize, this is not another form of writing but rather marking against writing, marking against the State and the law, marking that says "you will not have the desire for power; you will not have the desire for submission" (188).

The marks might be understood, then, as a sign of an individual's bond to the collectivity. The bond takes a specific form that serves to signify the political values of the collectivity. In this sense, the mark can be interpreted as a sign of the community itself, as a sign of the individual's willingness to accept the values and thereby participate in the life of the community.

In this understanding of the practice of scarification in ceremonies, rituals and dances such as the sundance, the State's actions take on a rather different intelligibility than that situated
within a discourse of humanitarian compassion. The State wrote
a law against this primitive law; it banned in writing the mark
against writing. In doing so it wrote in a language almost completely alien to the subjects of its discourse. It did so in order to
break down precisely those mechanisms that worked within Native societies to prevent the imposition of alienated power and to
materially embody the collectivity. The State then spent the next
fifty years ensuring that Native people could read the officially
sanctioned languages, English and French, so they would know
the law that prohibited marking against writing and they would
thereby lose the deep bonds of community. Once Native people
could read Western alienated inscription, it became safe to allow
the sundance to take place again. Just as once Native people in
British Columbia became relatively dependent on the capitalist
market it became safe to lift the ban on the potlatch. The possibility etched in the mark remains even where it is not read. Sun-
dances, including scarification, take place today. The pride taken
in her scars by one of my female colleagues in Native studies at the
University of Saskatchewan is for me a living reminder of this
message. These scars evoke the possibility of a society that continually resists alien powers and structures of domination, that
reasserts the value of community.

The Subversive Gesture: II

The dynamic relation between totalization and subversion
can be seen, not only in the historical struggles of aboriginal people and the State, but also in contemporary cultural conflict. In a
sense, Native peoples in Canada have been forced by history to
occupy a subversive position within the dominant society. Were
the term *nature* not in such disrepute, we might regard Native
peoples as natural subversives; instead, we must be satisfied with
more awkward constructions and suggest that they have placed
themselves and been placed in a structural position where subversion has become a crucial form of political activity.

In understanding contemporary Native cultural politics in Canada, then, it is particularly important to pay attention to the emancipatory potential of objects, structures and signs that on the surface may appear wholly in the realm of domination. The relation between totalization and subversion appears in culture as a relation between the ideological and the utopian. Jameson, in his recent careful reading of Adorno, has argued that we must "simultaneously insist on what is false and ideological and also on what is utopian in the work" (*Late Marxism* 221). The tendency today to focus on the ideological means that there may be a strategic value in shifting the emphasis toward the utopian/subversive, but a dialectical reading will not lose sight of either. This particular dynamic can be staged with reference to some paintings in the church at Colville Lake.

Colville Lake is a very small Dene community just north of the Arctic Circle in the western Arctic. When I visited Colville Lake in the summer of 1984 it was considered by the Dene to be one of their most traditional communities: small, isolated and without electricity. Certainly the rhythm of life there was as non-Western as we might find in North America: a daily pattern in the summer that revolved around setting and bringing in nets to catch fish that were then dried in the sun, stored and eaten. There were two prominent buildings in Colville Lake when I visited it: one was a fishing lodge run by a non-Native, the other the church. The church had a series of paintings[10] that were perhaps intended to localize Christian figures. One shows the image of a Native Mary and child-Jesus positioned within the northern lights over Colville Lake (Fig. 1).

Another painting that I want to briefly discuss shows our Dene Mary and Jesus in very uncharacteristic—indeed I am tempted to say strikingly un-Christian—poses (Fig. 2.). The Mary is tossing the child-Jesus in the air. Both are smiling or laughing. The position of the child, not relegated to parental subordination, is unusual, as is the whole "playful" tone of this painting. This is a Mary and a Jesus that we see infrequently if at all in the Western religious narratives and visual representations. It recalls the non-coercive aspects of child rearing that so many anthropologists have commented on with respect to primitive peoples. This representation of Mary and Jesus fits comfortably in Colville Lake:

Fig. 1. Interior view of front part of church. The painting is of a Native Mary and Jesus, highlighted against northern lights in the sky over Colville Lake. Photo by Peter Kulchyski, with the assistance of Rita Kakfwi.

what is remarkable about the painting for me is that it walks a tightrope. Is it to be taken as illustrating the ability of a totalizing religious discourse to adapt to local conditions or the subversion of that discourse by unrepentant (and ultimately unconverted) primitives?

The Western religious traditions have left many representations of Jesus and Mary; there are whole schools of thought and aesthetic/theological debates about various Jesus-Mary iconic positions. Nevertheless, for our purposes we need only acknowledge that the dominant trope, what could be described as the commodity Jesus and Mary, figures them as peaceful, even passive. This image as a commodity has become complicit with the establishment of economic relations based on commodification. These economic relations are in northern Canada associated with the "development" of nonrenewable resources, particularly the extraction of oil and gas. The Dene have consistently opposed the

Fig. 2. Interior view of back part of church at Colville Lake, with painting of Native Mary and Native child-Jesus. Photo by Peter Kulchyski, with the assistance of Rita Kakfwi.

imposition of these forms of economic development, most significantly in the last few decades through their struggle against the building of the Mackenzie Valley pipeline. Resistance to commodification takes place at many levels; the struggle over images, over the representation of spirituality, is not insignificant.

Another example, another question, might be appropriate: how are we to understand the inscription by a Native artist in the 1930s of a representation of Jesus on the ramparts of the Deh Cho (Mackenzie) River? The ramparts, a few miles upstream of Fort Good Hope, the Dene community that is the "center" in relation to Colville as its "periphery," form an important part of Dene mythology and are at least respected if not sacred. This Jesus bears resemblance to the many religious paintings, icons and figures described by Michael Taussig in his recent *Shamanism, Colonialism, and the Wild Man.*[11] The figure on the ramparts is clearly Christian. The gesture, invoking a mythical/religious figure as a source of protection by marking the land with His image, can only be understood in Dene terms.

If we acknowledge the viability of both readings and recognize simultaneously the power of totalizing discourse and the moment of subversion, I think we must also stress the latter. A Jesus that represents play over prohibition, the Native Jesus, serves somewhat better as a bearer of Native culture and values than the Western way of life. Nevertheless, the Native Jesus is still Jesus: I want to also point then to the way in which subversion takes place within totalization. It sometimes uses the language of power to represent something other than power, but this form of subversive gesture is not itself that other and, perhaps, not even that other language.

In contemporary practice, subversion lives more in the everyday than in any other sphere of existence. That is why, I believe, it so frequently escapes the notice of cultural critics: it often produces few artifacts. While objects, signs, even structures offer tangible evidence that can be decoded, gestures are lost in their moment. The anecdote, the story, is perhaps the only written form that tries to preserve subversive gestures. On this point I am in agreement with Greenblat, who has written that "the anecdote has at once something of the literary and something that exceeds the literary, a narrative form and a pointed, referential access to what lies beyond or beneath that form" (5). I offer up the following:

In the summer of 1977 I made two visits to the small Cree community of Shamattawa, located far to the northeast of Thompson in northern Manitoba. Shamattawa was a relatively recent settlement of Cree who had left larger Native communities because of the social deterioration they saw in the larger centers, a deterioration they blamed on alcohol abuse. Nevertheless, Shamattawa itself soon acquired a reputation as one of the most impoverished, miserable Native communities in northern Manitoba if not Canada, with a serious alcohol, violence and gas-sniffing problem. Geoffrey York has written of Shamattawa:

> The unemployment rate at Shamattawa exceeds 80 percent. Of the band's population of about seven hundred people, more than one-third are essentially homeless—sharing the overcrowded homes of friends or relatives, or living in shacks

or decaying houses that desperately need replacement. The people of Shamattawa get their water in buckets from the river, and their homes are heated by wood stoves constructed from old oil drums. The stoves are constant fire hazards, sometimes sparking fatal blazes. (2)

There are many such descriptions. Journalists and even academics seem to relish the opportunity that Shamattawa gives them for practicing the language of despair.

In my visit to Shamattawa, about a decade before York's, I saw both debilitating poverty and a community seriously working at reestablishing a traditional culture and economy. Because of its location Shamattawa could not receive signals from the Anik satellite that provides television to northern Canadians.[12] As well, there were no telephones in Shamattawa because of the expense of stringing a line from Thompson, the nearest center. The major contacts with the outside world were the biweekly plane and the community radio phone, operated by the local band.

The incident I want to discuss took place the spring before my first visit and was related to me by a white teacher; he and a nurse were the only non-Native residents of Shamattawa at that time. The teacher, a friendly fellow whose previous experience included training South Vietnamese army regulars in underwater espionage, had decided to purchase a personal radio phone because he was tired of having to make his personal calls in the public space of the community hall. He had, as a result, invested time, energy and money in going through the "red tape" and necessary bureaucratic process of ordering one. The difficulty was exacerbated by the fact that the northern climate of Shamattawa stunted tree growth: a special pole had to be flown in by helicopter from Thompson. The whole process, from initial application to pole delivery, took the teacher just over a year. However, one fine day in the spring of 1977, the pole was delivered and the teacher, on his way to school in the morning, walked by the official standard radio phone pole that lay in his backyard. It would be raised, and the radio phone ready to operate, later that day. On the short walk to the school he passed the town chief, industriously driving the only motorized vehicle, a small tractor with three or four platforms on wheels pulled behind. On his way back from school for lunch, a few hours later, he again absently waved at the chief as he scanned the horizon in search of the new marker, his pole. The chief smiled and waved cheerfully, on his way back to the community center with a pile of fresh-cut supplies for the wood stove, neatly stacked on the platforms, a pile of wood that began to look startlingly familiar . . .

The story was related to me by the teacher as an illustration of the town's backwardness: the chief had not been able to tell a radio phone pole from a source of firewood. The teacher, in good grace, gave in to fate and gave up on his project for personalized communication. The anecdote, I think, points beyond the chief's presumed naivete to the politics of small, Native communities.[13] What kind of culture insists on privatized communication? What kind of economy is structured around possessive individualism and insists on the so-called right to preserve unequal property relations? I think it is possible to read this anecdote politically. In doing so we have to acknowledge the different views of the different actors. The pole represented for the teacher a means of private communication with his loved ones who lived far away from his isolated post. It also represented modernization and progress, a step out of the backwater status he had chosen or was forced to choose. For the chief, the pole represented firewood. It may have also represented a political challenge of sorts. The pole could have been seen as a mark of separation, of the teacher's refusal to participate in the community life, or refusal of the social on the teacher's part. As such, this symbolically laden "pole" was a challenge to the community's culture and an explicit refusal of their values. The chief's responsibility in this roughly egalitarian setting was to cut the teacher down to size and cut up the mark of individual prestige (castration complex notwithstanding) that might stand against the mark of community solidarity, or at least equality.

We have no way of knowing exactly what the pole meant to the different actors of this event. I have related a story and constructed an interpretation in the hope of illustrating the degree to which subversion is most frequently a matter of micropolitics, a politics of everyday experience, of speech and gesture, a politics that leaves few traces, but may be passed on from generation to generation through stories or values and may also disappear into a backwater eddy of history, not even serving to inspire those who bear its spirit of constructive refusal.

Primitive Subversions

One of the premises of subversive practice is the disconnection posited in semiology between signifiers and signifieds. The opening created by this rupture is precisely the moment of subversion "because as ventured in action, the sign is subjected to another kind of determination: to processes of human consciousness and intelligence" (Sahlins 151). So argues Sahlins, who points to the "potentially inventive" possibilities raised by "interested" readings. Two of the three subversions I have discussed can be understood as conflicts of interpretation in which Native peoples have taken a sign—a visual representation of Jesus, a legal definition—and invested it with a reading grounded on and supportive of their own cultural values. In one case, the legal definition, the sign was constructed as a mechanism of totalizing power. But, as Sahlins argues, "nothing guarantees . . . that intelligent and intentional subjects . . . will use the existing categories in prescribed ways" (145). The same might be said for structures, signs, and objects.

This kind of subversion takes place when Native people make use of occasional wage labor to support their traditional economies rather than undermine them, or when advanced technology is adopted and incorporated by Native communities to affirm community structures rather than destroy them.[14] Minnie Aodla Freeman's *Life Among the Qallunaat* is another example of a subversive text that demonstrates and encapsulates my argument. Freeman's book describes her life as a translator for the government in southern Canada, and her reactions to the strange people and customs she encounters there. It can be read as an Inuit anthropological description of non-Natives: the strange habits of the *qallunaat*, "people who pamper their eyebrows." A passage called "So Close Together and Yet So Far Apart" illustrates this point:

> My first ride on a bus during rush hour made me wonder how the bus could move with all its passengers. When I travelled

with my family, the sled would not move if it was too full; the dogs could not budge it without help. But the bus, run by a motor, was something else. I was with a man and we were on our way to visit his family. I sat while he stood, but felt rather awkward as I was taught to let my elders sit, man or woman. Much later I learned that it was his custom to be a gentleman to a female, young or old.

No one spoke. Now and then I would hear a little bell and I learned that the bell meant that somebody was getting off. (I decided that I would never ride the bus alone because I would be too shy to ring the bell.) It occurred to me that people can be close together and yet far apart. No one seemed to know any other. I could not understand how people could ignore each other when they were sharing a bus, let alone one seat. While the bus lulled me into daydreams, making my mind drunk with the smell of gasoline, I thought of big gatherings at home. When a whale or seal was divided among the families, children laughed and threw stones into the water, dogs yapped and everybody enjoyed the food. I could hear the water at the shore and the merriment down the banks. (25)

The Inuit have a saying—"use what you have"—that in a sense provides a primitive justification for subversion if we read it to represent taking the structures and tools at hand to create what is possible in that context, rather than hoping for something else to come along or to create utopia from thin air. In this sense, subversion always works within totalization.

The other kind of subversion that I want to point to invokes the specificity of the "primitive" and is related to the example of the law against marking. It also points to the reason why the other kind of subversion is somewhat more radical than its description implies. The existence of peoples who attach themselves to forms of social organization that owe as much to the gatherer/hunter mode of production as to the capitalist poses a specific challenge to the established order. Societies structured around the active opposition to coercion cannot be tolerated in social contexts dependent on institutionalized coercion as a societal norm. Gatherer/hunters pose a threat to the modern world, to the State and to capital. They represent the possibility of egalitarian gender and social relations, of generalized affluence, of nonalienated labor, of all those aspects of everyday life which, Freeman's passage above reminds us, do not have to be organized around totalizing, serial exigencies.

In this context, finally, I would like to raise the question of my use of the word *primitive* as a conceptual tool in understanding Native politics in Canada today. The word takes on, I think, a negative connotation (by which I mean one that suits the interest of totalizing power) where it is read to represent a "simpler" or an earlier form of human society, barely distinct from nature. However, I think it is possible to subvert this reading today, to understand *primitive* in a way related to Marx's notion of primitive communism or, as Stanley Diamond once argued when he wrote: "the sickness of civilization consists . . . in its failure to incorporate (and only then to move beyond the limits of) the primitive" (129). The nature of incorporation is precisely the battleground of Native politics today. The established order draws its power from its expansive and absorptive exigencies. Resistance takes place both through direct opposition to these exigencies and through subverting the structures and signs employed by totalizing power.

Notes

This paper was first presented at Strategies of Critique II, York University, Toronto, March 1988. A subsequent draft was read at the 46th Annual Congress of Americanists, June 1988. I am very grateful to a number of friends and colleagues, including Shannon Bell, Edgar Dosman, Michael Gismondi, Gad Horowitz and Deborah Lee Simmons, for their helpful comments. I would like to extend particular thanks in this regard to Julia Emberley.

1. Sahlins has little to say about the degree to which these exchanges may have underwritten a patriarchal social order by being constituted at the expense of women or, alternatively, the degree to which the exchanges were a mechanism that challenged patriarchal power. Given that the text represents the Hawaiian social system as a generally less repressive alternative to the British/Western/Japanese regimes, and given such evocative comments later on in the text as "Maori say 'the genitals of women are killers of men'" (55), the question deserves a more systematic examination. For example, compare Christopher Hill's discussion of the implications of the puritan sexual revolution: "sexual freedom, in fact, tended to be freedom for men only" (319).

2. In recent years, Jameson's work has done the most to elaborate social analyses based on the concept mode of production, though his understanding of the gatherer/hunter mode remains somewhat contradictory and undertheorized. Compare *Postmodernism*, 337, with *Late Marxism*, 99–100, on this point.

3. See Jameson, "The Cultural Logic of Late Capitalism," in *Postmodernism* 1–54.

4. A similar perspective on the State and totalization has been developed more recently by Anthony Giddens in his *A Contemporary Critique of Historical Materialism*, where surveillance is seen as a critical dimension of totalizing power.

5. See John L. Tobias, "Protection, Civilization, Assimilation."

6. For an excellent discussion of this issue see Kathleen Jamieson, "Sex Discrimination in the Indian Act."

7. See LaCapra, Madame Bovary *on Trial*, 7, 18.

8. I have discussed Jenness's view of the sundance and the potlatch at greater length in "Anthropology at the Service of the State: Diamond Jenness and Canadian Indian Policy," forthcoming in *The Journal of Canadian Studies*.

9. Writing must here be seen in a more narrow sense than Derrida has proposed in *Of Grammatology* where he argues that "to say that a people do not know how to write because one can translate the word which they use to designate the act of inscribing as 'drawing lines', is that not as if one should refuse them 'speech' by translating the equivalent word by "to cry," "to sing," "to sigh"?" (123). Rather, Clastres here proposes two modalities of inscription: to the extent that one is separate from the body of the writer it is an alienated form that might be seen as writing in the narrow sense; the other may be seen in this context as nonalienated marks, marks not inscribed on a foreign material but rather inscribed on the body and, though subject to interpretation, a nonalienated form of inscription.

10. Authorship of the paintings is uncertain. I was told that the paintings were by a former Catholic priest, though other members of the community were suspicious and saw that story as speculation.

11. See his discussion of the Lord of Miracles, 164–70, the Three Potencies, 183–87, and especially the chapter on Our Lady of Remedies, 188–208.

12. This is what various residents told me. Although Shamattawa is quite far north even by Canadian standards, it was too far south to receive Anik signals, which were oriented to the Yukon and Northwest Territories. By now the people of Shamattawa have probably been blessed with television.

13. There seems at least a peripheral relation between my anecdote and Sahlins's discussion of Maori rebel Hone Heke's war with British flagpoles, as narrated in *Islands of History* 60–72.

14. My "Postmodern and the Paleolithic" deals with this issue respecting technology and, particularly, Inuit uses of television.

Works Cited

Clastres, Pierre. *Society Against the State: Essays in Political Anthropology.* Trans. Robert Hurley. New York: Zone, 1987.

Derrida, Jacques. *Of Grammatology.* Trans. Gayatri Chakravorty Spivak. Baltimore: Johns Hopkins UP, 1976.

Diamond, Stanley. *In Search of the Primitive: A Critique of Civilization.* New Brunswick: Transaction, 1987.

Emberley, Julia V. "'A Gift for Languages': Native Women and the Textual Economy of the Colonial Archive." *Cultural Critique* 17 (1990–91): 21–50.

Freeman, Minnie Aodla. *Life Among the Qallunaat*. Edmonton, AB: Hurtig, 1978.

Giddens, Anthony. *A Contemporary Critique of Historical Materialism. Vol. 1: Power, Property and the State*. Berkeley: U of California P, 1981.

———. *Vol. 2: The Nation-State and Violence*. Berkeley: U of California P, 1987.

Greenblatt, Stephen. *Learning to Curse: Essays in Early Modern Culture*. New York: Routledge, 1990.

Guattari, Félix. *Molecular Revolutions*. Trans. Rosemary Sheed. Markham, ON: Penguin, 1984.

Hill, Christopher. *The World Turned Upside Down*. Markham, ON: Penguin, 1984.

Indian Acts and Amendments, 1868–1950. Ottawa: Indian and Northern Affairs Canada, 1981.

Jameson, Fredric. *Late Marxism: Adorno, or, The Persistence of the Dialectic*. New York: Verso, 1990.

———. *The Political Unconscious: Narrative as a Socially Symbolic Act*. Ithaca: Cornell UP, 1983.

———. *Postmodernism, or, The Cultural Logic of Late Capitalism*. Durham, NC: Duke UP, 1991.

Jamieson, Kathleen. "Sex Discrimination in the Indian Act." *Arduous Journey: Canadian Indians and Decolonization*. Ed. Rick Ponting. Toronto: McClelland, 1988. 112–36.

Jenness, Diamond. *The Indians of Canada*. Toronto: U of Toronto P, 1984.

Kulchyski, Peter. "The Postmodern and the Paleolithic: Notes on Technology and Native Community in the Far North." *Canadian Journal of Political and Social Theory* 13.3 (1989): 49–62.

LaCapra, Dominick. *Madame Bovary on Trial*. Ithaca: Cornell UP, 1982.

Marx, Karl. *Capital: A Critique of Political Economy, Vol. 1*. Trans. Ben Fowkes. New York: Vintage, 1977.

———. *Grundrisse: Foundations of the Critique of Political Economy*. Trans. Martin Nicholas. New York: Vintage, 1973.

Poulantzas, Nicos. *Political Power and Social Classes*. London: New Left, 1978.

———. *State, Power, Socialism*. London: New Left, 1980.

Sahlins, Marshall. *Islands of History*. Chicago: U of Chicago P, 1987.

Sartre, Jean-Paul. *The Critique of Dialectical Reason I: Theory of Practical Ensembles*. Trans. Alan Sheridan-Smith. London: New Left, 1978.

Taussig, Michael. *Shamanism, Colonialism, and the Wild Man: A Study in Terror and Healing*. Chicago: U of Chicago P, 1987.

Tobias, John L. "Protection, Civilization, Assimilation: An Outline History of Canada's Indian Policy." *As Long as the Sun Shines and the Water Flows: A Reader in Canadian Native Studies*. Ed. Ian A. L. Getty and Antoine Lussier. Vancouver: U of British Columbia P, 1983. 39–55.

York, Geoffrey. *The Dispossessed: Life and Death in Native Canada*. London: Vintage, 1990.

The Author in Court: *Pope v. Curll* (1741)

Mark Rose

On 4 June 1741 Alexander Pope, represented by his friend William Murray, later Lord Mansfield, filed a complaint in Chancery against his ancient enemy the bookseller Edmund Curll. At issue was a volume of letters Curll had published five days earlier entitled *Dean Swift's Literary Correspondence* that contained letters to and from Pope and Jonathan Swift as well as further letters from Dr. John Arbuthnot, Lord Bolingbroke, John Gay, and others. Pope filed his complaint under the terms of the Statute of Anne (8 Ann. c. 19), the world's first copyright statute, and he claimed the rights, curiously enough by modern thinking, both in his own letters and in those sent to him by Swift, seeking an injunction to prevent Curll from selling any further copies of the book. The injunction was issued and, after a response from Curll moving to dissolve, it was continued by Lord Chancellor Hardwicke but only for those letters written by Pope, not for those sent to him by Swift.[1]

Pope v. Curll, in which the rule was established that copyright in a letter belongs to the writer, remains a foundational case in English and American copyright law. *Pope* is also one of the first cases in which a major English author went to court in his own name to defend his literary interests. What *Pope* records, I shall suggest, is an important transitional moment in the concept of authorship and of authors' rights, and a transitional moment, too, in the conception of literary property.

It is a striking fact that in England the legal empowerment of the author as a proprietor preceded the social formation of professional authorship, a development that as Alvin Kernan has argued is to be associated with Samuel Johnson. In the first part of the eighteenth century the values of the patronage culture of early modern England were still prevalent among respectable authors. Pope may have had commercial reasons for pursuing his action against Edmund Curll under the provisions of the new copyright statute, but he presented the issue less as a matter of commerce than of privacy. The unauthorized publication of a gentleman's private letters was, he felt, a violation of basic social principles. *Pope* suggests how from the very beginning of the story of authors' rights in England, issues of "propriety" in the moral sense became inextricably entwined with issues of "property" in the sense of economic interest.

Pope also records an important moment in the production of the concept of intellectual property. Who owns a letter, the writer or the receiver? In the court's response to this question, the notion of the essentially immaterial nature of the object of copyright was born. This was at the time a novel doctrine. But the potential for its production was latent from the beginning in the provision of the Statute of Anne that made authors as well as booksellers into possible owners of literary property, for booksellers are concerned with material objects—books—whereas authors are concerned with compositions, with texts. If the author was to be a proprietor and an agent in the literary marketplace, if the author was to appear in court in his own person to protect his own interests, then inevitably the conception of the property owned would be affected.

Before turning to the case proper and considering its significance by looking at it both in the context of Pope's life and career and in the context of the development of legal doctrine, some discussion of the Statute of Anne and of the rights of authors in the period prior to its passage is necessary. After this I wish to consider the complex nature of Pope's motives in initiating this lawsuit. Finally I shall discuss the case itself and the significance of the Lord Chancellor's decision.

I

Entitled "An Act for the Encouragement of Learning, by Vesting the Copies of Printed Books in the Authors or Purchasers of such Copies, during the Times therein mentioned," the Statute of Anne, which came into effect on 10 April 1710, was not quite the landmark recognition of authors' rights it has often been claimed to be. As Lyman Ray Patterson has emphasized, the statute was essentially a booksellers' bill, a legislative continuation of the ancient trade regulation practices of the Stationers' Company, the London guild of printers and booksellers that had long controlled the book trade in Britain (143–50). But unlike the traditional guild practice in which ownership of a "copy" continued in principle forever, the statute limited the term of copyright to fourteen years with a possible extension for a second fourteen-year term if the author was still living at the expiration of the first. And in a second departure from traditional guild practices, the statute established authors as the original holders of the rights in their works, thereby explicitly recognizing the author for the first time as a fully empowered agent in the literary marketplace.

Prior to the passage of the statute authors could not be said to "own" their works. Indeed, the very notion of owning a text as property does not quite fit the conception of literature in the early modern period in which it was usual to think of a text as an action rather than as a thing. Texts might serve to ennoble or immortalize worthy patrons, and in the process perhaps to win office or other favors for their authors; they might move audiences to laughter or tears; they might expose corruptions or confirm the just rule of the monarch or assist in the embracing of true religion, in which case their authors were worthy of reward. Alternatively, they might move men to sedition or heresy, in which case their authors were worthy of punishment. Thinking of texts in this way, valuing them for what they could do, was commensurate with the traditional society of the sixteenth and seventeenth centuries dominated by patronage structures, just as, later, treating texts as aesthetic objects was commensurate with the advanced marketplace society, founded on the notion of private property, as it developed in the eighteenth century.[2]

A sixteenth- or seventeenth-century author did, of course, own his manuscript, and this might be sold to a bookseller or to a theatrical company, but once the material object left his possession his rights in it were at best tenuous. Still, to say that authors owned nothing more than the ink and paper of their manuscripts is not to say that they had no literary rights at all. In the early modern period there seems to have developed in connection with the individualization of authorship—the transformation of the medieval "*auctor*" into the Renaissance "author"—a general sense that it was improper to publish an author's text without permission. In sixteenth-century Venice, for example, the Council of Ten decreed that printers must not publish works without the author's written consent (H. Brown 79–80), and in sixteenth-century France there were several law cases in which the author's right to control publication was successfully asserted (C. Brown 1: 117n37; Dock 78–79). In England, according to an edict proclaimed by the Long Parliament in the context of the flood of anonymous controversial publication that followed the abolition of Star Chamber, the Stationers' Company was required to see that all books identify the author on the title page and that no book be published without the author's consent. If any printer failed to secure the author's consent he would be treated as if he were the author himself (*Commons Journal* 2: 402).

Issued in a moment of anxiety at the prospect of an uncontrolled press, the Long Parliament's decree was essentially an instrument for establishing criminal responsibility for books deemed libelous, seditious, or blasphemous. And yet the House of Commons was aware that an unscrupulous printer might publish a book against the author's wishes, and therefore to protect authors from such printers the clause concerning authorial consent was included. Parliament's concern was not with authors' economic rights but with their potential vulnerability to prosecution merely for having held offending ideas, which was not in itself a crime.

The nature of the English decree suggests that in discussing the development of authors' rights it is important to distinguish between issues of "property" and issues of "propriety." The acknowledgment of the author's personal right to control the publication of his texts, a principle based on concepts of honor and reputation that are commensurate with the traditional patronage society, was not necessarily the same as the acknowledgment of a property right in the sense of an economic interest in an alienable commodity. In practice, of course, the right to control first publication had economic implications and therefore it could easily be treated as a property right. Indeed, in practice English booksellers of the sixteenth and seventeenth centuries seem to have recognized an obligation to pay authors for their "copies" (Patterson 64–77).

The parliamentary decree of 1641/2 is so far as I know the only state affirmation of any kind of authorial right in England earlier than the Statute of Anne, and it is essentially a criminal edict. It is probably not an inaccurate generalization, then, to say that before the statute an English author effectively had no place in court except as a criminal defendant charged with libel, blasphemy, or sedition. Despite assertions in the eighteenth century about authors' ancient common law property rights, no such right was ever established or even so far as I know asserted by an author (Abrams; Rose). Indeed, what legal standing—other than the edict of 1641/2, which was only briefly in force—an English author might have had to take action against a bookseller is unclear. To my knowledge no author ever did.

In 1704 Daniel Defoe called for a change, complaining in his *Essay on the Regulation of the Press* (1704) that there was "no Law so much wanting in the Nation, relating to Trade and Civil Property" as one that would provide for authors. If an author could be punished for a libelous or seditious book, Defoe said, then it was only just that he also be permitted to reap the benefit of an excellent book: "For if an Author has not the right of a Book, after he has made it, and the benefit be not his own, and the Law will not protect him in that Benefit, 'twould be very hard the Law should pretend to punish him for it" (27–28). In the course of the seventeenth century England had become essentially a marketplace society and the values of possessive individualism had been defined and promulgated. Defoe's call for the establishment of authorial property bears witness to the potential for the extension of the ideology of possessive individualism to authorship, but we should note that his claim is not based on the modern principle that the author is entitled to exploit the product of his labor so much as on the notion of the complementarity of punishment and reward. Defoe was still thinking within the framework of the traditional society in which authority, transmitted through punishment and reward, was conceived as descending from above.

II

The provision in Statute of Anne establishing the author as the first proprietor of his works opened the way for the author to appear in court in the novel role of plaintiff in a civil action, but in fact nearly all the early litigation that arose under the statute involved booksellers seeking determinations against other booksellers rather than authors defending their rights against booksellers. The explanation is simple: authors in this period were still in large part sustained by the ideology of the traditional patronage society in which gentlemanly honor was the crucial value and reward rather than profit was what one expected for worthy works. The early eighteenth-century conception of respectable authorship as a learned and polite activity that existed, at least in principle, apart from the marketplace did not encourage authors to rush into litigation in defense of their literary properties.[3]

Alexander Pope was an exceptional figure, for more than any other writer of his day he behaved like a literary entrepreneur and he made a fortune from his verse. Pope's prominence gave him enormous bargaining power, which he used to secure unusually favorable terms from his booksellers. Despite his involvement in the literary marketplace, Pope characteristically presented himself as a gentleman and a scholar rather than as a professional, and he was almost obsessively concerned with what we would today call image management. It was as part of his concern with image management that Pope in the latter part of his career resolved to make his correspondence public in order, as Maynard Mack puts it, among other things, to "erect a monument to himself and the gifted writers he had known" (660). But for a gentleman to publish his own letters would have seemed inexcusably vain, and Pope had to arrange matters so that publication would seem to occur against his wishes. In 1735, therefore, Pope tricked Curll into publishing his correspondence, thereby creating a situation that would allow him to protest against the indignity of being exposed in print and would at the same time open the way for an authorized version.

So much is familiar knowledge. As reconstructed by James McLaverty, however, the evidence suggests that Pope had a further purpose in the 1735 affair with Curll, one that illuminates his goal six years later in filing suit against Curll over the correspondence with Swift. In the spring of 1735 the London booksellers were campaigning for a bill that would extend the statutory term of copyright. Pope does not appear to have been particularly concerned with the term of copyright, but he was concerned that no such bill for the benefit of booksellers should be passed without also including a clause to protect authors, and therefore he contrived to have the surreptitious edition of his letters appear while the bill was pending. Thus Curll would serve as an example of an irresponsible bookseller in order to dramatize the bill's limitations and defeat it. The 1735 bill was indeed defeated, although not necessarily because of the affair of the letters as Pope claimed. Shortly after, Pope expressed the hope that if the booksellers' bill was again brought in, Parliament would not increase the term of copyright without also doing something for authors "Since in a Case so *notorious* as the printing a Gentleman's PRIVATE LETTERS, most Eminent, both *Printers* and *Booksellers*, conspired to assist the Pyracy both in printing and in vending the same" (*Narrative* 345).

The incident of 1735 bears witness to Pope's genuine concern that there be a legal remedy for unauthorized publication of letters, but we should observe that the issue as he presents it is a matter of personal right rather than of economic interest. Pope's point is that the unauthorized printing of a gentleman's "PRIVATE LETTERS"—the outraged capitals are expressive—is an offense against decency. And he makes exactly the same point again in 1737 in the preface to the authorized edition of his correspondence. The unauthorized printing of private letters is, he says, a form of *"betraying Conversation"* and is damaging to the social fabric:

> To open Letters is esteem'd the greatest breach of honour; even to look into them already open'd or accidentally dropt, is held ungenerous, if not an immoral act. What then can be thought of the procuring them merely by Fraud, and printing them merely for Lucre? We cannot but conclude every honest man will wish, that if the Laws have as yet provided no adequate remedy, one at least may be found, to prevent so great and growing an evil. (*Correspondence* 1: xl)

What I would suggest is that in the suit against Curll in 1741 Pope was seeking to achieve in the courts the same goal that he had failed to achieve in Parliament—that is, to secure protection for himself and for others against the unauthorized procuring and printing of private letters.

The correspondence with Swift was a set of letters that Pope particularly wished to see published, and for many years he had sought to get Swift to return his letters to him. When at last he succeeded, Pope arranged through an elaborate ruse to have the letters printed in Dublin. This made it possible for him to publish an authorized edition as part of his collected works (Mack 665–71). Six weeks after Pope's edition appeared, Curll brought out his volume, which he claimed was a reprint of the Dublin edition, and Pope, who had been anticipating Curll's action (Letter to R. Allen, *Correspondence* 4: 343), immediately brought suit. No doubt commercial considerations figured in Pope's suit, for Curll's cheap piracy represented a threat to the expensive authorized edition (Letter to R. Allen, *Correspondence* 4: 350). No doubt, too, Pope may have derived vindictive pleasure from making Edmund Curll once again his target. But, whatever his other motives, the history of his passionate concern over the previous six years with the impropriety of unauthorized printing of letters suggests that in suing Curll in 1741 Pope was trying to answer his own call to find an "adequate remedy" for "so great and growing an evil" by establishing that letters fell under the statute. In *Pope*, then, a commercial regulatory statute was being employed to pursue matters that had as much to do with "propriety"—with authors' personal rights—as with authors' economic interests. In the context of the developing marketplace culture questions of authorial honor and reputation were becoming entwined with questions of commercial law.

Let us return for a moment to Pope's preface to the 1737 edition of his letters. This preface is dominated by the genteel discourse in which Pope represents his outrage as a man of honor against unauthorized publication. But what we can call the "discourse of property" makes itself felt as well, as for example when Pope complains that the booksellers' practice of soliciting copies of authors' letters leads to petty thievery: "Any domestick or servant, who can snatch a letter from your pocket or cabinet, is encouraged to that vile practise" (*Correspondence* 1: xxxix). Moreover, if the quantity of material procured falls short, the bookseller will fill out the volume with anything he pleases, so that the poor author has "not only Theft to fear, but Forgery" (xl). And the greater the writer's reputation, the greater will be the demand for the books and so the greater the injury to the author: "your Fame and your Property suffer alike; you are at once expos'd and plunder'd" (xl). The blending of the discourse of propriety (marked by such terms as "honor," "generosity," and "fame") with that of property (marked by such terms as "theft," "snatch," and "plunder") produces a certain instability in the preface that is evidence of the way it inscribes a transitional moment in cultural history. My point is that Pope's suit against Curll is equally a mingled affair, an action that takes place between two worlds, the traditional world of the author as a gentleman and scholar and the emergent world of the author as a professional.

On 16 February 1742/3, a year and a half after the decision in *Pope v. Curll*, Pope was again in court filing complaints against booksellers, this time employing the statute in two actions that clearly pertained to his right to exploit his works for profit. Neither of these cases is reported, and neither seems to be as fascinating as *Pope v. Curll*, but they do remind us that although Pope always presented himself as a gentleman, he was also in practice an aggressive professional and the first major author to use the Statute of Anne repeatedly to pursue his professional interests in court.[4]

III

Let us turn now to the issues litigated in *Pope v. Curll* and to their resolution. Pope's Bill of Complaint begins by invoking the Statute of Anne and its provision for authors. He states that between 1714 and 1738 he wrote various letters to Swift and he specifies by date twenty-nine, asserting himself to be the sole author and maintaining that, having never disposed of the copyright, he possesses the sole right of printing or selling them. He states that during the same period he also received various letters from Swift, and again specifies twenty-nine by date, saying that he hoped that neither those letters in which the property was vested in himself by virtue of being their author nor those other letters which were addressed and sent to him would ever have been published without his consent. He charges Curll with knowingly conspiring with certain unnamed confederates to defraud him of his rights by publishing these letters and complains that he is without remedy by common law. He waives the penalties allowed by the statute but asks for a disclosure of all agreements made with respect to the book and an accounting of the profits, which are to be paid to himself. Any unsold copies are to be delivered to the court and disposed of as the court shall direct. Meanwhile Curll and his associates are to be restrained by an injunction from any further sales.

Pope's Bill of Complaint was entered on 4 June 1741, and shortly thereafter the requested injunction was issued. Curll swore his Answer on 13 June, moving that the injunction be dissolved. In this document Curll acknowledges the statute and admits printing five hundred copies of the book and selling sixteen, but he makes three principal points in his defense. First, he argues, that since

> all the letters mentioned in the Complainants said Bill of Complaint were as this Defendant verily believes Actually sent & delivered by and to the several Persons by whom & to whom they severally Purport to have been written & Addressed . . . the Complainant is not to be Considered as the Author & proprietor of all or any of the said letters.[5]

Second, he raises the question of whether, in any case, familiar letters fall under the terms of the statute, saying that he is advised "that the said letters are not a work of that Nature & sole Right of printing whereof was Intended to be preserved by the said Statute to the Author." Third, he says that he has reprinted the letters in question from the Dublin edition printed by George Faulkner under the direction, as he believes, of Dr. Swift, and it is his understanding that any book first published in Ireland may be lawfully reprinted in England.[6] In addition, responding to particular assertions in Pope's complaint, Curll makes various other statements including denying that he has any direct knowledge of whether Pope is the sole author and proprietor of the letters purported to be signed by him or that he has any direct knowledge of whether Pope has ever disposed of whatever rights in the letters he might have. He denies that he has made any agreements with anyone about the book except with his printer, and he points out that the part of the published book to which Pope is laying claim comes to only one-fifth of the whole. Curll therefore asserts that he has done nothing illegal in publishing the book and he maintains that Pope is not entitled to an account of his profits.

Lord Chancellor Hardwicke's decision, handed down on 17 June 1741, takes up each of the principal points that Curll makes in his defense. The first question, he says, is whether letters, not being intended for publication, come within the grounds and intention of the statute, the purpose of which was defined, we recall, as the encouragement of learning. Hardwicke cites as a parallel the instance of sermons, "which the author may never intend should be published, but are collected from loose papers, and brought out after his death," and he rules in the affirmative, saying that "it would be extremely mischievous, to make a distinction between a book of letters, which comes out into the world, either by the permission of the writer, or the receiver of them, and any other learned work" (Atkyns, *Pope*). In response to Curll's argument that an author is no longer to be considered the owner of a letter if it has actually been sent—or, as Hardwicke summarizes the point, "that where a man writes a letter, it is in the nature of a gift to the receiver" (Atkyns, *Pope*)—Hardwicke again overrules the objection, doing so by making a distinction between the physical letter and the copyright. "I am of opinion," he says, that it is only a special property in the receiver, possibly the property of the paper may belong to him; but this does not give a licence to any person whatsoever to publish them to the world, for at most the receiver has only a joint property with the writer. (Atkyns, *Pope*)

In response to the question of whether a book originally printed in Ireland, where the statute did not reach, was "lawful prize," Hardwicke points out that an answer in the positive would have pernicious consequences, for it would establish an easy way for booksellers to evade the statute by sending books over to Ireland to be printed first. Finally, returning to the initial matter of whether the contested material falls under the statute, Hardwicke notes that the defendant's counsel has insisted that the exchange of letters between Swift and Pope "does not come within the meaning of the act of Parliament, because it contains only letters on familiar subjects, and inquiries after the health of friends, and cannot properly be called a learned work." Again he decides in the affirmative:

> It is certain that no works have done more service to mankind, than those which have appeared in this shape, upon familiar subjects, and which perhaps were never intended to be published; and it is this makes them so valuable; for I must confess for my own part, that letters which are very elaborately written, and originally intended for the press, are generally the most insignificant, and very little worth any person's reading. (Atkyns, *Pope*)

On the basis of his judgment that familiar letters do indeed fall under the statute, together with the distinction he has made between the receiver's tangible property in the physical letter and the writer's intangible property in his copyright, Hardwicke rules that the injunction be continued, but "only as to those letters, which are under Mr. *Pope*'s name in the book, and which are written *by him*, and not as to those which are written *to him*" (Atkyns, *Pope*).

Hardwicke's decision on the question of Irish publication is comparatively straightforward and requires little comment. More interesting is his decision on the question of whether the Swift–

Pope letters fell under the terms of the statute. What we should observe here is that the issue in the case had led to a circumstance in which a legal question—were letters on familiar subjects protected?—involved a judge in making a literary critical proclamation from the bench. If there were to be a statute protecting certain kinds of writings, those that contributed to the advancement of learning, then judges would perforce find themselves, like Hardwicke, making pronouncements on generic matters and on literary value. Hardwicke's judgment is rendered in the somewhat pompous language of refined taste, but the issue is nevertheless also one of commercial value. Under the aegis of the statute, literary and legal questions were converging in such a way that significant sums of money might depend upon whether a particular kind of text was deemed "worth protecting" and admitted to the privileged category. Two senses of value—the literary and the commercial—were becoming entangled.

But perhaps the most interesting aspect of Hardwicke's ruling was the distinction that he made between the receiver's special property in the physical letter and the writer's property in the copyright. The Statute of Anne, let us note, prescribed specific and concrete penalties for the invasion of literary property, providing that all offending books were to be forfeited to the rightful proprietors of the copy to be destroyed, and furthermore that every offender was to forfeit one penny for every offending sheet found in his custody. Precisely what kind of property, material or immaterial, Parliament supposed it was protecting in the statute is unclear, for in all likelihood such metaphysical questions about the nature of literary property never occurred to the legislators. As Benjamin Kaplan has remarked, the draftsman of the statute was "thinking as a printer would—of a book as a physical entity; of rights in it and offenses against it as related to 'printing and reprinting' the thing itself" (9). So, too, the defendant's counsel was thinking of a letter as a physical entity, an object which once "Actually sent & delivered" (Curll, Answer) passed wholly to the recipient. But Lord Chancellor Hardwicke's judgment involved an important and novel abstraction of the notion of literary property from its material basis in ink and paper.

It is perhaps significant that it was in the years immediately preceding Hardwicke's decision that the new term "copyright" first came into general use. Indeed, appropriately enough, one of the earliest recorded uses of "copyright" occurs in a letter that Pope wrote to John Gay in 1732 in which Pope speaks of the bookseller Benjamin Motte together with some other "idle fellow" having written to Swift "to get him to give them some Copyright" (Letter from Gay to Swift, 28 August 1732, quoting Letter from Pope to Gay, in Swift, *Correspondence* 4: 64–65). The old stationers' term "copy" was related to the use of copy as the term for an original manuscript from which copies were made, and it thus retained some feeling for "copy" as a material object, the manuscript on which the printed edition was based. The new term "copyright" suggests an attenuation of the sense of the material basis of the property. Its appearance at this moment is worth noting as part of the context in which Hardwicke's decision was rendered, for in that decision the author's words have in effect flown free from the page on which they are written. Not ink and paper but pure signs, separated from any material support, have become the protected property.

When they entered titles in the Stationers' Register, the English booksellers of the sixteenth and seventeenth centuries spoke of "their copies" and "their books," but they could not really be said to own texts in the absolute sense of property articulated for the marketplace society by John Locke. Rather what the stationers of the old order were doing was participating, as guildsmen of various kinds had done for hundreds of years, in a community defined in terms of reciprocal rights and responsibilities. When disputes between stationers arose they were settled by the guild court, which generally tried to arrange compromises rather than lay down principles. Now, however, with a statute on the books, the need for interpretation and for the articulation of principles would inevitably arise. Furthermore, with the shift in jurisdiction from the guild to the public courts, literary property would tend to be treated like any other form of private property, which was, after all, what the courts were most familiar with. But in order to do this a new and abstract concept of what precisely it was that an author owned would have to be constructed. In Hardwicke's decision we can see this process at work. We should observe, however, that Hardwicke's judgment on this matter is couched in cautious language: "possibly the property of the paper" may belong to the receiver, who "at most" has "only a joint property with the writer" (Atkyns, *Pope*). The tentativeness with which Hardwicke proposes the distinction between the receiver's tangible and the author's intangible property is to be attributed, no doubt, to the fact that the notion of copyright as a wholly intangible property was still at this point novel and the theory of a property that inheres in words alone had not yet been worked out.

Could a text—as distinguished from a book—be a property? Did authors really have a "property" in their works, in which case they would be entitled to general relief at common law, or did the statute merely grant them an exclusive privilege, a limited monopoly with penalties to give it force? In 1743, two years after the decision in *Pope v. Curll* and a year before Pope's death, a group of seventeen London booksellers, invoking the Statute of Anne, initiated a suit in the Scottish Court of Session against a group of twenty-four booksellers of Edinburgh and Glasgow in which precisely these questions figured.[7] It was in the context of this long-drawn-out case that in 1747 William Warburton, Pope's friend and literary executor, published his *A Letter from an Author to a Member of Parliament Concerning Literary Property* in which he provided the earliest theorization of copyright as a wholly intangible property.

At the heart of Warburton's *Letter* is an analysis of the nature of property that is designed to demonstrate that texts can indeed be property. Property, he says, can be divided into two classes, movables and immovables. Movable properties can in turn be divided into those that are natural and those that have been artificially made. And artificially produced movables can be still further divided into products of the hand and products of the mind, for example, "an *Utensil* made; a *Book* composed."

> For that the Product of the *Mind* is as well capable of becoming Property, as that of the *Hand*, is evident from hence, that it hath in it those two essential Conditions, which, by the allowance of all Writers of Laws, make Things susceptible of Property; namely common *Utility*, and a Capacity of having its Possession *ascertained*. (7)

We should note that Warburton never actually demonstrates that literary property has "a Capacity of having its Possession *ascer-*

tained," but this point might be lost in the smooth development of his analysis, which, proceeding by progressive division into familiar binary oppositions (movable/immovable, artificial/natural, body/mind), makes the notion of intellectual property seem natural and inevitable.

What was the nature of the author's property? According to Warburton, property that was the product of the hand was "confined to the individual Thing made." Like the instrument of its creation, the property was wholly material.

> But, in the other Case of Property in the Product of the Mind, as in a *Book* composed, it is not confined to the Original MS. but extends to the *Doctrine* contained in it: Which is, indeed, the true and peculiar Property in a Book. (7–8)

The essence of the author's property was thus wholly immaterial, consisting solely of the "doctrine" or ideas that were the product of his mental labor. Six years earlier Lord Chancellor Hardwicke had tentatively distinguished between the receiver's property right in the material basis of a letter and the author's property right in the words. Now, in Warburton's *Letter*, the notion of a property in pure signs abstracted from any material support was being systematically developed and promulgated.

The clincher in Warburton's argument was his treatment of the relation between literary property and patents. Warburton was arguing that since copyrights were property rights and not merely privileges, literary properties, unlike patents, were perpetual. But why should an author's rights be treated any differently from the rights that an inventor might have in a new and useful machine? Warburton's approach was to demonstrate that inventions were of a mixed nature, partaking of the characteristics of both manual and mental products. Thus insofar as a machine was a kind of utensil it was appropriate that the maker's property be located in the individual material object and be perpetual. Nevertheless, because the operation of the mind was so intimately concerned in inventions, it was appropriate to extend to inventors a patent, a grant that reached beyond the individual material object, but only for a term of years. Thus patent protection, which by long-established principle was limited to a specific term of years, was a special category of limited rights designed to accommodate the mixed nature of mechanical inventions as opposed to the purely intellectual nature of literary compositions. Rhetorically, then, the introduction of this third, mixed, category of property situated between products of the hand and products of the mind helped to confirm the idea of literary property as wholly immaterial.

The year after Warburton's *Letter* appeared, the Court of Sessions issued a decision that in effect denied that a text could be a property (see note 7). But the legal debate over the nature of literary property was only beginning and Warburton's theorization of copyright was to influence William Blackstone, who, arguing for the plaintiff in *Tonson v. Collins* (1760), a suit between two booksellers over the right to print the *Spectator*, developed the notion of copyright still further. "I must maintain," Blackstone said,

> that "a literary composition, as it lies in the author's mind, before it is substantiated by reducing it into writing," has the essential requisites to make it the subject of property. While it thus lies dormant in the mind, it is absolutely in the power of the proprietor. He alone is entitled to the profits of communicating, or making it public. The first step to which is clothing our conceptions in words, the only means to communicate abstracted ideas. (Blackstone, *Tonson* 180–81)

Words might be either spoken or written, Blackstone continued, but in any case the words were merely the vehicles of the author's sentiments. "The sentiment therefore is the thing of value, from which the profit must arise" (181).

Joseph Yates, arguing for the defendant in *Tonson*, accepted the principle "that the author has a property in his sentiments till he publishes them" (185), but he insisted that from the moment of publication the author's ideas ceased to be private property, and he cited the limited protection afforded inventors under patent law as a parallel. Blackstone in reply invoked Warburton's *Letter* on the difference between mechanical inventions and literary compositions, and reaffirmed the immaterial nature of literary property:

> Style and sentiment are the essentials of a literary composi-
> tion. These alone constitute its identity. The paper and print
> are merely accidents, which serve as vehicles to convey that
> style and sentiment to a distance. (189)

And six years later, in the second volume of his *Commentaries*,
Blackstone refined the formulation he had made in *Tonson*, discussing copyright as a species of property and insisting that, whatever might be the material method of conveying a text from one
person to another, the identity of the composition itself "consists
intirely in the *sentiment* and the *language*; the same conceptions,
cloathed in the same words, must necessarily be the same composition" (2: 406).

We should note that in the process of developing Warburton's theory of copyright—and under pressure from Yates's rejection of the notion that ideas might remain property once published—Blackstone significantly shifted the conception of literary
property from Warburton's "doctrine" or his own equivalent "sentiments" to the conception of the essence of the property as a
fusion of idea and language: "the same conceptions, cloathed in
the same words." Not ideas alone but the expression of ideas: this,
to put Blackstone's point in the familiar modern form which it
anticipates, was what copyright protected. What was the nature of
literary property as Blackstone formulated it? Paper and print—
the material basis of publication—were to be regarded merely as
"accidents." The bearer of meaning through which the writer's
ideas were realized was language. Clothed in words, which Blackstone treated as if they were a kind of substance, the writer's
sentiments became property. In the early modern period, it was,
as I have noted, usual to think of a text as an action, as something
done. Now, in the context of the developing marketplace society,
the text was being represented as a kind of thing.

Warburton and Blackstone were arguing the case for copyright to be regarded as a common law property right and thus for
copyright to be perpetual. The debate over this issue continued
until 1774, when perpetual copyright was rejected by the House
of Lords. But, even if the claim for perpetual copyright was finally
rejected, nevertheless their representation of literary property as
essentially immaterial—a representation that may be understood

as an exposition of Lord Chancellor Hardwicke's opinion on the question of the ownership of letters—endured and of course endures to this day.

Pope v. Curll, then, represents a significant transitional episode both in the history of authorship and in the conception of literary property. Pope himself is of course fascinating as a transitional figure: on the one hand, the last of the great poets in the Renaissance tradition and as such the courtly transmitter of received wisdom and the jealous guardian of his own and others' honor; on the other, the first of the moderns and as such a professional who was immersed in the production and exploitation of literary commodities and the jealous guardian of his financial interests. And the case, with its complex blending and enfolding of motives and its fascinating dissolving of matters of propriety into matters of property, refracts both the peculiar nature of its eminent plaintiff and the earliness of its moment in the history of the author as a legally enfranchised figure.

Hardwicke's decision in *Pope v. Curll* has gone down in legal history as establishing that letters are subject to copyright and that an author has the right to withhold his texts from publication if he chooses. But perhaps even more fundamental than the ruling about letters coming under the statute was the distinction that Hardwicke drew between the receiver's property in the paper and the writer's property in the words, for in this moment the concept of literary property as a wholly immaterial property in a text might be said to have been born.

Notes

Portions of this essay were delivered at public sessions at the Interdisciplinary Humanities Center at the University of California, Santa Barbara, the Stanford Humanities Center, and the University of California Humanities Research Institute at Irvine. I am grateful for the responses offered on those occasions. For comments and assistance of various kinds I am particularly indebted to Robert Burt, Robert Folkenflik, Paul Geller, Peter Haidu, Richard Helgerson, Robert Post, Ruth Warkentin, and Everett Zimmerman.

1. *Pope v. Curll* is reported by J. T. Atkyns. Pope's Complaint and Curll's Answer are in the Public Record Office in London. The case has been discussed by Ransom, who reports on *Pope* and the later case involving the posthumous

publication of Lord Chesterfield's letters, *Tompson v. Stanhope*, and then explores in a series of hypothetical cases the complications that arise from the establishment of letters as copyrightable; and by Rogers, who reports on the materials in the Public Record Office. Foxon provides an appendix on "Pope and Copyright," which draws together much useful information on Pope's contracts, lawsuits, and plans for litigation.

2. On occasion an early modern author might be granted a state printing privilege in his own work, an exclusive right to print for a limited period of term. But these privileges should be thought of as versions of patronage rather than as private property—that is, as rewards for notable services rendered.

3. The only case preceding *Pope* that I am aware of in which a specifically literary figure sued in his own name is *Gay v. Read* (1729) in which John Gay obtained an injunction to protect his rights in *Polly*, the sequel to *The Beggar's Opera*. For information about the case see Sutherland.

4. Both suits were related to the publication of the four-book version of the *Dunciad* in 1742. In one suit, Pope sued Henry Lintot in order to establish that after the initial fourteen-year period the rights in the original version of the *Dunciad* reverted to himself as author. In the other Pope sued Jacob Ilive, claiming that he had pirated the enlarged *Dunciad*. See the accounts in Vincent and in Feather.

5. The phrase "Author & proprietor" is, I take it, to be understood in the conjunctive: Curll is certainly not denying that Pope actually wrote the letters that he sent to Swift but only that he can claim a property in them.

6. In fact Curll used Pope's own edition as copytext. Rogers observes that Pope probably did not realize this because it might have been an effective point to make in court (329).

7. The fullest report of this complex case, known variously as *Booksellers of London v. Booksellers of Edinburgh and Glasgow* or *Midwinter v. Hamilton* or *Midwinter v. Kinkaid* or *Millar v. Kinkaid*, is in Kames 154–61.

Works Cited

Abrams, Howard B. "The Historic Foundation of American Copyright Law: Exploding the Myth of Common Law Copyright." *Wayne Law Review* 29 (1983): 1119–91.

Atkyns, J. T. *Pope v. Curll. English Reports*. 176 vols. Edinburgh: W. Green, 1900–30. 26: 608.

Blackstone, William. *Commentaries on the Laws of England*. 4 vols. Oxford, 1765–69.

———. *Tonson v. Collins. English Reports*. 176 vols. Edinburgh: W. Green, 1900–30. 96: 169–92.

Brown, Cynthia J. "Du manuscrit a l'imprime en France: le cas des Grands Rhetoriqueurs." *Actes du Ve Colloque International sur le Moyen Age Français*. 3 vols. Milan: Universita Cattolica del Sacro Cuore, 1985. 1: 103–23.

Brown, Horatio F. *The Venetian Printing Press, 1469–1800*. London, 1891. Amsterdam: Gerard Th. van Heusden, 1969.

Curll, Edmund. Answer to Pope's Complaint. C11/1569/29. Public Record Office, London.

Defoe, Daniel. *An Essay on the Regulation of the Press*. London, 1704. Oxford: Blackwell, 1948.

Dock, Marie-Claude. *Etude sur le droit d'auteur*. Paris: Pichon et Durand-Auzias, 1963.

Feather, John. "The Publishers and the Pirates: British Copyright Law in Theory and Practice, 1710–1775." *Publishing History* 22 (1987): 1–32.

Foxon, David. *Pope and the Early Eighteenth-Century Book Trade*, rev. and ed. James McLaverty. Oxford: Clarendon, 1991.

Great Britain. Parliament. *The Statutes at Large*. 18 vols. London, 1763–1800.

———. ———. *Journals of the House of Commons*. London, 1803.

Kames, Henry Home, Lord. *Remarkable Decisions of the Court of Session*. Edinburgh: A. Kincaid and J. Bell, 1766.

Kaplan, Benjamin. *An Unhurried View of Copyright*. New York: Columbia UP, 1967.

Kernan, Alvin. *Printing Technology, Letters and Samuel Johnson*. Princeton: Princeton UP, 1987.

Mack, Maynard. *Alexander Pope: A Life*. New York and New Haven: Yale UP, 1985.

McLaverty, James. "The First Printing and Publication of Pope's Letters." *The Library* 6th ser. 2 (1980): 264–80.

Patterson, Lyman Ray. *Copyright in Historical Perspective*. Nashville: Vanderbilt UP, 1968.

Pope, Alexander. *The Correspondence of Alexander Pope*. Ed. George Sherburn. 5 vols. Oxford: Clarendon, 1956.

———. *A Narrative of the Method by which Mr. Pope's Private Letters were procured and published by Edmund Curll, Bookseller*. 1735. *The Prose Works of Alexander Pope*. Ed. Rosemary Cowler. Vol. 2. Hamden, CT: Archon–Shoe String, 1986. 317–56.

———. Bill of Complaint against Edmund Curll. C11/1569/29. Public Record Office, London.

Ransom, Harry. "The Personal Letter as Literary Property." *Studies in English* 30 (1951): 116–31.

Rogers, Pat. "The Case of *Pope v. Curll*." *The Library* 5th ser. 27 (1972): 326–31.

Rose, Mark. "The Author as Proprietor: *Donaldson v. Becket* and the Genealogy of Modern Authorship." *Representations* 23 (1988): 51–85.

Sutherland, James R. "'Polly' Among the Pirates." *Modern Language Review* 37 (1942): 291–303.

Swift, Jonathan. *The Correspondence of Jonathan Swift*. Ed. Harold Williams. 5 vols. Oxford: Clarendon, 1963–65.

Vincent, Howard P. "Some *Dunciad* Litigation." *Philological Quarterly* 18 (1939): 285–89.

Warburton, William. *A Letter from an Author to a Member of Parliament Concerning Literary Property*. London, 1747.

Turns of Emancipation:
On Rahel Varnhagen's Letters

Liliane Weissberg

I

Emancipation, the "deliverance from bondage or controlling influence,"[1] is a term that has its origin in the Roman family and describes not just the liberation of slaves but also the freeing of children from paternal power. It developed into a political term associated with contracts and laws and with the declaration of civil rights, and its use is highly charged ideologically. The eleventh edition of the *Encyclopaedia Britannica*, for example, does not list the term; the American *Webster's* dictionary, on the other hand, refers to its own country's history by listing Lincoln's proclamation. The German *Brockhaus* deflects attention away from German history and cites instead the end of American slavery as well as the French Revolution, and points to a general history that seems to defy all national boundaries: to the emancipation of women and of Jews.[2]

Perhaps, however, it is precisely this deflection that marks German historical writings, even more so than the account of the legal constructs by which "women" or "Jews" were established as emancipated objects within the national tradition. Moreover, the

---

question arises as to how "women" or "Jews" have viewed the definitions of emancipation that have formed a discourse from which they have been excluded, even when their desire to participate in that discourse has been presupposed.[3] The present essay tries to reflect on this desire by choosing a particular historical moment in which it is often said to have articulated itself. The place and time chosen is Berlin at the turn of the nineteenth century.

Obviously, one cannot assert the equality of women in late eighteenth- and early nineteenth-century Berlin, or discuss the emancipation of Jews during a time when different Prussian laws took and gave various rights without establishing an equal status for the Jewish population. The democratic influence of the French Revolution had its limits, even in French-occupied Berlin. If I were to write about a Jewish woman author in Berlin during this period, I would have to shift the discussion of emancipation from a statement of paternal will to the question of daughterly wishes, private acts, and reflections, but perhaps not of an unpolitical kind. How could one be equal? Rahel Varnhagen seems to ask, and to whom should one be equal? Under which conditions, moreover, is this equality at all desired?

In his study of Jewish female authors in Berlin in the late eighteenth century, Gert Mattenklott identifies a relationship between the conditions of their literary production and the possibility of their own aesthetics.[4] The double "marginality" of being a woman and a Jew, he writes, creates a secondhand way of living for them. For these Jewish women, there could not have been any life beyond their participation in another's—and there could not have been any "free" life at all. Art, it seems, however, is possible only after emancipation. The impossibility of leading a free life therefore makes the development of one's own aesthetics impossible:

> Surely art could not flourish here. Art presupposes freedom. A Jewish, a female aesthetics, this is a contradiction in itself, and the women of this circle were much too clever not to discover this. Art by Jewish women would presuppose a sovereignty over their sex and birth, nature and history, and this, as it were, had to be illusory. ("Aufbruch")

The writings of these Jewish women were structured by their general lack of sovereignty; and they had to choose, as Mattenklott insists, a medium that lacked sovereignty as well. Examining the relationship between gender and genre, he focuses on the essay and the letter: "These are forms that flourish when something can be disposed with, independent of any direction, or in which the hindrance, the inability, or the resistance to conform to the representational forms of the old culture would find its expression" ("Aufbruch"). Texts by Jewish women appear here not only as writing that replaces action, but also as the replacement of proper literature,[5] despite the fact that the letter and the essay are, paradoxically, precisely genres that mark, like no other, the official literary discourse in the eighteenth century.[6]

Mattenklott repeats the statements of many other literary critics and sketches further consequences of this thesis. The growth of these semipublic literary forms, made possible through resistance and the inability to choose other genres, itself indicates the deficiencies of the female and Jewish demimonde. There is only one response to these deficiencies. Because a "free life" is impossible for Jewish women, the letter and essay have to produce alternative lives and to reflect utopian autobiographies. But any critic who censures the essay and the letter as improper literary genres has to censure the sketch of an imaginary life as well.[7] The hopeful alternative is therefore doomed to appear deficient. Here, as before, life meets art.

Perhaps, however, the issue may not be whether these Jewish women discover their sovereignty *over* their gender, but whether they find the sovereignty *of* their gender; perhaps we are dealing here with the paradox of a sovereignty that has to establish itself in the very moment of writing—even if they are writing as women and as Jews. The object/subject distinction of author and text, which has to be established in any kind of judgment, must be called into question. The sovereignty that can be discovered in these women's writing, and the sovereign nature of their writing, have to be different from that other, masterful discourse of literature.

In her letters, and by writing several letters a day, Rahel Varnhagen tries to establish herself, to describe herself as an individual. Rahel, the hostess of a well-known Berlin salon, receives numerous guests, many of whom become her correspondents. The concept of friendship and *Geselligkeit* [sociability] as established by the culture of the salons, and the oral discourse, influence the style of her letters and often their content as well. Paradoxically, Rahel writes about her self by reporting about others and by aiming her letters to her addressees, who become partners in a dialogue.

Moreover, her production of tens of thousands of letters reveals a strange fact. While letters are denied inclusion in established literary history, Rahel's letters do not even conform to the official rules of the letter. She does not follow epistolary guides, style manuals, or dictionaries. One is not always sure which qualifications of the "letter" they fulfill. Which description and definition can capture the abundance of her writings? And what "life" can we deduce as a result of Rahel's text?

In order to read and to find a descriptive term to characterize her letters, the critic must find similarities in, and make comparisons to, other texts. For Rahel, similarities are as crucial as differences. There are, for example, the similarities that Rahel recognizes between herself and the men of her circle of acquaintances: Christians, German bourgeois or bourgeois aristocrats, the authors of philosophical lectures or *Bildungsroman*. To remark on similarities implies, however, that one thing is comparable to another, and that they are established by the act of comparison; therefore, such a gesture is a means for discerning and articulating difference. The reader today, who would like to trace this gesture of comparison in Rahel's statement about her writing and in Rahel's writing itself, compares literary products. Are we able to understand these letters as a special, different literature; do we have indications of the possibility of another evaluation, another aesthetics? How can this gesture made by the female, Jewish author be compared to the gesture made by the reader herself today? How can the possibility of another kind of writing be compared with that of another kind of reading, without blurring the distinction between the conditions of writing and those of reading within this comparison?

II

In 1806, Napoleon's army moved into Berlin, beginning a period of French domination. During this time, between 1807 and 1809, the Prussian government devised a program of administrative and economic reforms, initiated by its secretary Freiherr von Stein. These reforms had no effect on lessening social differences, however. Prussia's precarious situation as a truncated state between France and Russia engendered a new feeling of patriotism. As a consequence, new tensions arose between Jews and gentiles. It was difficult to view the Jew, whose emancipation French revolutionary thought promoted, as a supporter of Prussian national ideas.

In May 1809, Karl August Varnhagen introduced his friend Alexander von der Marwitz to Rahel Levin. Rahel, who had begun to call herself Rahel Robert, or even Rahel Robert von Tornow, was living alone and was experiencing financial difficulties. Marwitz was the descendant of an old and established aristocratic family. He administered his family estate and was soon to join the Austrian army in its desperate revolt against the French. Rahel, at this time thirty-eight years of age, was very taken with Marwitz, sixteen years her junior, but their friendship was based primarily on an exchange of letters. Five years after their first meeting, Marwitz was killed in battle in France. At the time of his death, Rahel had already begun her relationship with Varnhagen; she converted to Christianity and married him in 1814. The handsome soldier Marwitz was, however, remembered by Rahel in many of her letters, and especially in her correspondence with Varnhagen. She wrote about him with fondness and with praise, and described Marwitz, who did not paint, or play any music, or write any poetry, as an "artist" (*Briefwechsel* I: 248).

Rahel's correspondence with Marwitz tells the story of their relationship. Her letters are filled with questions, reports, and descriptions of her own life and adventures. Marwitz in turn reads her letters many times, finding them agitating in a way that prevents his immediate reply.[8] Rahel calls Marwitz's description both of his reaction and of her letters flattering, and she calls his letter a *Schmeichelbrief* [letter of flattery]. By rejecting his flattery, however, Rahel also comments on her own letters. A few years earlier (October 16, 1794), in a letter to her Jewish friend David Veit, Rahel describes them as the *Confessions de J. J. Rahel* (*Briefwechsel zwischen Rahel und David Veit* I: 240). Here, in her letters to Marwitz, she speaks again of her confessions:

> You should know that this letter of flattery has flattered me
> indefinitely; do you know that it is quite true that I need to be
> calmed down about my quite terrible letters; that I could not
> suspect that you would deal with them [*verführen*] in this way?
> Do you also know that I wish quite different ones for you, to
> deal with them like that; but, on the other hand, that I do not
> think my own unworthy? And you should hear, first of all,
> what I have decided for myself: I will continue to write such
> letters to you; these are true *confessions*, I have thought about
> it and decided; and you should see my soul as only I can
> capture it. (17 Nov. 1811; *Briefwechsel* I: 129–30)

Rahel, the author and heroine of a text in Rousseau's tradition,
offers her letters as a confession, as a form of purifying autobiography. The gesture of offering her letters is ambiguous. Only
after some thought do her confessions reveal themselves to the
reader as those of a soul that may not be beautiful but that wants
to be true. The "truth" of these confessions will make Rahel's soul
visible, on the other hand, and this becomes the justification for
her letters.

Both an offering and a retraction are thematized here and
are acted out through the exchange of these letters. Only true
confessions and multiple avowals may prevent the replacement of
Rahel's letters with those other, nameless ones, those that are not
present here but that would be more deserving of a flattering
reading and response. A foreign word, the French *confessions*,
enters her letter seductively. It indicates a polite tone as well as a
literary tradition, which is, despite the stress on "truth," important
here as well. After all, the reader's eye should not just capture the
letters, but Rahel's soul—a soul that is in view only fleetingly, as if
the reader would have to trace it in the act of reading and find a
meaning that is in danger of escaping. The letter serves as a
mirror, and it casts a double reflection. The reader captures the
view of Rahel's soul, just as the author herself can view it—and
only while it is passing by. Rahel's picture appears in this reflection, in the moment when her soul is offering itself: in its "truth"
in Rahel's writing.

In Rahel's letters, this moment is always at stake; it is a moment that she has to produce by writing constantly, so as to be able
to hope for its elusive appearance. The text should function as a

mirror, but it cannot reflect her exact image from a smooth surface. This would presuppose a notion of an intact and stable image to which Rahel's "truth" cannot subscribe. Hannah Arendt
describes Rahel's writing as a putting together of the disconnected
and compares it with the technique of the joke (42). Connecting
the disconnected, Rahel searches for her moment as one outside
any linguistic order. If truth can be revealed in Rahel's dialogue
with a reader, Rahel has, at the same time, to put into question
what seems to be fundamental to every introspective narrative
and every autobiography: a constant, defined self.

Autobiographical reflection presupposes a paradox; a stable
"I" who narrates, and the transformation of the "I" in time. In this
process the other—the reader or the addressee—is necessary.
Jean Starobinski writes:

> [Autobiography] only requires that certain possible condi-
> tions be realized, conditions which are mainly ideological (or
> cultural): that the personal experience be important, that it
> offer an opportunity for a sincere relation with someone else.
> These presuppositions establish the legitimacy of "I" and au-
> thorize the subject of the discourse to take his past existence
> as theme. Moreover, the "I" is confirmed in the function of
> permanent subject by the presence of its correlative "you,"
> giving clear motivation to the discourse. I am thinking here of
> the *Confessions* of St. Augustine: the author speaks to God but
> with the intention of edifying his readers. (288)

Rahel sees the "truth" of her *confessions* as sufficient reason for
their formulation. Her confessions are beyond any judgment,
even the aesthetic one: "If truth is coarse or not, nobody can
question it as such; it corresponds to its being, if it is true; and
where it settles on, this is the place that transforms it into coarse-
ness or courtesy" (21 Feb. 1809; *Buch des Andenkens* I: 405). One
cannot criticize Rahel's "truth," only the site in which it produces
itself. "Truth" itself does not change because of the condition of
its appearance. For Rahel, the Jewish woman who can choose
neither an "acceptable" social place nor the "acceptable" form of
literary expression, this may be a concept offering hope.

While truth does not orient itself according to the concretely
placed subject, the legitimacy of that "I" and its authority are put

into question by the structure of the representation itself. The separation between addressee, reader, and writer undermines in Rahel's letter the integrity of the self and the stability of the "place." Her soul exists only while it passes quickly by. In her dialogue with the reader, truth does not become anything constructive or edifying, although it is the aim and object of her discourse. It becomes the third, fleeting, and never quite articulated side of a triangle that links writer and reader; one that separates them, as any message would, but also reflects this separation in itself. Rahel needs Marwitz not only to be a reader of her missive but to be a reader who makes the writing of truth possible and who makes the truth of her lines appear.

"[T]hat you would deal with them in this way?" Rahel asks. The subjunctive *verführen* [to seduce] derives from *verfahren* [to follow a procedure], to deal with, and hints at a procedure; but it is also the infinitive of the verb *verführen*, to seduce. Procedure and seduction, here ambiguously stated, are a necessary part of Rahel's writing. The letter that is her *confessions*, message and narrative of what can never be fully or permanently present, will finally also have to remove itself from that presence that insists on contemporary time. To be able to make herself understood by Marwitz in the future, at the time of his receipt of her letter, Rahel does not write what "is," but about that which has made her what she is. She describes what makes her view of the world possible. Rahel comments on it elsewhere, in a letter to Friedrich de la Motte Fouqué:

> I am, therefore, observing the world. Life, nature, are here for me. Calculate the *lutte* of my life, therefore; the big, the small and bitter moments. With the sharpest knowledge (*Bewußtsein*) about myself. With the opinion that I should be a queen (no reigning one, however), or a mother: I discover that there is just   n o t h i n g   that I am. No daughter, no sister, no lover, no spouse, not even a burgheress. (26 July 1809; *Buch des Andenkens* I: 436)

Rahel observes the world. The happiness that she sees in others seems only to highlight what she lacks: properties, positions, places that she should have occupied. The subjunctive "should be" constructs an alternative position for her, however, that does not resemble a sketch of a dream world, but leads her to record her dreams. To record them, and to make the analysis of her writing possible, Rahel needs the other: "Please calculate," she addresses her reader. The "sharpest consciousness" takes shape without a stable subject, between the author and the reader in the act of reading.

III

Rahel's first salon folded at the turn of the nineteenth century. The French occupation and the following war provided a political context in which Berlin's social life changed. Just after 1809, when Rahel was not able to keep even her position as hostess, she often writes down her dreams in her letters to Marwitz. These narratives, presented as gifts, function as signs of the greatest intimacy, and at the same time they provoke distance. As evidence of their friendship, Marwitz asks Rahel to show the narrative of her dreams to his friend Henriette Schleiermacher. With this presentation, he wants to seal his new friendship with his old one, and he encourages, moreover, the friendship between the women themselves and their exchange of dreams.[9] Following this request, Rahel's letters to Marwitz become more cautious; she is not sure if she would really like to be part of this triangle and present her dreams. Later, however, she records the dreams for a second time, this time for Varnhagen, who will later marry her: *Verfahren* and *Verführung*, procedure and seduction, are here at play as well. With her help, Varnhagen prepares Rahel's letters for publication.[10] He heads his copy of Rahel's dream narrative only with a date, "July 1812." He selects dreams from those Rahel had copied into a notebook and introduces these excerpts into his printed edition of Rahel's correspondence with Marwitz. The dream that had been narrated as a letter is then returned as a narrative to the epistolary exchange.

Varnhagen's editorial procedure points to the special status of the narrated dream that would function as a letter. The reader—Marwitz or, later, Varnhagen—relates to this other world that Rahel would like to encounter, even if she could only do so voyeuristically. Strangely, though, the relationship between the reading of her text and her view of the other generates a double blindness: "Do you know," she writes to Marwitz, "that your presence has become to me like the eye of the world? I see it, even if you are not there, but I cannot look into her [the world's] eyes: I also don't know if she [the world] is seeing me" (16 May, 1811; *Briefwechsel* I: 36). This blindness is marked by a sense of strangeness as well as by gender. It is a blind sight, which love demands, and is likened to that writing which directs itself blindly, and some distance away from the person who makes her search for truth possible. Without addressing Marwitz, the world outside cannot perceive her.

Several critics have pointed out that Rahel's writing calls for a psychoanalytic reading and that the writing itself bears out the structure of psychoanalytic discourse.[11] Fritz Ernst concludes his article "Rahels Traum" with a quotation from one of Rahel's dreams which he uses to try to trace her "wishes" and "longings." At the center of her monograph on Rahel Varnhagen, Hannah Arendt places a chapter ("Night and Day") in which two of Rahel's dreams are used as objects of biographical interpretation; Arendt cares not about the process of analytical reading itself but about a reading that attempts to stabilize the individual in the process of analysis. Not the act of reading is of importance, but the interpretation of symbols. Arendt can therefore proceed to make a thematic selection. Rahel's dreams become for her biographical keys to her relationships with the German Count Karl von Finckenstein or the Spanish diplomat Raphael d'Urquijo and become "silent and consuming complaints of the night," "shadow images," which repeat themselves, and "assault, as memories, the waking person" (Arendt 129). The night, however, which is calling for these ghosts, also repeats another dream that can be found in Rahel's letters, but that is neither quoted by Arendt nor copied by Varnhagen for reproduction, and that is therefore censored from the chain of repetitions, much in the same way dreams themselves exercise censorship and repression.

This censored dream tries to confront art and life. It is not without obvious biographical references. Indeed, in many ways it resembles another dream that Varnhagen and Arendt record and which places Rahel in a castle, observing a gathering of people who are unable to see her. Here, in this second dream, Rahel finds herself in a big and festively lit hall on whose walls are hung "the portraits of all sculptors and painters who have ever lived or still live" (650).[12] Painters and sculptors are forming crowds to look at these portraits and to evaluate them in "a kind of last judgment of art" (651):

> I saw men of every . . . age, from about 17 years on; . . . expression . . . of the face from all nations which art, imagination and reality had ever shown me . . . men with and without beards, with great ones and with moustaches, with moustaches without long beard; and again the other way around. (651)

Rahel's attention is concentrated on the artists, not the paintings, and on the room itself. It is a ballroom that bears resemblance to a church:

> But also the large room I had to look at a lot, and I could not understand the light, it was very friendly in its *decoration*, above, and with its pointed arches; and the many colors, of the many people and pictures, the colors of the room even above, the very light yellowish reddish light, all of this seemed to produce a crowd before the eyes, and gave the whole no cut up or petty look, but the impression remained large and joyful. (651)

Rahel presses through the crowd of people, "carried dragged on between coats, dresses, backs and arms" (651), and ventures forward, to see the Ideal, who has arrived and who is greeted with awe by the gathered artists. The language of awe, that of the judging people who are present, is a silent hiss, like that of the seductive serpent itself:

> [T]he Ideal, some said quietly, silently hissing; and an astonishment moves like a quiver through the room where we are: I, however, center my glance on him, a young man of about 20 years, in common clothes, without a hat . . . who tries to suppress his laughter: the others do not see it; I, however, call, but he is a human being, he lives, he cannot refrain from

> laughter. . . . I come closer and search directly for this per-
> son's eyes which he keeps covered, but he smiles more. (652)

Rahel is the only one who recognizes the joke and unheard laughter. And while she begins to waltz uninhibitedly with "this human
being" (652), the artists step back.

Blindness and sight, important for Rahel's description of her
confessions, are thematic here. Now it is the Ideal who covers his
eyes and needs Rahel in order to be seen properly. She is the only
one who realizes that he is a young man and human being. While
the audience looks on, Rahel can join with him in dance. The
reader, however, knows that Rahel is the only one who would
have been able to dance with him. Despite the fact that some
sculptors have freed their arms "like women" (651), Rahel is the
only woman present. By virtue of being a woman, she alone is able
to report that the Ideal lives and laughs, and that she alone may
dance with him. The Ideal is not only seductive, but can be se-
duced to dance as well; in view of this, the other artists, who know
nothing about life, have to withdraw. Here ends Rahel's dream.
She reports it to Marwitz, who has chosen to read her letters and
whom she thinks of as an artist whose flattery she likes both to
accept and to reject.

Rahel often mentions waltzing in her early correspondence
with David Veit, for whom she describes her dancing master and
her lessons, as well as the education that is necessary for accul-
turation and *Bildung*—for example, the French language of the
confessions.[13] In all of these letters, waltzing becomes the metaphor
of that seductive and dizzying common movement that she de-
signs as an image for her writing, the movement of giving and
withdrawing—a linguistic dance. To dance happily with the Ideal
could indeed be a proper alternative to the established judgment
of art, whose criteria Rahel can fulfill neither through her letter
writing nor with her own life.

IV

While she records this dream, however, Rahel is also engaged in a matter of aesthetic judgment herself. She exchanges

letters with Varnhagen about Goethe's works. Varnhagen substitutes letters for the names of authors and addressees, and therefore transforms their exchange into an anonymous discussion. In this form he shows his and Rahel's letters to the master, Goethe, himself. Rahel, who idealizes Goethe, is curious about his judgment, and Goethe answers positively. In conferring his opinion, Goethe reads the letter of the alphabet that identifies Rahel's letters, *G.*, as an initial substituting for the name of a male author; and Rahel's letter does indeed correspond to the one beginning his own name. Did Rahel want to be anything else but Goethe's well-meaning mirror? For her, Goethe's reaction is flattering, but it has disturbing consequences for her calculation:

> Much as this event pleases me and flatters my self and my heart, I am so terribly sorry that Goethe has to see now which person of really no importance this G. is, in the world as well as in literature; and although he has probably never thought about it, he will not experience it as new that I love him, and in counting those who wish him well there will be one less now. (Letter to Marwitz, 26 Dec. 1822; *Briefwechsel* I: 146)

Letters of flattery circulate now as well, and Rahel is again afraid of an exchange of judgment and affection. Her reaction to Goethe's reading parallels her reaction to Marwitz's response, and this is not accidental. Goethe is not only an object of Rahel's admiration and love, but also a constant theme in her correspondence with Marwitz. It is precisely in this movement of giving and withdrawing, exemplified by the exchange of letters itself, that the master of all *Bildung* and poetry can reveal himself. Rahel writes to Varnhagen about the instigation for her own words and correspondence:

> In *one* thing I have followed my innermost depth, I held myself in distance from Goethe shyly. God, how right this has been! How chaste, how safe from profanation, as if it would have been safeguarded throughout a whole and unblessed life, I could now be able to show him the adoration in my heart. It passes through everything that I have ever expressed, *every* written word nearly does contain it. And he, too, will be the one to take count of this for me, understand-

ing how difficult it is to keep such loving admiration silently throughout one's whole life hidden in oneself. How embarrassedly I had to fall silent two years ago, when Bettina told me once of the object of her greatest passion, fiery and beautiful, in a Monbijou that turned shiny and silent in the autumn sun! I pretended that I did not even know him. This happened to me quite often; and, at another time, *I* am willing to talk. You know this. Now, Marwitz has to suffer it. All of our conversations begin with him, and end with him. (25 Dec. 1811; *Briefwechsel* I: 183)

While her aristocratic friend Bettina von Arnim talks freely about her love of Goethe, Rahel hides her admiration of him. Rahel resists any competition which would also presuppose that their positions are the same. Rahel denies her own confession the aesthetic scenery, moreover; no autumnal sun keeps shining on her words. Her confessions appear only sometimes, and they cannot always be expected. Goethe, and the confession of her admiration of him, form, however, the beginning and the end of every talk with that other partner, Marwitz. Her confessions about Goethe are a necessary part of her letters to Marwitz, of those special conversations that communicate her dreams as well. But as her letters to Marwitz deal with Goethe and—as *confessions*—with her own truth as well, Goethe's words themselves will have to speak an ambiguous language, one that not only tells a story but that can tell Rahel's life. The special relationship between Rahel and Goethe thus becomes understandable. It is a relationship that produces Rahel's admiration of the master:

You [Marwitz] were smiling the other day in such a way, when I told you that all of Goethe's words appear to me so totally different, when he is saying them, than when other people have said the same: such as hope, faith, fear, etc. You smiled, judged my observation as correct, and proceeded to explain my words. But now, listen to the unheard of. It seems to be the same for me in regard to my own life. I always think, in the first sense, which is taken from the bloodiest and liveliest heart, that the other people do nothing. I have been thinking this way, if not quite so clearly, for a long time now. And in this way I am telling you this, too. Therefore, I am able to

recognize Goethe's words, and every truth of men. (5 Jan.
1812; *Briefwechsel* I: 153)

Rahel's letters are confessions that deal with herself and speak
about Goethe; they are aimed at Marwitz, herself, and Goethe.
Goethe, on the other hand, pursues a writing that offers for his
reader Rahel the special significance of her own life. Goethe
writes a language that becomes immediate metaphor; he writes
with the same letter but differently. The metaphor articulates
Rahel's view. Goethe is able to write like this because there is a
"truth" in his writing, and this truth is offered by him in words
that cannot be his own. Goethe, with his *Bildungsroman*, the masterful *Wilhelm Meister*, writes the "unheard of" because he can
hear. Rahel, the reader, comments:

> Yes, I would be a real part of this book (as you [Veit] say: "as
> if this is a great loss!"). Although he may have invented ev-
> erything, even Aurelie, the speeches that she gives he must
> once have h e a r d, this I know, this I believe. Namely, the
> princess of Tasso says the same; only in a different tone. How
> great is t h i s! But he must have heard it. The women no-
> body can argue with me about. Either one thinks this a s
> woman, or one hears it from a woman. One cannot invent
> this. Every other humanly possible thing I grant him. But
> t h i s I know as I. (Letter to David Veit, 1 June 1795; *Buch des
> Andenkens* I: 264)

By listening to a woman, and by writing Rahel's life specifically,
Goethe finds words for a life that Rahel cannot describe except by
comparison, in a paradox that is her truth. This truth appears
unexpectedly, and it is unexpected because it always appears in
another place. As a "thoroughly witty" similarity and likeness, it
can even appear in Goethe's letters themselves (Letter to Varnhagen, 19 Feb. 1809; *Buch des Andenkens*, I: 264). Just "like this,"
Goethe describes her life. While Rahel is unique in comparison to
him, she produces with her life a balance to his work. This balance
is needed, not only for any comparison, but for any counting and
calculation as well. She herself cannot appear differently except in
the "image":

> I am as unique as the greatest appearance on earth. The artist, philosopher, poet does not stand above me. We are of the same element. We are of the same level [*Rang*], and we belong together. And he who wants to exclude one, is only excluding himself. I am, however, appointed to the life; and I remained as a germ, until my century, and I am totally buried from outside, therefore I say it myself. Because one image should end the existence. (Letter to David Veit, 1 June 1795; *Buch des Andenkens* I: 264)

With the statement of this comparison, the irony as well as the "truth" of another dream becomes apparent, which Rahel, in her dialogue about hearing and true silence, adds to her dream about art and the Ideal. This other, shorter dream is older, but it is one that she "loves still" (652). It is presented as an appendix to the earlier one and recounts an aesthetic judgment. In this dream, Rahel is again among men. Men visit her father and refer, among other topics, to the Duke of Weimar. Rahel provokes a smile, although not suppressed laughter, because she herself knows the "unheard of" this time:

> The talk about war ended, and the men dispersed, at that point, I asked somebody who came together with an officer, if Goethe is with the Duke, and how he is doing. "Goethe?" said the man, "who is that?" What? You don't know Goethe? I answered; our foremost poet. Goethe is your foremost poet, this may not quite be the case; the man smiled; this I have never heard. After a pause, in which I could not confront the man, and could not find any answer, nor any evidence, I said: listen! He *is* the greatest poet; because if God would come down from heaven and tell me that this is not the case; well I say, then I no longer understand His world. (652)

V

Bettina von Arnim published her memoirs of the ennobled Johann Wolfgang von Goethe as a collection of letters that, while not without erotic impact, are entitled *Goethe's Correspondence with a Child*.[14] For Rahel, Goethe is a paternal figure who has to be worshiped but who undergoes a peculiar secularization. Goethe's writings represent all that a German *Bildung* should strive for, the desired social position and style that Rahel is unable to attain. In her dream, the uniform of military men gives entrée to the House of Weimar, and it is an entry that neither Rahel's person nor any of her letters are ever able to obtain. Venturing from a native Yiddish, and trying herself with the established pen, her writing mirrors the military order as anarchy. She writes to the poet Fouqué:

> Something else! And something quite different! Quite! When I am writing myself into the Fouquéan writing house, it is quite honest and naive of me! I know very well that I am writing things that are worthwhile reading; but my words and yours! Like exercising soldiers in beautiful uniforms everything of yours is standing there; and mine, they look like run together rebels with sticks! (Letter to Fouqué, 31 Dec. 1811; *Buch des Andenkens* I: 585)

Neither Rahel nor her writing wear the proper "uniform," but this may not necessarily imply any deficiency on her part. In contrast to a man's world, it may simply be "something else." Rahel's descriptions designate failure as well as success: to lack particular properties but to be of the same level, and to produce a balance by the absence of the proper place. Unlike Bettina von Arnim, Rahel is neither child nor daughter in her relationship to her male correspondents. While her writing lacks the "uniform," and therefore the authority, of Marwitz or Fouqué or, above all, Goethe, her Jewish mother tongue is an origin of more than an alternative discourse. Rahel can only write differently under Goethe's image. But Goethe's writings themselves are "true" only inasmuch as they offer a metaphor for Rahel's existence.

This dialogue offers a peculiar paradox. By its ability to liberate, to open one's powerful hand to let go, emancipation presupposes an established ownership. Goethe's paternal hand, however, can only offer emancipation by writing what is already not his own, the truth of Rahel's life and conversation. Far from being barred any access to literature and aesthetics by her lack of social freedom, Rahel undermines in turn the structure of emancipation itself—with her writing. Neither the positions of master and

dependent student seem stable, nor does any delineation of gender that would conform to and confirm this configuration of
power—Rahel can turn, indeed, into the author *G*. Her letters,
linking the dependency of life with art, give birth to a mastery that
transgresses the relationships of mother and son, and of father
and daughter. Here, the search for any Jewish and feminist aesthetics has to begin.

Notes

This paper was first presented at Cornell University, November 1988. It is
part of a longer work on Rahel Varnhagen and Dorothea Schlegel that will
appear in German in a special volume of the *Deutsche Vierteljahrsschrift, Perspek-
tivenwechsel.*

1. See *Webster's New Universal Unabridged Dictionary.*
2. See *Der Grosse Brockhaus.*
3. This is taken for granted in all the studies dealing with Jewish emancipation; see, for example, Reinhard Rürup, "Judenemanzipation und bürgerliche
Gesellschaft in Deutschland," or Arno Herzig, "Das Problem der jüdischen Identität in der deutschen bürgerlichen Gesellschaft." Jewish resistance towards the
adoption of the German language, for example, is generally seen as a mark of
the pre-emancipatory era, and the pre-Mendelssohn time; see, for example,
Alexander Altmann, *Moses Mendelssohn: A Biographical Study.*
4. See Gert Mattenklott, "Aufbruch in neue Lebensräume oder Der ungestillte Hunger." The following quotations are taken from this article. All trans-
lations from the German, here and elsewhere, are mine.
5. The thesis that literature serves as a replacement for actions continues a
traditional opposition of art and life. It can often be found in the secondary
literature on Rahel Varnhagen, and seems to answer her own complaints about
her limitations to act. See, for example, even the discussion of Varnhagen in a
feminist study like that of Silvia Bovenschen, *Die imaginierte Weiblichkeit.*
6. See Kay Goodman, "Poesis and Praxis in Rahel Varnhagen's Letters." She
refers to Jürgen Habermas's *Strukturwandel der Öffentlichkeit.*
7. Indirectly, Mattenklott himself criticizes his representation of Jewish
women writers as women without properties later in his essay, by correcting
Wilhelm von Humboldt's similar assertion. In another essay, Mattenklott also
touches on the fact that the letter may not be such a "marginal" genre. It is an
essay on the letters and epistolary novels of a non-Jewish woman writer, Bettina
von Arnim: "Romantische Frauenkultur."
8. Compare Alexander von der Marwitz's letter to Rahel Varnhagen, 12 Nov.
1811; *Briefwechsel* I: 125.
9. See letter to Alexander von der Marwitz, 8 Dec. 1812 (*Briefwechsel* I: 217–
21), and the following letters.
10. For this reference, I am grateful to Ursula Isselstein, who was able to
consult Rahel's corrections on the original letters. The copy of the dream narratives has not been censored any further by Rahel or Karl August Varnhagen,

however. See "'daß ich kein Träumender allein hier bin!'" esp. 650. See Issel-stein for a history of the publication of Rahel's dream narratives. Friedrich Kemp gives these narratives the heading "Aus Rahels Tagebuch" [From Rahel's diary] (*Briefwechsel* I: 202).

11. See, for example, Goodman 133; Isselstein, 653n12; and Liliane Weiss-berg, "Writing on the Wall."

12. Rahel Varnhagen's dreams are quoted from their first publication by Is-selstein; the page references follow the quotations in the text.

13. See, for example, the letters to David Veit, 13 and 17 Dec. 1793, and David Veit's letter to Rahel, 24 Dec. 1793; *Briefwechsel zwischen Rahel und David Veit* I: 78 and I: 85–86.

14. In German, *Goethes Briefwechsel mit einem Kinde. Seinem Denkmal.*

Works Cited

Altmann, Alexander. *Moses Mendelssohn: A Biographical Study.* Tuscaloosa: U of Alabama P, 1973.

Arendt, Hannah. *Rahel Varnhagen: Lebensgeschichte einer deutschen Jüdin aus der Romantik.* Munich: Piper, 1959.

Arnim, Bettina von. *Goethes Briefwechsel mit einem Kinde. Seinem Denkmal.* Berlin, 1835.

Bovenschen, Silvia. *Die imaginierte Weiblichkeit: exemplarische Untersuchungen zu kulturgeschichtlichen und literarischen Präsentationsformen des Weiblichen.* Frank-furt: Suhrkamp, 1979.

Ernst, Fritz. "Rahels Traum." *Essais.* 2 vols. Zurich: Artemis, 1946. I: 211–27.

Goodman, Kay. "Poesis and Praxis in Rahel Varnhagen's Letters." *New German Critique* 27 (1982): 123–39.

Der große Brockhaus. Wiesbaden: F. A. Brockhaus, 1953.

Habermas, Jürgen. *Strukturwandel der Öffentlichkeit.* Darmstadt: Luchterhand, 1962.

Herzig, Arno. "Das Problem der jüdischen Identität in der deutschen bürger-lichen Gesellschaft." *Deutsche Aufklärung und Judenemanzipation,* Ed. Walter Grab. *Jahrbuch* Beiheft 3. Tel-Aviv: Institut für Deutsche Geschichte, 1980. 243–64.

Isselstein, Ursula. "'daß ich kein Träumender allein hier bin!': Zwei unbekannte Träume Rahel Levins." *MLN* 102 (1987): 648–50.

Mattenklott, Gert. "Aufbruch in neue Lebensräume oder Der ungestillte Hun-ger: Überlegungen zu Briefen der Henriette Herz," *Frankfurter Allgemeine Zeitung* 33 (8 Feb 1986, *Beilage*).

———. "Romantische Frauenkultur: Bettina von Arnim zum Beispiel." In *Lite-ratur—Frauen—Geschichte: Schreibende Frauen vom Mittelalter bis zur Gegenwart.* Ed. Hitrud Gnüg und Renate Möhrmann. Stuttgart: Metzler, 1985. 123–43.

Rürup, Reinhard, "Judenemanzipation und bürgerliche Gesellschaft in Deutsch-land." *Emanzipation und Antisemitismus: Studien zur "Judenfrage" der bürgerlichen Gesellschaft.* (ser.) *Kritische Studien zur Geschichtswissenschaft* 15. Göttingen: Van-denhoeck und Ruprecht, 1975. 11–36, 134–35.

Starobinski, Jean. "The Style of Autobiography." *Literary Style: A Symposium.* Ed. Seymour Chatman. New York: Oxford UP, 1971. 285–96.

Varnhagen, Rahel. *Briefwechsel.* 4 vols. Ed. Friedhelm Kemp. Munich: Winkler, 1979.

_____. *Briefwechsel zwischen Rahel und David Veit.* 2 vols. Ed. from the papers of Karl August Varnhagen. Leipzig: Brockhaus, 1861. Rpt. in *Rahel-Bibliothek.* 10 vols. Ed. Konrad Feilchenfeldt, Uwe Schweikert, and Rahel E. Steiner. Munich: Matthes und Seitz, 1983.

_____. *Buch des Andenkens.* 2 vols. Ed. Karl August von Varnhagen. Berlin: Duncker und Humblot, 1834. [*Rahel-Bibliothek* I.]

Webster's New Universal Unabridged Dictionary. 2nd ed. New York: Dorset, 1983.

Weissberg, Liliane. "Writing on the Wall: Letters of Rahel Varnhagen." *New German Critique* 36 (1985): 157–73.

BOOKS RECEIVED

Anisfield, Nancy, ed. *The Nightmare Considered: Critical Essays on Nuclear War Literature.* Bowling Green, OH: Bowling Green State U Popular P, 1991.

Bakhtin, M. M. / P. N. Medvedev. *The Formal Method in Literary Scholarship: A Critical Introduction to Sociological Poetics.* Trans. Albert J. Wehrle. 1978. Baltimore: Johns Hopkins UP, 1991.

Benjamin, Andrew. *Art, Mimesis, and the Avant-Garde: Aspects of a Philosophy of Difference.* New York: Routledge, 1991.

Birringer, Johannes. *Theatre, Theory, Postmodernism.* Bloomington: Indiana UP, 1991.

Black, Joel. *The Aesthetics of Murder: A Study in Romantic Literature and Contemporary Culture.* Baltimore: Johns Hopkins UP, 1991.

Boothby, Richard. *Death and Desire: Psychoanalytic Theory in Lacan's Return to Freud.* New York: Routledge, 1991.

Cameron, Sharon. *The Corporeal Self: Allegories of the Body in Melville and Hawthorne.* New York: Columbia UP, 1991.

Clayton, Jay, and Eric Rothstein, eds. *Influence and Intertextuality in Literary History.* Madison: U of Wisconsin P, 1991.

Corner, John, ed. *Popular Television in Britain: Studies in Cultural History.* London: British Film Institute, 1991.

Davis, Lennard J., and M. Bella Mirabella. *Left Politics and the Literary Profession.* New York: Columbia UP, 1990.

Davis, Tracy C. *Actresses as Working Women: Their Social Identity in Victorian Culture.* New York: Routledge, 1991.

Day, Holliday T., ed. *Power: Its Myths and Mores in American Art, 1961–1991.* Indianapolis: Indianapolis Museum of Art, 1991.

DeJean, Joan. *Tender Geographies: Women and the Origins of the Novel in France.* New York: Columbia UP, 1991.

Epstein, Julia, and Kristina Straub, eds. *Body Guards: The Cultural Politics of Gender Ambiguity.* New York: Routledge, 1991.

Forsas-Scott, Helena. *Textual Liberation: European Feminist Writing in the Twentieth Century.* New York: Routledge, 1991.

Fort, Bernadette, ed. *Fictions of the French Revolution.* Evanston, IL: Northwestern UP, 1991.

Frosh, Stephen. *Identity Crisis: Modernity, Psychoanalysis and the Self*. New York: Routledge, 1991.

Gandelsonas, Mario. *The Urban Text*. Cambridge: MIT Press, 1991.

Garber, Marjorie. *Vested Interests: Cross-Dressing and Cultural Anxiety*. New York: Routledge, 1992.

Gilman, Sander. *The Jew's Body*. New York: Routledge, 1991.

Gilroy, Paul. *"There Ain't No Black in the Union Jack": The Cultural Politics of Race and Nation*. Chicago: U of Chicago P, 1991.

Gramsci, Antonio. *Selections from Cultural Writings*. Ed. David Forgacs and Geoffrey Nowell-Smith. Trans. William Boelhower. Cambridge: Harvard UP, 1991.

Handelman, Susan A. *Fragments of Redemption: Jewish Thought and Literary Theory in Benjamin, Scholem, and Levinas*. Bloomington: Indiana UP, 1991.

Hill, Geoffrey. *The Enemy's Country: Words, Contexture, and Other Circumstances of Language*. Stanford: Stanford UP, 1991.

Holub, Robert C. *Jürgen Habermas: Critic in the Public Sphere*. New York: Routledge, 1991.

Huyssen, Andreas, and David Bathrick, eds. *Modernity and the Text: Revisions of German Modernism*. New York: Columbia UP, 1991.

The Institute for Contemporary Art. *David Hammons: Rousing the Rabble*. Cambridge: MIT Press, 1991.

Kastan, David Scott, and Peter Stallybrass. *Staging the Renaissance: Reinterpretations of Elizabethan and Jacobean Drama*. New York: Routledge, 1991.

Kubiak, Anthony. *Stages of Terror: Terrorism, Ideology, and Coercion as Theatre History*. Bloomington: Indiana UP, 1991.

Lang, Berel. *Writing and the Moral Self*. New York: Routledge, 1991.

MacPherson, Pat. *Reflecting on the Bell Jar*. New York: Routledge, 1991.

———. *Victorian Subjects*. Durham, NC: Duke UP, 1991.

Minh-Ha, Trinh T. *When the Moon Waxes Red*. New York: Routledge, 1991.

Modleski, Tania. *Feminism without Women: Culture and Criticism in a "Postfeminist" Age*. New York: Routledge, 1991.

Mücke, Dorothea E. von. *Virtue and the Veil of Illusion: Generic Innovation and the Pedagogical Project in Eighteenth-Century Literature*. Stanford: Stanford UP, 1991.

Nordquist, Joan, comp. *Jürgen Habermas (II): A Bibliography*. Social Theory: A Bibliographic Series 22. Santa Cruz, CA: Reference and Research Services, 1991.

Rancière, Jacques. *The Ignorant Schoolmaster: Five Lessons in Intellectual Emancipation*. Trans. Kristin Ross. Stanford: Stanford UP, 1991.

Roof, Judith. *A Lure of Knowledge: Lesbian Sexuality and Theory.* New York: Columbia UP, 1991.

Rustin, Michael. *The Good Society and the Inner World: Psychoanalysis, Politics and Culture.* New York: Verso, 1991.

Sawicki, Jana. *Disciplining Foucault: Feminism, Power, and the Body.* New York: Routledge, 1991.

Silverman, Hugh J. *Gadamer and Hermeneutics: Science Culture Literature.* Continental Philosophy IV. New York: Routledge, 1991.

Witte, Bernd. *Walter Benjamin: An Intellectual Biography.* Trans. James Rolleston. Detroit: Wayne State UP, 1991.

Xue, Can. *Old Floating Cloud: Two Novellas.* Trans. Ronald R. Jansen and Jian Zhang. Evanston, IL: Northwestern UP, 1991.

CONTRIBUTORS

Amanda Anderson teaches in the department of English at the University of Illinois, Urbana. She has published essays in *Genders* and *Diacritics* and is completing a book on depictions of fallenness in Victorian literature and culture.

Michael Eric Dyson is assistant professor of ethics and cultural criticism at Chicago Theological Seminary. His work has appeared in numerous books and in the *New York Times Book Review, Tikkun, The Nation, Social Text,* and *Cultural Studies.* He is also author of *Pursuing the Horizon: Essays in African-American Cultural Criticism.*

Henry A. Giroux is currently professor of education and director of the Center for Education and Cultural Studies at Miami University. In the fall of 1992, he will assume the Waterbury Chair in Secondary Education at Penn State University. His most recent book is *Border-Crossings: Cultural Workers and the Politics of Education.*

Martin Jay teaches in the history department of the University of California, Berkeley. Among his books are *Adorno, The Dialectical Imagination: A History of the Frankfurt School and the Institute of Social Research, 1923–1950,* and *Fin de Siècle Socialism: And Other Essays.*

Peter Kulchyski is acting chair of the department of Native studies at Trent University, Peterborough, Ontario, Canada.

Jeffrey T. Nealon teaches in the English department at Loyola University, Chicago. He has published essays in *Modern Drama, PMLA,* and *boundary 2* (forthcoming). He is also author of the forthcoming *Double Reading: Literary Criticism and the "Logic" of Postmodernism.*

Paula Rabinowitz teaches American studies, women's studies and English at the University of Minnesota. She is author of *Labor and Desire: Women's Revolutionary Fiction in Depression America* and coeditor of *Writing Red: An Anthology of American Women Writers, 1930–1940.*

Mark Rose is director of the University of California Humanities Research Institute at the University of California, Irvine. He has written books on a range of subjects from Shakespeare to science fiction.

Liliane Weissberg is associate professor of German and comparative literature at the University of Pennsylvania. Her publications include *Geistersprache: philosophischer und literarischer Diskurs im späten achtzehnten Jahrhundert* and *Edgar Allan Poe*. She is completing an edition of early Romantic letters for the Deutscher Klassiker Verlag.

boundary 2 an international journal of literature and culture

Paul Bové, editor

New Americanists 2: National Identities and Post-National Narratives

19:1 (Spring 1992), a special issue edited by Donald E. Pease

National Identities, Postmodern Artifacts, and Post-National Narratives / Donald E. Pease

Engendering Paranoia in Contemporary Narrative / Patrick O' Donnell

Technoeuphoria and the Discourse of the American Sublime / Rob Wilson

The Politics of Nonidentity: A Genealogy / Ross Posnock

Nationalism, Hypercanonization, and *Huckleberry Finn* / Jonathan Arac

On Becoming Oneself in Frank Lentricchia / Daniel T. O'Hara

Resisting History: *Rear Window* and the Limits of the Postwar Settlement / Robert J. Corber

Failed Cultural Narratives: America in the Postwar Era and the Story of *Democracy* / Alan Nadel

Queer Nationality / Lauren Berlant and Elizabeth Freeman

As I Lay Dying in the Machine Age / Jack Matthews

_____ Institutions,$40

_____ Individuals, $20

_____ Single issue price, $14

Please enter my subscription to **boundary 2** for 1992. (Include $6 for postage if outside the U.S.)

Payment options:

_____ I enclose my check or money order payable to Duke University Press.

_____ Bill me. (No issues can be sent until payment is received.)

_____ Charge my _____ VISA or _____ MasterCard

No. _____ Expiration _____

Signature _____

Or call (919) 684-6837 between 8:00 and 4:00 with VISA or MasterCard orders.

Name _____

Address _____

Send this coupon to: **Duke University Press** Journals Division, 6697 College Station, Durham, NC 27708

BERKELEY
JOURNAL OF
SOCIOLOGY
A Critical Review

Bell: The Misreading of Ideology

Rose: One-Dimensional Man at 25

Naderi: Max Weber and the Middle East

Luff: Witchcraft as Feminist Spirituality

Stoecker: Taming the Beast

–Review Essays–

Brooks: Political Economy of Professions

Manza: Critical Legal Studies

Stephen: The Tourist Eye

Teske: Sources of the Self

Delaney: Genetics and Eugenics

Nichols: Creative Initiative

Students: $6.00   Domestic Institutions: $15.00
Individuals: $8.00   Overseas Institutions: $18.00

Volume 35/1990

Papers are solicited for publication on a continual basis.
Also, please inquire about discount rates on back issues/multi-volume orders.
All inquiries and submissions should be addressed to:

The Berkeley Journal of Sociology
458A Barrows Hall/University of California, San Diego
Berkeley, CA 94720